THE CONSULTANT'S GUIDE TO WINNING CLIENTS

THE CONSULTANT'S GUIDE TO WINNING CLIENTS

Herman Holtz

WILEY

John Wiley & Sons

New York   Chichester   Brisbane   Toronto   Singapore

*In dedication to the memory
of a beloved brother,
Solomon Martin Holtz*

Copyright © 1988 by Herman Holtz.
Published by John Wiley & Sons, Inc.

This publication is designed to provide accurate and
authoritative information in regard to the subject
matter covered. It is sold with the understanding that
the publisher is not engaged in rendering legal, accounting,
or other professional service. If legal advice or other
expert assistance is required, the services of a competent
professional person should be sought. *From a Declaration
of Principles jointly adopted by a Committee of the
American Bar Association and a Committee of Publishers.*

Library of Congress Cataloging in Publication Data:

Holtz, Herman.
    The consultant's guide to winning clients / by Herman Holtz.
        p.   cm.
    Bibliography: p.
    ISBN 0471-62759-3
    1. Business consultants.   2. Consultants.   I. Title.
HD69.C6H623   1988
658.4 ′ 6 − dc 19   87-24945
                                                     CIP

Printed in the United States of America
10 9 8 7 6 5 4 3 2 1

PREFACE

Most independent consultants are highly competent in providing their professional services and solving their client's problems. But many, if not most, independent consultants are in almost desperate need of help in marketing—in winning those clients. In fact, it is the lack of success in marketing that is responsible for the many failures of consulting practices.

That was the underlying premise of my first book on the subject of consulting, *How to Succeed as an Independent Consultant*, and many readers of that book reacted by confirming that premise rather emphatically. That is the underlying cause for writing this book, for marketing continues to be a problem for many independent consultants. Marketing anything, but especially marketing professional services, requires first finding prospects, not always the easiest thing to do but probably the most critical factor in the marketing process.

As in many other things, we run into problems of definition here. Just as we have had many problems and many conflicting opinions on how to define consulting, so we have similar problems in defining prospecting. Bill Good, a consultant who offers his own seminars on selling consulting services, defines prospecting as "The art of finding someone who may need your product, possibly wants it, and is most qualified to buy it." He goes on to say that prospecting is an act of disqualification, discarding those who are clearly not interested in and/or unable to buy what you sell.

I find it hard to quarrel with the gentleman, for prospecting does mean screening out those individuals and/or organizations who are definitely not likely ever to become your clients. But that strikes me as rather negative. I prefer a more positive elaboration of the definition: prospecting is screening to select those who appear most likely to become clients. That is, I try to discriminate between prospects and sales leads. (Some other sales experts, obviously with a sardonic sense of humor, have said the same thing more cleverly by declaring that they try to discriminate between prospects and suspects!) A prospect is anyone or any organization who appears to be someone you might reasonably expect to sell your services to. For example, you might reasonably expect to sell a security survey to almost anyone owning a home or office building—but dwellers in secure, highrise buildings are not likely to be interested; they would not normally be prospects.

In any case, prospecting, the first stage of finding clients, is most difficult for so many consultants. Following up and closing good sales leads is not nearly as difficult when and if the prospecting is handled well, for that means that an abundance of sales leads are being developed and they are good sales leads. That is the purpose of prospecting, and so prospecting becomes the key to sales.

In recognition of this, the bulk of the content here is devoted to prospecting and the planning that must go into prospecting successfully and efficiently.

HERMAN HOLTZ

Wheaton, Maryland
December 1987

CONTENTS

PART III: THE METHODS FOR ACHIEVING CONSULTING SUCCESS

PART I

THE FUNDAMENTALS OF INDEPENDENT CONSULTING SUCCESS

What constitutes success for the independent consultant, for *you* as an independent consultant? Is it a growing practice that will eventually scoop in many associates or employees to constitute a large consulting firm? Is it professional innovation, setting new standards in your special field? Is it a growing professional reputation that enables you to charge several thousand dollars a day for your services and to be invited to address large groups for equally munificent fees? Is it the amassing of a great deal of wealth? Is it a position of power? Is it "showing them"—friends, relatives, acquaintances, former employers, former associates—what you can do?

The fact is that success, whether in independent consulting or elsewhere, is a very personal matter, subject to your own personal definition. However, perhaps you have not given a great deal of thought to what success as an independent consultant really means to you. In these pages we are going to explore the question and suggest what success as an independent consultant is—what logic suggests it is—and how you can achieve it, at least on that scale.

CHAPTER 1

SUCCESS: WHAT IS IT?

The secret of success is constancy to purpose.
—Benjamin Disraeli

SUCCESS IS NOT A STRANGER
NOR A RARE OCCURRENCE

We talk a lot about success, but there is no widely accepted definition of the word. Probably many, if not most, individuals have some vague concept that wealth equals success, as a first definition, and with it comes prestige, power, and whatever other trappings the individual likes to think are the spin-offs or evidence of wealth. But that is only one definition of success, and a quite broad and generalized one at that; there are many others, even broader. There are also more narrow definitions, referring to success in a more limited and usually more personal sense. For example, on December 17, 1903, Wilbur and Orville Wright wired the Reverend Milton Wright from Kitty Hawk, North Carolina as follows:

Success. Four flights Thursday morning. All against twenty-one-mile wind. Started from level with engine power alone. Average speed through air thirty-one miles. Longest fifty-nine seconds. Inform press. Home Christmas.

Calling that day's achievements success might appear a bit ludicrous in today's world of jet airplanes, supersonic speeds, rocket ships, and space travel. But what it reported was indeed a great success under the circumstances of that time and in the face of all the sneering skeptics who confidently predicted that heavier-than-air flight was a misbegotten fantasy and the Wrights a pair of misguided fools. (In fact, in the face of those circumstances the telegram was an example of a low-key and somewhat laconic report of what was really a sensational achievement.)

Thomas Edison is reported to have tried some 10,000 different materials in his quest for something to serve as an incandescent filament for his electric light. And, it is reported, he regarded each test a success because he had successfully eliminated another possible material and was one step closer to the eventual success he knew would be his one day.

Many successful salespeople who know that they average a sale on one out of every five calls regard each call a success for the same reason: each no-sale is another obstacle overcome and a step closer to their next sale; it is a 20-percent success, at the least.

But there are many other kinds of successes. There are, for example, successes in academic achievement—winning an undergraduate degree, an advanced degree, a doctorate, being Phi Beta Kappa, graduating Magna Cum Laude, and otherwise distinguishing yourself educationally. Even putting yourself through college, when you come from a family that cannot afford to pay your tuition and sustenance, is a success.

Those are all notable accomplishments, reasons to be proud of what you have done, reasons to make others proud of what you have done. And they may very well pave the way and contribute substantially to other, later successes in the professional and business worlds of the independent consultant. Despite that, and with no thought of making light of those very real achievements, these are preliminary successes, usually realized at an early, pre-career stage. The best and in a large sense more significant successes are yet to come. Success is not some singular or rare occurrence, a pot of gold at the end of the rainbow. We face problems and challenges throughout our lives, so that life is a lengthy series of successes and failures—hopefully more of the former than of the latter. But even then, failure need not be a final state of affairs, but only a way station, a learning experience that will help us achieve final success on the next try . . . or the one after that.

A FEW TYPICAL PROBLEMS AND CHALLENGES IN INDEPENDENT CONSULTING

As an independent consultant you are both a professional and an entrepreneur, a professional practitioner and a businessperson. That is an immediate bifurcation in the assessment and definition of success. Success as a professional and success as a businessperson may well be regarded in entirely different terms and usually are, for they are measured by different standards entirely.

Speaking broadly, with reference to standards, success as a businessperson is usually linked to the balance sheet and the profit and loss statement—to business success, that is, to making sales and earning profits on those sales. But attainment as a professional is generally judged in terms of recognition by peers, as well as by clients, with prestige a mark of that recognition and professional success. And even that tends to subdivide into a number of activities generally associated with professionals, including writing, speaking, and active participation as a member in whatever are the leading societies of the profession. Active consultants must generally belong to a minimum of two professional societies or associations: one that gathers in consultants generally as members and one that gathers in members of the professional discipline, who may or may not be consultants representing that discipline. For example, the marketing consultant is likely to be a member of a marketers' association, while being also a member of a consultants' association. And many, perhaps most, consultants find it necessary or at least judicious to belong to several associations, for image and visibility are among the several important factors in success as an independent consultant.

The typical successful independent consultant is, then, usually a successful mixer, mover, public speaker, and writer, as well as a successful executive and marketer. These qualities all fit together and are mutually interdependent in a number of ways. Success spelled with a capital S is the sum of many successes spelled with a small s.

Some individuals choose to sneer at financial success as being beneath their professional dignity even to recognize, much less openly aspire to. Unfortunately, without success in winning enough income as an independent consultant to pay your bills and provide an acceptable salary for your own survival any other kinds of success will not mean much, for you will then be unable to survive as an independent consultant. We are therefore compelled to regard and define success as an independent consultant to mean success in the marketplace, selling whatever you offer as a consultant.

But there is even a simpler rationale for equating success generally with success in the marketplace. The very purpose of establishing an independent consulting practice is to serve clients with your analyses and counsel, so you cannot carry out your most basic objectives without having those clients—without success in wooing and winning clients in sufficient number and with adequate frequency.

By just about any standards we can conceive or develop, then, we must regard success as meaning *marketing* success. And that is what we will explore and expound on in the pages to follow.

CHAPTER 2

WOOING AND WINNING CLIENTS: A BRIEF STUDY OF THE PROBLEM

Before a problem can be solved it must be understood, and defining it successfully is the first step in understanding it.

CONSULTING IS A BUSINESS, BUT NOT A ONE-CALL BUSINESS

Consulting is not a one-call business. That term, while perhaps cryptic to some, is actually both colorful and highly definitive. In consulting you will rarely win a client and assignment instantaneously as a direct result of an initial sales call or other single sales appeal. Prospective clients for your consulting services will not ordinarily retain you as casually as they might buy razor blades or shoes. They usually buy consulting services much as they would buy an automobile or a house — after extensive shopping, many inquiries, and at least a few comparative evaluations, at a minimum.

What this means, from your viewpoint as the marketer of your own services, is that each client must be wooed and won as you might woo and win a hard-to-get sweetheart. Clients and consulting assignments or contracts are won only after, and as a result of, successful sales *campaigns*—numerous "calls" in pursuit of that client/assignment. Hence that apt and well-merited characterization of consulting as "not a one-call business." But are there not exceptions to this? Certainly; there are exceptions to the rule in every field and in every activity, but that does not make the rule less valid. You may even get unlucky and win a first client or two that way. *Un*lucky? Yes, unlucky, because if you happen to win your first clients without a struggle you may easily be deceived into believing that you can build a practice without serious marketing perspiration. It has happened to many, and often they have found themselves forced to close up shop before they learned the lessons of their too-early success. In fact, more than a few independent consultants decided to enter the profession only after, and a result of, acquiring a client or two through some pure chance or stumbling into an initial consulting project or two and deducing from this that it must be easy to succeed as an independent consultant. (I have again and again met newly established independent consultants who were inspired to enter the profession for such reasons and met with ultimate disappointment and disillusionment only after they had completed that first project or two and sought others in vain.)

There is still another, perhaps even more insidious drawback to this kind of early and unearned success: The victim of such a calamity decides that it is not necessary to market—to seek other clients—as long as he or she is busy; time enough to market later, when the current project is over and there is time to decide which client will be favored next! Some cheery and optimistic consultants are even foolish enough to believe that the initial clients will have new assignments to offer indefinitely, and that word-of-mouth-advertising by satisfied clients will bring hordes of other clients knocking on their door. In any case, the happy but deluded consultant seeks a next client and assignment only after the current assignment has ended. And then comes the bitter disillusionment, the slow and painful revelation that the independent consultant cannot afford to ever stop marketing. Then comes the realization that marketing means seeking clients and pursuing assignments when you are busy and do not need new clients—at the moment. For even the most successful marketing usually produces results that do not materialize in work for many months, after persistent effort. That is what "not a one-call business" really means, and the time to learn it is "up front," before the disaster strikes.

THE "CALLS" ARE REALLY PHASES OF ACTIVITY

Consulting service is a multi-call business, and that means that the marketing is carried out in three major steps of finding sales leads as a necessary first step and converting those leads to sales through follow-up and closing as second and third steps. In fact, it is even misleading to refer to these as "steps," for that implies three discrete and single actions, whereas each of these "steps" consists of multiple and repetitive actions. They are, in fact, more accurately described as phases of activity, within each of which there may be many steps. The three phases are, however, easily identified functionally as follows:

1. Prospecting.
2. Following up.
3. Closing.

Those simple terms are highly meaningful to sales professionals for they encompass, in a kind of cryptic shorthand, the body and the essence of what we have already referred to here as multi-call marketing. They explain, in principle, all marketing for businesses that are not one-call businesses. The pattern of those three phases is the general pattern for marketing almost everything that requires repeated and extended sales effort.

This book will expand steadily on those phases—what they mean and how they must be accomplished, especially that most important first step of prospecting for sales leads, for marketing success overall depends heavily on that first phase. Let's have a brief look now at each of these phases.

Prospecting

Sales begin with sales leads—with prospects, and a most important part of marketing is the prospecting to produce those sales leads. These sales leads are generated in a great many ways. The person who walks into a retail store is a sales lead—a prospective customer and "hot" lead, who can usually be sold without as much effort as a "cold" lead because he or she entered the store ostensibly to buy something. Even if that prospect did not have some specific need in mind, he or she was probably in a buying mood.

A great many individuals entering the store represent sales leads that were the result of the store's advertising, of its being in a location where shoppers stroll past a display in the window, or even by pure chance because it is an emporium open to the public. Retail stores do their prospecting—generating sales leads—by whatever means will bring prospects into their stores.

Prospecting for potential buyers of automobiles is another matter. For the most part, it begins also by inducing prospects to visit the showroom through advertising appeals in newspapers, radio, and television. Still, a large percentage of those vistors are "just looking," and may or may not be seriously considering the purchase of a new automobile. Nevertheless, since they have entered the showroom, they are prospects, and the salesperson who is "next up" (most such establishments operate by permitting their salespeople to take turns trying to sell prospects) will approach such a visitor and attempt to follow up the lead represented by a presumed legitimate prospect for a new car.

Consulting is a bit different, of course. Consultants don't operate out of retail locations with doors open to the public, and most consultants do business with others in business, rather than with off-the-street consumers. Prospects don't usually visit the consultant (although there are exceptions to this), so it is up to the consultant to seize and keep the contact initiative. Overall, prospecting by consultants is an entirely different matter than any other kind of prospecting discussed here yet, and it is to be a major topic of discussion in this book.

Following Up

Once a sales lead is established, follow-up is essential. That means making serious efforts to fan the initial interest of the prospect into a flame of desire for the benefits you can bring. To a large degree the success of the follow-up depends on how well the earlier marketing has been done—on how good the sales leads are. That means how seriously the prospects are considering retaining you or any other consultant, perhaps. It means that sales success will depend to a large extent on the effectiveness of the prospecting. I will have a great deal more to say about that as we proceed.

Closing

Closing is a very much misunderstood term by those who are not familiar with sales and marketing, and even by some who are in sales positions. Those who are not in a position to know better believe that closing is winning the sale—getting the order—and they often speak of "closing the order" or "closing the sale" with that in mind. The sales professional knows better. He or she knows that closing means asking for the order through gentle nudges and suggestions. The sales professional knows that even prospects who are sold and want to buy will often not say "I'll take it" without being guided and induced to make the decision. The truly successful sales professional must *help* the prospect make the decision and place the order.

That isn't all of it. Closing has other uses, valuable uses that we will explore in great depth. Closing is a major sales tool, a "secret weapon" for sales experts. It's a well-known fact that many salespeople do a great job up to the point of closing and then lose sales because they have never learned how to close. But that really means that they have never learned how to *use* the great power of closing to win the sale. All really great sales professionals are expert closers. They couldn't be great sales professionals without being great closers. But there are many other related factors to study and learn. Let's preview a few of them here.

THE SUBTLE INFLUENCES

Just as buying a house or an automobile is a major commitment for most individuals, so is the retention of a consultant a major commitment for most executives. In fact, there is even more at stake for the prospective buyer in the latter case, for he or she may be risking even more than money. Consulting services are usually what retailers are likely to think of as "big tag" items, sales costing enough to represent risk to the buyer and compel him or her to think long and hard before making the commitment. But there is usually even more at risk: The risk may very well be the well-being of the entire company. Upon the consultant's recommendation may rest a major marketing commitment, an investment in a large-scale computer system, or some equally important outcome. Moreover, the executive responsible for the decision to retain you is probably quite conscious of personal risk—that is, that the success of his or her personal *career*—may very well depend directly on how well you do your job.

Of course, the reverse is also true: an outstandingly successful performance by you might do wonders for the career of that fortunate executive who was wise enough to retain you! The individuals to whom you must make your appeals and with whom you must ultimately negotiate cannot help but be concerned with the possible personal consequences to them of any business decision they make, and you must always be conscious of this important factor in your marketing.

Emotion Versus Reason

Under the circumstances described you can hardly expect casual decisions for any but perhaps an occasional small and not very important consulting task, at least with prospects who have no direct knowledge of you, what you can do, and how well you do it. The decisions will almost always be carefully reasoned ones. At the same time, that does not mean that the decisions will be based on reason alone. As you will soon see, that is a quite rare occurrence. There are emotional influences at work always in decisions to buy—or not to. We can see the phenomenon in the many cases of public figures—politicians, entertainers, sports figures, and even executives, occasionally—who remain popular, if they were well-liked and respected to begin with, despite scandalous revelations about them. Consider, for example, some who could or can do no wrong in the eyes of most of the general public— Franklin D. Roosevelt, Dwight Eisenhower, Ronald Reagan, and Lee Iaccoca, to name only a few. There is an almost instinctive reluctance by a great many people to believe ill of someone who is likable enough or commands great respect. At the least, the tendency is to be forgiving and regard any transgressions by such people more with humor and tolerance than with anger and resentment. On the other hand, the reverse is true also: We find it relatively easy to believe ill of those whom we regard with some distaste. Richard Nixon, in his greatest distress, won little sympathy from the public generally because he had never exhibited the warmth or charisma of many of those who became public heroes. A rather militant and combative personality, he commanded some degree of respect, but earned little affection, at least from the public. Nor does this factor of emotion versus reason apply to public figures alone; the phenomenon functions equally well with regard to anyone you know personally.

In your efforts both to market your personal consulting services (or anything else you offer for sale) and to carry out commitments resulting from sales, your clients will inevitably be influenced to a large degree by their personal impressions of and feelings toward you—by your very personality. If you are fortunate enough to have a charismatic persona, or at least are able to radiate warmth and charm, while inspiring respect, your tasks in both selling and satisfying clients with your performances will be greatly lightened.

Charisma is probably a fortunate accident of birth, a subtle aura, a talent or personality characteristic that is entirely instinctive and cannot be acquired. However, other traits of almost equal importance can be acquired, and we will consider them as we proceed.

Credibility

Credibility is a most important consideration in your marketing. It applies to both you, as a professional consultant, and to the individual project or set of services you propose to a prospective client. Note in TV commercials and all other advertising the concerted effort to persuade prospective buyers of the validity of the claims made, to make both the claims and the seller believable through a wide variety of devices.

Credibility is not achieved by logic and reason alone, nor even primarily on a rational basis. Again, your credibility depends largely on the prospect's emotional reaction to you, on whether the prospect *wants* to believe you and to find your claims and promises easily believable. It is a general truth that all of us tend strongly to believe what we wish to believe, what we would like to find true. (It is for that reason that arguments over religion and politics, subjects that are usually highly charged with emotion, virtually never change anyone's mind and so should probably be avoided.) "Proof" is generally in our individual perceptions far more than in our objective and rational judgment. That is the point of using popular public figures to endorse products: The assumption is that people will *want* to believe them.

The Confidence Factor

These factors add up to something that, for lack of a better term, we might call the *confidence factor*. It is the necessary ingredient in any sale that involves substantial risk for the purchaser. One large insurance company features a pair of cupped hands as its logo to signify that the prospect is in good hands and may have confidence in the company. Another uses the Rock of Gibraltar as its logo for much the same reason, as a symbol of absolute stability and strength.

Consider just a few of the many goods and services you buy where having confidence in the seller and in the seller's claims and promises is a major consideration in your buying decision:

Choosing a bank.
Buying a home.
Buying insurance.
Enrolling in college.
Selecting a physician.
Selecting a dentist.
Having expensive furniture upholstered or refinished.
Having your automobile repaired (especially major repairs).
Building an addition to your home.

It is not only the major purchases that involve risk or otherwise influence you to seek a seller in whom you can feel confidence. Even choosing a dentist or physician for an ordinary dental or physical checkup requires confidence. Choosing a consultant — and often the seminal decision to utilize consulting services — is in that same category.

Your Professional Image

To a large degree we are really discussing and considering your *professional* image. Roosevelt's image as a leader in difficult times inspired enough citizens to vote him into unprecedented third and fourth terms in office. Other public figures rise and fall on their images. The right image is a must for success in many undertakings. Just as Eisenhower won two terms—and could have won more, had the law allowed it— primarily because of his image. Gerald Ford was unable to win a full term because he had developed an unfavorable image. His successor, Jimmy Carter, fell victim to his own unfavorable image at the expiration of his single term. Opponents of Barry Goldwater succeeded in making him appear to be a hawk bent on making war, creating an image that destroyed his chances of winning the Oval Office. We are speaking entirely of image here—what people *appear* to others to be, which may or may not be reality.

Image is important to everyone who aspires to influence others in any way. In your marketing, and in your consulting work generally, your image translates to a large degree into the confidence factor, helping to lend credibility to you as a consultant generally as well as to your specific claims and promises. And your image becomes a prime factor for success in the prospecting activity that we will deal with as the first and probably most important element in your marketing activities overall.

Credentials

Closely related to all the foregoing factors and especially to *image* is that somewhat intangible set of records, characteristics, and other somewhat subtle factors referred to most commonly as *credentials*. In fact, in considering credentials and image together, their relationship is by no means certain—that is, whether your image stems in part from your credentials, as a reflection of your credentials, or the reverse. Certainly, they do relate to each other, in a kind of symbiosis, and certainly your image is often judged by others as one of your important credentials.

Credentials are of two classes. You lay claim to and establish certain *personal* credentials, those factors that qualify you as a consultant expert in your general field. They may include such factors as formal education and degrees earned, awards and honors, personal experience, publications, and other achievements in your field. But you often need to claim and establish *special* credentials as qualifications for special projects you pursue, where you must compete with other consultants specifically for a given contract. These may include any of your personal credentials that are germane, but they may also include facilities, resources, and special experience.

From the prospect's viewpoint, credentials are viewed and evaluated *rationally* and *emotionally*. Your possession of certain academic credits—degrees from colleges and universities—may be judged rationally, for example, but the identity of the college or university where you earned those degrees may have an emotional value. A degree from Harvard, Yale, or Massachusetts Institute of Technology carries a great deal more weight with many prospective clients than does a similar degree from Podunk U. In fact, the latter might actually be a decidedly negative factor. Unjust? Irrational? Certainly, but still a fact. That, you must live with. Most of us, including all those potential and prospective clients, are far less rational and far more emotional in our judgments than we care to admit even to ourselves. I once did work for a client who was a "self-made man," and he was slightly suspicious and mistrustful of anyone with a degree! (It was probably resentment, but he rationalized his prejudice in various ways.) I knew of another executive who would give short shrift to a man who smoked a pipe. He was convinced that pipe smokers are slow thinkers and lethargic individuals. And of course there are men who resist accepting women as competent in consulting and in perhaps most other fields, persuading themselves that women are too emotional and otherwise unqualified for professional and executive positions.

Each of these is a *perception*, a factor that we will discuss only briefly here, but one that will surface as an important consideration in discussions of all aspects of marketing. If we speak of *image* from the consultant's viewpoint, we must also consider *perception* from the client's or prospect's viewpoint.

Perception

Despite all efforts to make truth an absolute quantity, it remains inevitably a subjective factor. We all have our own truths, arrived at by the evidence of our senses, our reasoning, and our emotions. Perhaps we rely over much on the evidence of our own senses, since we are easily deceived into believing that we saw something we did not, in fact, see. When it is obvious that our senses have been tricked, as in the case of the professional magician's legerdemain, we accept that; we "know," via our logical analysis—which really means via our past everyday experience—that the beautiful assistant on stage could not have truly vanished, so we know that our eyes—our senses—were deceived.

On the other hand most of us accept many things as true because we know that people generally accept them—for example, that the earth orbits the sun, and that we are compelled to maintain a large military organization for our survival because we are faced with a strong and determined enemy.

We believe that we arrive at these and other perceptions of truth by exercising reason. The fact is that emotions play a large part in the process, although we may deny it. We accept as true that which we have been taught is true through our basic education, through our observations of what the world generally accepts as true, and through learning what recognized authorities state is true because we would certainly look foolish challenging this accepted body of knowledge. And although most of us might be quick to deny that we permit emotions to color our perceptions, even the denial is an emotional reaction because we are most reluctant to admit even to ourselves, much less to others, that we are less than totally logical in our thinking.

On the other hand, we know very well what is "safe" to challenge, what subjects we may think, opine, and argue about without being considered somewhat odd, if not brain-damaged. And in those areas— politics, for example—we are truly emotional in our perceptions. We even admit—at least occasionally—to emotional bias about some of these subjects.

This is a vital consideration in marketing. Your image and your credibility are very dependent on the perceptions of the prospective client. Truth is whatever the prospect regards as truth. Perhaps a court of law would not accept a sports star's assurance that some brand of beer is fun to drink or some advertised brand of golf ball is superior to all others, but prospects do regularly accept such assurances as proof, and they demonstrate that acceptance by buying the product.

THE FACTORS THAT AFFECT PERCEPTION

You have it in your power to influence the perceptions of your prospective clients. That, in fact, is one of the major objectives of advertising, an objective often referred to as "positioning."

Positioning

There appears to be a great deal of uncertainty as to what *positioning* is and what it means, but it is a simple, not an especially complex idea. It is simply shaping the prospect's perception of what you and your product or service are—creating a (perceived) *position* in the marketplace for yourself or your product/service. Maytag, through an extended TV campaign featuring the "lonely" Maytag repair man, has worked hard at building a position of reliability and rare failure of their product. Ford Motor Company, with their "better idea" campaign of a few years ago, was working hard at building an image of creative innovation and latest ideas in their cars. Chrysler Corporation works at building a position of complete confidence in the quality of their product by offering unprecedented extended guarantees. United Airlines "friendly skies" campaign has been working for a long time to create a position as the courteous, cheery host among airlines.

There are many aspects or parameters along which to establish a position or *set of positions*. Here are some general classes or categories into which you will inevitably fit, with or without your deliberate effort:

- Price.
- Quality.
- Exclusivity.
- Popularity.

The world of prospective clients will fit you into positions in these categories, no matter what you do. You can permit your image for each of these to be established by chance—by spontaneous judgment of prospects and perhaps by fallout from competitive advertising—or you can go about engineering your image vis-à-vis each of these (and other) parameters, so that your position is what you want it to be. Consider just a few of the basic elements and choices.

Price: You can go high or low, depending on your overall marketing strategy and business philosophy.

Quality: In the minds of many, price and quality are linked directly to each other. If you shoot for low price you have an uphill battle to establish a perception of quality. It is difficult to separate the two.

Exclusivity: Again, linked to price. If you are so high priced as to exclude all but the "carriage trade," you will probably have some snob appeal—if you take care that the rest of your image fits the position. It's perhaps a bit risky, but it works very well—and profitably—for some.

Popularity: Popularity is the opposite of exclusivity. A certain kind of prospect is influenced by numbers, and will follow the crowd. Popularity, however, normally goes with low price; it's hard to separate the two.

These are by no means the only positioning choices and decisions to make, although they are basic ones. Here are a few other characteristics you may or may not wish to establish for you services and/or products, if you offer consulting products also:

- Bold innovation.
- Aggressive pioneering.
- Cautious conservatism.
- Rockbound reliability.
- Take-charge services.
- Close liaison (handholding with client).

Aside from the general image you pursue, you have specific claims of results (benefits). These, like your general image or position, may be conservative and modest or they may be extreme and dramatic.

You can't be all things to all prospects. If you try to be, you are on an almost sure road to failure. You must make choices. That does not mean that you must choose one of the extremes of each case, however; you can middle-road it, if you prefer. You will be in good company, if you do so; by far the majority choose that middle road. That means maximum competition, of course, one of the drawbacks of that route. On the other hand, middle-roadism also suggests mediocrity, and your position may be so read by many prospects. You many find it desirable to occupy a position at one of the less-crowded extremes that are available.

You can, of course, be middle road in some respects and extreme in others; there is no requirement that you be extreme or middle road in all parameters. Consider this, however: the more extreme or dramatic your claim of superiority or benefit, the more difficult it is to prove your case and thus the more evidence you must produce. At the same time, bear in mind that the more exciting and desirable your promised benefit is, the more the prospect *wants* to believe it, and people tend quite strongly to believe what they earnestly want to believe. That is why the late Joe Karbo was successful in selling a reported 600,000 copies of his little paperback book, *The Lazy Man's Way to Riches* for $10 a copy: Readers of his full-page advertisements were eager to believe that Karbo could show them the way to acquiring wealth of their own, and he was an expert enough copywriter to help them rationalize their desires and gamble $10 with him. Nor was Karbo the only one who managed to achieve great success with extravagant promises and skillful appeals to the desire to believe; it has been done again and again by others, and the principles are as sound today as they ever were: A promised benefit that the prospects are eager to believe in, and help in finding the promised benefit credible. Those are the major ingredients of all selling.

WORKING ON YOUR IMAGE

As a consultant you are not selling snake oil or get-rich-quick schemes. Quite the contrary, you must scrupulously avoid the appearance of huckstering, unctuous platitudes, and high-pressure tactics. Your objective must be to establish a conservative, dignified, and professional image. You must come across to others as enthusiastic and highly competent, but still low-key and confident in your own abilities. You must not "protest too much," and you must not try to be the font of all knowledge and wisdom; an outsized ego can be fatal. There is nothing wrong with saying, "I don't know," to some questions, and it is usually helpful to exhibit a little humility.

Always avoid the extremes. You must try to somehow strike a balance between the extremes of excessive modesty or humility—which shows up to others as a total lack of confidence in your own abilities—and excessively large ego, which is likely to come across to others as bluff and bravado. Bear in mind that strangers will tend to accept you as being what you appear to be. Therefore, be careful that you do not "protest too much"—try too hard, and thus too obviously.

DEVELOPING THE RIGHT SELF-IMAGE

Undoubtedly the easiest image to project is the one you have of yourself. (Your self-image tends to show through ultimately no matter how hard you work at trying to appear to be other than the person you think you are.) Therefore, working on your self-image ought to be a high priority. It is not easy for most of us to develop an accurate self-image, and probably a majority of us tend to cheat ourselves in this. (Some psychologists have noted that even among the most successful people there are many who secretly believe that they have been given much too much undeserved credit and success, and they fear that they will ultimately be "found out" as frauds or impostors!)

A poor self-image is a common ailment. It reflects or is caused by a number of feelings. Scan this list and see if you recognize any of these or their variants in your own feelings:

Lack of confidence in your own abilities.
Lack of faith in your own eventual success.
Suspicion that you do not deserve recognition and success.
Feeling that you have been given credit you don't deserve.
Feeling that you can't live up to others' expectations of you.
Feeling that you will eventually be found out to be less than you
    appear.
Belief that your competitors are more competent than you.
Fear that you will never be an unqualified success.
Fear that you will never fully satisfy a client.
Suspicion that others know you are not as good as they are.
Fear that others do not truly respect you.
Fear that you are aiming too high.
Feeling about a current or past success of "getting away" with it.

Such doubts and fears are as common as they are irrational. One of the most effective weapons for combating them is the knowledge that such fears and doubts are extremely common, experienced by a great many people, even those you most admire as successful and competent individuals. Exceedingly few people do not or have not in the past had many such feelings. It is important to know this and to remember it; if such fears trouble you, you are most certainly not alone, and the mere knowledge that you are not alone is a great help.

You must judge yourself—for self-image is your appraisal of your-self—by comparison with others or with whatever you believe to be the norm. But you must estimate that norm on realistic grounds, as what most people in your profession actually are. The fact is that prob-ably most of those you admire as highly successful and highly able are not more able than you but have managed to overcome their own self-doubts (although probably few ever put those doubts completely to rest) and have developed a comfortable feeling of confidence in them-selves. When that feeling exists, it radiates and shines through in all your actions.

Try to see yourself through others' eyes (especially those of strang-ers, who can be totally unemotional and thus objective about you) and bear in mind that they are probably far better judges of you and what you are than you are yourself. If you speak publicly and are greeted with applause when you finish, for example, accept that as a sincere gesture of appreciation for a good presentation. If you are compli-mented on a piece of work or advice, accept that in the same spirit. If you did exceptionally well academically or won special honors and awards, remind yourself of those achievements as evidence of com-petence. All successes you have had in the past or are having currently ought to be used to reassure yourself of your own competence and right to success.

PART II

THE PRACTICAL CONSIDERATIONS IN CONSULTING SUCCESS

There is often a vast difference between theory and practice, as experience soon teaches. Moreover, what has been an effective practice for one individual in one place and time may not be as effective for another individual in another place and time. The doctrine is a simple one: Whatever works is right.

CHAPTER 3

THE FIRST STEP: PROSPECTING

Is there such a thing as "a born salesman?" Maybe. But most top salespeople get their results through logical and methodical processes.

WHAT IS PROSPECTING?

There are prospects and then there are prospects. More precisely and cogently, there are prospects and then there are sales leads. Anyone and everyone who could possibly become your client is a prospect, but only those who have given you some indication of interest in becoming clients are true sales leads. Even then the quality of each sales lead is in direct proportion to how serious the interest and possibility of an order are. In any case, only true sales leads merit the time and effort you must invest to try to make clients of the prospects. Prospecting is therefore the quest for sales leads among all prospects, in search of those few who are most likely to become clients.

KNOCKING ON DOORS

There are many ways to prospect, to seek sales leads, and to follow them up. A door-to-door salesperson prospects by knocking on doors and making a statement designed to arouse interest in his or her product. If the reaction of the prospect brought to the door by the knock is totally negative then the prospect is never elevated to the status of sales lead. The salesperson moves on to the next door, to seek out another prospect to turn into a sales lead and a sale. Door-to-door selling is a viable way of seeking sales leads and generating sales because, (1) almost everyone living in a house or apartment is a prospect; (2) this prospecting can be carried out with enough efficiency to make it practicable; and (3) either the sale is small enough that it can be consummated or plans can be made for a positive sale followup. If the salesperson is effective enough, door-to-door prospecting and selling can be done with adequate efficiency.

"Effective enough" means several things here. Different salespeople operate on different premises, often with equal results, as I have learned by knowing and observing a number of experts at door-to-door selling. The almost diametrically opposed methods of two experts I knew illustrates this well.

Expert Harry L. was persistent, patient, quick-witted, and had a most pleasant, upbeat personality. He truly believed that every day was the best day of the year, and everything in his manner showed it. Harry did not give up until the door was virtually slammed in his face. He got through the door and made a sale in many cases where another salesperson would have given up and looked for another prospect. Moreover, once Harry had turned a prospect into a customer, he pressed on with all kinds of spontaneous "special deals" and promotions to maximize the size of each sale. Where almost anyone else would have been pleased to sell a quart of furniture polish or a floor sweeper, Harry would try—and often succeed—in selling cans of furniture polish by the dozen and two or even three sweepers to the same customer. He worked hard at selling—at making sales and building the size of each sale—and he succeeded.

Expert Tom W. didn't look or act like an expert at all. Rather laconic, he greeted people casually and told them briefly what he was selling, then ambled on cheerfully and without hesitation to the next door if confronted with the slightest sales resistance. He knocked on many doors every day, far more than Harry L. did, saw many more prospects, spent less time in closing and negotiating sales with those who became customers, yet achieved net results about on a par with Harry's sales.

Tom W. could never have operated the way Harry L. did. But then Harry was not constitutionally suited to Tom's style. Harry felt that every prospect he failed to convert into a sales lead and then a customer was a lost opportunity, a personal failure on his part. Tom thought of prospecting as a direct and swift way to separate the prospects from the sales leads—and to find the customers. He therefore never hesitated to say goodbye and go on to the next prospect.

Harry's premise was that efficiency meant maximum selling effort, while Tom's premise was that efficiency meant knocking on the greatest number of doors every day—by screening the most prospects to find true sales leads and close the sales. Both theories worked.

Knocking on doors is one way of prospecting, and probably the bulk of professional selling in the United States is done that way. Selling is literally knocking on doors, although most of it is only figurative, represented by the millions of salespeople who call on offices, retailers, wholesalers, and others. And some "knocking on doors" is done by using the U.S. Postal Service to do the knocking via mailed sales literature. Still more "knocking" is done by telephone and even by general advertising via newspapers, magazines, radio, and TV. All of this is prospecting—generating sales leads to follow up—and is based on these common concepts:

1. Identifying the prospects.
2. Screening the prospects to find or generate the sales leads.
3. Screening the sales leads to find or generate the customers and sales.

IDENTIFYING PROSPECTS

Identifying prospects is usually easy enough. Men are the main prospects for products used and worn by men. But how about all the women who buy men's products for husbands and male friends? It is the buyers, not the users, who are the prospects, and they are not always the same individuals. This is especially true when you are selling gift merchandise. But it is also true in many other cases. Purchasing agents for corporations, buyers for department stores, and procurement officials for government agencies are prospects although they buy for others' use.

There is rarely a single class of prospects. If you sell medical equipment you have one class of users—medical specialists—but you have several classes of buyers. For some medical equipment items you also have the public at large, because some items are suitable for use in the home: thermometers, crutches, bedpans, and numerous other items fit that dual description. But even among those items that only physicians and other medical specialists use, some are personal equipment—stethoscopes, for example—while others may be sold for the office of the private practitioner, and still others would be purchased only for and by the large clinic or hospital.

Analyzing Needs

Identifying prospects begins with noting the obvious ones. But if you stop after that you may be severely short-changing your marketing. Not all prospects are obvious. Even a brief analysis often reveals that.

Users Versus Buyers

First, discriminate between users and buyers. Those who use your services are not necessarily those who pay for them. Consider the case of selling seminar registration and attendance, for example. When I offer to impart the secrets of independent consulting success in a seminar, the usual buyer is the individual attendee, who is the usual user of the service. But when I conduct a seminar on how to write better proposals for government contracts, many of those attending—sometimes all—are the users of the information and products dispensed in the seminar, but their employers are the buyers. Both the attendees and the employers are among my prospects; I must attract both. In some other cases the seminar will be on a custom basis for a single buyer, who may be a government agency, a college division or department, an association, or a privately-held corporation. So all of these are among my prospects, whether I am offering my prospects an open-registration (open to the public) seminar or a custom-designed, in-house seminar.

Who, Finally, Is the Prospect?

So far, the analysis is a simple one. It addresses only two questions: Who can make good personal use of what we are selling and who benefits most from it? But there is a third question, too: Do the answers to these questions point to the same individual or organization? Yes, *organization*, for that is sometimes the critical question, as, for example, when the federal government spends huge sums of money to produce and provide products or services to state and local governments (a fairly common situation in government contracting).

What Does What We Sell *Do* for Prospects?

Somehow, we must make a sensible reconciliation of prospect and benefit. Consider whether what we are selling has other, less obvious uses than those immediately apparent. If so, does that change the definition(s) of our prospects?

That question may be linked to how you define and identify what you are selling. For my first seminar offered to the public in proposal writing, I chose to mail to high-technology firms. These were generally electronics-based organizations that I knew to be government contractors. I picked that pool of prospects because they reflected my own background, the type of firm and business environment I knew best. I did well with that group, too. That first seminar drew 54 attendees in response to a modest mailing. This was a surprising result and more significant than I realized at the time. Later I saw how shortsighted my original identification of my prospects was. Most of what I had to say on the subject of writing winning proposals could be generalized with only slight changes and thus made suitable for *anyone* pursuing government contracts — not only for high-tech firms. This opened up — and identified — a much wider range and larger pool of prospects. Subsequent seminar attendees represented organizations offering products and services in a significantly wider range of activities — training, health services, publications, and others.

In time I also diversified the presentation and further broadened the appeal — and numbers of prospects — by stressing other aspects of government marketing in addition to proposal writing. I soon found that attendees also displayed great interest in cost analyses, in bidding strategies, and in sundry other aspects, such as marketing in general. The growing experience in conducting the seminars, as well as in marketing them, influenced my marketing philosophy and helped it to mature. Later, when I began to present these workshops on a custom basis for various kinds of organizations, I put this experience to good use.

Without the gradual broadening of the presentation so that it built up
the benefits delivered and thus widened the appeal, it is doubtful that
I would have made many custom presentations.

My success in prospecting and in closing was in direct proportion
to my understanding of the prospects' needs and interests. The degree
to which your presentations reveal and appeal to the prospects' most
urgent interests is the same degree to which those prospects are inspired to respond. You must either manage to gain a true understanding of the needs and interests of the prospects you have chosen, or
select a class of prospects whose needs and interests you already understand. The adage about the difficulty of selling refrigerators to Es-
kimos or carrying coals to Newcastle is as true as ever.

First Steps in Marketing

The first step in marketing is to decide what you are selling; the second
is to pin down who is most likely to buy what you are selling. That is
how most entrepreneurs approach marketing, whether consciously or
instinctively. But that is not necessarily the way to do it. You can reverse that sequence: identify first the buyers you are best able to reach,
and then decide what you can sell them. That is also practiced widely.
Many consultants become consultants primarily on that basis—whom
they know and whom can they reach with their own services or on
behalf of clients. Henry Kissinger, for example, set up a consulting
service after leaving the government. He could hardly help but trade
on his principle assets: his international reputation as a diplomat, and
a mover and shaker who could reach, influence, or advise clients on
how to influence the heads of state of many governments—a kind of
super lobbyist/consultant/advisor. Many former Congress members
choose to remain in Washington as political consultants and/or lobbyists, since they have the personal contact capability for reaching those
still seated in the legislative bodies. Presumably, they can also influence those who enact the national legislation and make national policy.
That is the perception of those who wish to influence members of
Congress. So, many former members of Congress choose to stay in
Washington as registered (and paid) lobbyists because they can do the
double selling job necessary—selling their services to client organizations and selling their clients' arguments and appeals to current
members of Congress.

More common is a hybrid of the two approaches. In probably a majority of cases the entrepreneur, especially the consultant, decides on something to sell, identifies prospects, and begins to sell, but in the face of accumulating experience finds it necessary to modify what he or she sells and/or to whom he or she sells it. All ventures inevitably change, some gradually, some abruptly. Part of that change is due to external influences—most businesses would be obsolete in five to ten years if they did not adjust and grow—but much is also due to the improved vision and wisdom that come with growing experience. Sometimes the change is gradual and subtle; in other cases it is abrupt and radical. Bernard Gallagher, a New York seller of stocks and bonds, launched a free newsletter as a marketing tool. He soon discovered that readers valued it highly enough to pay for it and began to charge a modest subscription fee. Eventually he found his newsletter far more profitable than the original business he had intended to market with it and abandoned that original enterprise in favor of newsletter publishing. Another entrepreneur, Matthew Lesko, founded Washington Researchers, Inc., a firm dedicated to aiding organizations searching for information available from government sources, sold that portion of the enterprise—research services—to another organization and devoted more time to training clients in how to do their own searching in government files. Later he progressed (or digressed) to writing books and newsletters on where and how to find all sorts of information in all kinds of media, operating as both a free-lance writer and as Information USA, which is also the title of one of his several successful books.

In the first case, entrepreneur Gallagher stuck with his list of prospects, but changed what he was selling. Instead of selling stocks and bonds he sold information, tips, and suggestions or advice—consultative services in the form of a newsletter (and ultimately more than one newsletter). In the second case, entrepreneur Lesko stuck with his original concept—information and how/where to find it—but to different prospects, to individuals (book and newsletter readers) for the most part, rather than organizations. Both entrepreneurs were, or became, consultants, each in his own manner, selling a service—information and advice—in the form of products: books and newsletters.

Prospecting is tied closely to what you are selling. If you change what you are selling, for any reason, you must consider what it does to your prospecting—whether it changes the definition of your proper prospects.

The Service Aspect of All Enterprises

The distinction or dividing line between services and products is by
no means clear-cut. A sound argument is made by many that all businesses are service businesses. That is not difficult to demonstrate quite
logically, because all customers buy whatever they buy for what their
purchases *do* for them rather than for what they *are*. That consideration lies at the heart of prospecting. It is at the heart of the question:
What are you selling? In the end you can only answer this usefully by
responding to another question, What does it do for the buyer? Never
forget that people buy for their reasons, not yours, and those reasons
are always a belief that their self-interests are served by the purchase.

Individuals who attend my seminars on how to succeed as an independent consultant are motivated by the desire for success in an independent enterprise. But as prospects they fit a variety of descriptions
or definitions. Some are in positions they wish to leave in favor of
launching their own independent ventures. Others are unemployed at
the moment and have decided that consulting represents a tempting
opportunity. Some are already in a related enterprise and want to diversify into consulting. Still others are already consulting but are in
need of greater success in it. The common denominator is that these
people want to earn more money via building an independent consulting enterprise. To make contact emotionally with all prospects it is
necessary to appeal to more than the desire to make money as an independent consultant. It is necessary to help each prospect "identify"
with the appeal, to recognize himself or herself as one to whom the
message is addressed. To do that it is necessary that you have thought
out all those definitions of your prospects.

Prospects into Sales Leads: The Metamorphosis

To turn those prospects into sales leads you must not only have defined
them, but you must include each in your appeal: Each prospect must
recognize that he or she is being addressed directly. It is important not
only to understand the motivations of the prospects, but also to list
them. For example, that consultant who is already established but who
needs more success may feel the need for help and guidance in winning clients. So the appeal ought to mention this as a feature of the
seminar. Another prospect may be attracted by the idea of diversifying

his or her existent practice through launching a newsletter or undertaking speaking engagements. Still another individual wants to know
more about how to negotiate contracts. While each attendee may sign
up to learn how to earn more money, each has his or her own idea
about what he or she prefers to do to make more money as an independent consultant. I love to present seminars and speak to groups, but
others are terrified at the thought of mounting the speaker's platform.
I enjoy writing, but there are others who detest it. On the other hand,
I love to market but do not like cold selling. Others have no hesitancy
about knocking on doors and finding ways to get into inner offices in
quest of clients. This is why your prospecting must be based on a
thorough analysis and understanding of motivation, and appeals to the
right "hot buttons" that work for different prospects. Here are just a
few ideas that would generate the interest of some prospects if they
read them in your initial appeals. Remember that each of these is a
promise to the prospect, and you must be prepared to deliver what you
promise. These items are almost sure to appeal to some prospects for
a seminar on how to succeed as an independent consultant:

- How to diversify for greater profits.
- Generating new-client leads without leaving your office.
- Newsletters for direct and indirect profits.
- Money-making seminars.
- 7 ways to increase your income.
- Mail-order-bookstore profits.
- Getting clients to recommend you to others.
- 3 ways to increase the size of your contracts.
- How to work successfully from your own home.
- How to incorporate yourself.
- Do-it-yourself legal procedures for consultants.
- How to make your clients love you.

Some of these are generalizations; others are quite specific. It is
useful to have both. Some prospects will translate generalizations into
their personal terms; others require specific items. All are motivated
by personal considerations.

On the other hand, when an employer sends employees to a seminar on marketing to the government and/or on writing proposals in quest of contracts, the primary and overall motivation is more profitable operation, but the recognized route to that is increased success in winning contracts. The employer will send to the seminar those employees who are involved in writing proposals and otherwise contributing to the effort to win new contracts. The appeal must therefore help the employer perceive who should attend the seminar. Possible lines to sharpen perception are these:

- How to write winning proposals.
- How to *appear* to be the low bidder (even when you are not)!
- How to overcome typical proposal problems.
- The common deadly errors you must avoid.
- Contracting hazards: how to cope successfully with them.
- Taking advantage of being a small business.
- The bid/no-bid analysis: saving your time and money.
- The public bid opening: Should you be there?
- Best and final offers: What are they? What should you do about them?
- The contracting officer: friend or foe?
- Marketing intelligence: how to gather it.
- Freedom of Information Act: how to use it effectively.

Again, we use a mix of generalizations and specific statements to maximize the appeal, to help turn prospects into sales leads.

What, Then, *Is* a Sales Lead?

A prospect is anyone who (according to your logic) *ought* to be interested in your offer. A sales lead is anyone who has given you any reason to believe that he or she *is* interested in your offer. It is that simple and that complicated. Even then the question arises as to whether it is truly a sales lead.

The problems and potential problems with what appear to be legitimate sales leads are several. In marketing we are all most eager to find positive results from our prospecting—sales leads, that is—and we sometimes grasp at straws, eager to change prospects into sales leads. We tend therefore to interpret mild curiosity as sincere interest, and waste a great deal of time pursuing the idly curious who are not truly potential buyers—or trying to sell those who are sincerely interested but who cannot become customers because they do not have the power to purchase. This includes staff people in organizations—even executives—who do not have the funds available in their budgets and/or cannot get funds authorized for one reason or another. Sometimes even those who appear to you to be senior executives and officials because they occupy luxurious offices have neither the authority to make deals nor enough influence to persuade their seniors to do business with you. Even worse, sometimes such people are not very busy and so are delighted to squander time. That can easily lead you to believe that you are making great progress toward a sale when you are simply wasting valuable time with someone who has nothing better to do and regards chatting with you as a break in the routine of a dull day! (This is especially a hazard in large government agencies and companies big enough to have become almost as bureaucratic as is the government.)

There are remedies for this kind of problem. The first is to be aware that the problem exists. The second is to guard against permitting yourself to be deceived by outward appearances. Some highly-placed and truly senior executives function in quite small, modestly furnished offices. Many dress quite simply as well, while relatively junior people work hard at trying to win impressive offices and dress "for success." The third is to work hard at learning as much as you can about the individual. Try to discover what his or her job title and duties are, and try to judge the relative authority of the position. See if you can learn how high in the organization they report, for example. Be aware that junior people are sometimes assigned impressive titles. Ask discreetly if you can see an organization chart, professing deep interest, for example.

There are other tactful ways to find out whether you are pursuing serious business or wasting your time. These measures are known as *qualifying* the lead or prospect, which means simply determining whether you are following up a true sales lead.

Qualifying Leads

Fortunately, the method used to find out the most important thing about the sales leads also happens to be the most effective way to qualify the lead. To many sales professionals the only thing necessary to find out is: *Can* the prospect make the purchase?

If the prospect is an individual or represents a very small business, the question may come down to whether the prospect can afford you and your services. In the case of the larger organization, where there is no serious financial doubt that the organization can retain you, there is still the question of whether your contact has the budget, authority, or influence necessary to retain you. So it is, in the end, the same question: *Can* the prospect do business with you? Asking this significant question usually tells you what you want to know rather quickly.

You must ask the question diplomatically, not abruptly, even though you don't want to wait too long to find out whether you are wasting your time. So, after a decent interval—enough time to get acquainted and discuss the possibility of a contract—it is time for the question. You can ask it tactfully by a casual, matter-of-fact inquiry along the lines, "Has this project been budgeted yet?" or, "Are funds presently available for this work?"

If the answer is no, the next question is, "Have you any idea when this is likely to be funded?" or, "Is there some way I can help you get authorization for this?" In some cases it may be, "Would we have to get approval from some other folks to go ahead with this?" "We" is far more tactful than "you" in this example because it doesn't challenge the person's image and prestige. "You" might easily be taken as a sneering assumption that the prospect is an employee of little authority and importance. It also recognizes the truth that you must be ready to help an individual sell you and your services to others in his organization. (In many organizations even people at fairly high levels are quite limited in what they can do entirely on their own authority.) I have run into this situation on many occasions, and found many prospects understandably reluctant—perhaps a bit embarrassed—to raise the subject on their own initiative or at a loss as to how to raise it. Frequently I have found them grateful that I anticipated and understood their problems. This can launch a cordial relationship that will turn out to your advantage ultimately.

Answers to such questions tell you what the true status of the situation is, what authority your contact has, and how good the chances are for a contract. Frankly, a negative answer to the first question is usually—but not always—an indication that you should say goodbye quickly. There are cases where you can persuade the individual to introduce you to someone who will prove to be a much better prospect, or you may get information that you can use to pursue a more promising prospect in the same organization. In any case you must qualify the leads. If a lead seems too good to be true, it probably is. Don't guess: *qualify*. And don't be too quick to give up on the organization when the individual proves to be an unqualified prospect. He or she may be the key to a payoff prospect in the organization. When you believe that to be the case, be especially diplomatic. See if you can't make a useful sales ally — an asset — out of the lead that did not qualify.

CHAPTER 4

THE METHODS OF PROSPECTING

There are right and wrong ways to do everything, and prospecting for sales leads is no exception to this. Still, there are few absolutes in the world, and prospecting is not an exception to this, either.

KNOCKING ON DOORS

A majority of prospecting is, in its initial stage, a kind of knocking on doors — philosophically, if not literally. Nearly all prospecting is a kind of knocking on doors, with the proviso that it is often *selective*. Unless what you are selling is of potential interest and value to virtually every household, you don't waste your time, energy, and money knocking on the doors of those whom you know or can judge to be most unlikely to be good prospects. Instead, you seek one or more means to reach those whom you have identified as proper prospects. There are a number of ways in which you can do this. Exploring these is the objective of this chapter. Dividing the methods of prospecting into the two classes of general knocking on doors and selective knocking on doors is only one way of separating and classifying methods of prospecting. In this chapter we will be looking at other philosophical approaches to prospecting, as well as other methods.

PROACTIVE VERSUS REACTIVE

The world's best known and most successful sales professionals are all believers in and practitioners of proactive sales methods. They do not wait for prospects to come to them, but actively and energetically seek out potential buyers and work aggressively at turning as many as possible into sales leads. Unlike the typical retail merchants, who open their doors and wait for prospects to enter, these sales experts pursue prospects by mail, telephone and in person, in quest of sales.

Even retailers are not totally reactive and passive in their prospecting. They advertise, sponsor various promotions, and exercise some initiative in bringing prospects to and through their doors. However, so that we may make the main points entirely clear, we are going to pretend that it is a black-and-white issue and that all prospecting is either proactive/aggressive or reactive/passive. We define proactive/ aggressive prospecting as going out to find the prospects, whereas reactive/passive marketing is inducing prospects to approach you.

For example, the siding salesperson who walks around looking at houses that appear to need siding and then sees if he or she can arouse the owner's interest in new siding is being proactive and aggressive. The siding merchant who runs newspaper advertisements and/or broadcast commercials inviting people to call and get more information is practicing reactive/passive prospecting, at least by our definitions here.

You may infer from these statements that proactive prospecting is absolutely and unexceptionally the right way—the positive way—while reactive marketing is wrong—the negative way. Certainly, many sales professionals have implied that clearly enough or stated it specifically in their many books on the subject. It is not my intention to pass judgment, although I will confess to a personal bias in favor of aggressive marketing. That bias is strictly philosophical, an expression of my own tendencies to what I consider to be positive action. I recognize, rationally if not emotionally, that the issue is not quite as clear-cut as I have suggested. There are hybrid methods that fall somewhere between the extremes suggested by these definitions, and we will look at all methods that have any applicability to selling your consulting services and related products, if any. In the final analysis, I still believe what I once was taught quite forcefully in the Infantry School at Fort Benning, Georgia: Whatever works is right. Isn't that the final test?

WHATEVER WORKS. . .

The world houses a great many individuals who will never hesitate to tell you that you are doing things in an entirely wrong way, that what you are doing will never work, and/or that they can show you the right way. (They even imply that only *they* know the right way!) Many, if not most, achievements of note have been made not only in spite of such self-appointed experts with unfailing wisdom and vision, but also by ignoring conventional wisdom and other people's rules. Somehow those experts knew that railroads would never carry people at speeds higher than 30 miles per hour because it would be impossible to breathe while traveling at high speed. Similar experts knew that the steamboat, the electric light, the telephone, television, and the automobile self-starter, among many other inventions, were impossible dreams, and they could "prove" it by their logical analyses. They condemned inventors as fools, as they did Montgomery Ward when he created the unconditional money-back guarantee in mail order merchandising, setting a new standard for business in general as well as for the direct mail business.

In the face of this, common sense dictates that we keep our minds open in marketing, as in other activities, and accept success or the lack of it as the final arbiter of what is right and what is wrong. And it is this attitude that I urge on you, despite my own admitted predilection for the more aggressive means of finding or creating clients. (The question of whether we *create* or *find* clients merits some discussion later.) A few case histories illustrate the folly of being sure that we know in advance with any certainty what will and what will not produce good results.

A FEW FOR-INSTANCES

A "for instance" is not a proof, and these examples are not offered as proof of anything except that human behavior, generally is quite unpredictable. That is why marketing in general and prospecting in particular can never be an exact science but must always remain far more art than science.

Mail order, also called *direct mail*, is an excellent example of this, largely because it has perhaps more than its share of experts who con-

stantly utter their wisdom as immutable truth. In my early ventures
into this field, offering my consulting services via mail (I started in
direct-mail consultation by offering help to executives in devising effective résumés), I sat patiently and attentively at the feet of those
experts I could find and listened to whatever pearls they had to offer.
My mentors assured me that the summer months, starting as early as
May, were a dead loss in mail order. They said I would almost surely
lose my shirt if I risked my capital in warm-weather promotions. The
right time was fall and winter, starting immediately after Labor Day.
I was assured by all. One, in fact, was all but rubbing his hands together exultantly as he spoke of "settling down to a long winter of
making money" with his own mail order business.

These sages were not completely wrong. They were right—in some
years. In others—they were dead wrong. In some years the summer
months were highly profitable, while the post-Labor Day surge of
business often did not materialize at all. One year, January was my
best month of the year; another year I "died" in January and came back
to life in February or March. Some years the best month was June or
July.

The belief that business always dies in the summer is rooted in business tradition. But today many people have air conditioning in their
homes and in their cars. Almost all stores and shopping malls are air
conditioned, so the basic reason for the summer slump of years ago—
it was too hot to shop or even to hang around town—simply does not
exist anymore.

In one case I compiled my knowledge of, and advice in, marketing
to government agencies into a book that I published myself and titled
Anyone Can Do Business with the Government and began to promote it
via direct mail. I combined that book, a directory of government agencies, and a subscription to a newsletter I published on the same subject
for a package price of about $89.95. I made up a two-page circular and
had one of my expert friends review it. He immediately condemned it
as totally unsuitable and doomed to total failure. Unfortunately—or
perhaps it was really fortunately—I had already had a considerable
number of these circulars printed and was too niggardly (that is my
nature!) to waste them, so I gambled the postage. To my delight, they
were quite effective, bringing in many orders and producing a surprisingly profitable venture.

What is to be learned here? We really do not know. Perhaps the copy was inspired. Perhaps the success was an accident of timing. Perhaps "doing business with the government" was so appealing that it succeeded despite being done "all wrong." Or maybe—probably—the lesson is simply affirmation that we are dealing in art, not science, and that no one can predict how the public will react to any given stimulus. There is another lesson, which we will get to later, that teaches us the need to *test*, if we want to minimize risk and maximize success.

On the other hand, I found the maxim that says "The more you tell, the more you sell" to be a basic truth. A promotion in which I used a simple letter to follow up the inquiries—to try to convert the sales leads into sales—produced rather poor results until I added a circular and a brochure. Then, orders picked up rather briskly. The art, however, is not in knowing the truth but in knowing how much you need to "tell." Too much "tell" can produce adverse results, too.

Prospecting for leads in the examples discussed here was accomplished in two ways: Mailing to lists of names rented or acquired by some other means, and running print advertising to solicit inquiries. Some prospecting was also accomplished by PR methods, which produced notices in various publications, tantamount to free advertising. The idea is to induce readers to inquire, thereby producing the leads to follow up.

In theory, every inquiry is a lead. Unfortunately, many inquiries are leads of poor quality, if we are justified in calling them leads at all, especially when they are responses to print advertising. They may be idle curiosity seekers, competitors scouting you, children gathering materials for school projects, or others who are not truly legitimate prospects for your sevice and, hence, not bona fide sales leads.

QUALIFYING PROSPECTS

Prospects must be qualified, just as leads must be, if you are to use your marketing time and money effectively. Consider prospecting by mail. Suppose that your consulting service is based on helping clients set up efficient desktop computer systems in their offices, and that you offer an entire range of services, from initial survey of their needs, through recommendations for hardware and software systems, to overall work flow and system design, and training of personnel. That gives you a wide range of potential prospects, including virtually all large and small businesses, and professionals' offices as well. If you wish to reach everyone in every organization meeting that general description, your basic prospecting is fairly easy. You can rent mailing lists of such organizations and individuals without great difficulty, although if you turn to inquiry advertising, you will have to structure it in such a way as to attract responses from the chosen class. With as general a set of specifications as those suggested here, that should present little difficulty.

Let us suppose that your experience has taught you that the bulk of your practice has proved to be helping clients who have gone out and bought computer hardware and software but who really do not know how to make the best use of their systems. They need both a plan of usage and training of the staff. That means that you must study their operations and define their needs in terms of what can be and should be converted to computer operation, and you must design at least a general system of flow and control. But you have also learned that the bulk of your clientele consists of professionals with small offices. So you are in a position to draw a pointed profile of your typical client. That profile will serve you well as one of a typical prospect representing a high degree of success probability—a profile of a good sales lead, in fact.

For the most effective prospecting, if your goal is to increase your volume quickly (as compared with slower expansion through diversification), steer your prospecting exclusively to small professional offices with systems already in place but also in need of expert help in using the system gainfully—to those matching the profile of your average and typical prospect/sales-lead/client. The closer you come to making your appeal draw responses (inquiries) from a population of prospects who all meet those specifications, the higher your percentage of successful closes will be. Certainly it will be much higher than if you made your appeal to the general population of computer-owning businesses and professionals. That will also tend to maximize your marketing efficiency, which should then maximize your income, an end-result that is certainly to be desired!

Obviously no list broker can rent lists of names guaranteed to meet those specifications. These brokers can use their computers to sort lists for you according to characteristics, such as demographics, industries, businesses, and professions, but not to match a specific profile beyond those limits. What you must do is rent those lists that come close to your needs—that meet your base specifications (business and professional offices, in this case)—and then tailor the lists and appeals you send out for further qualification or screening that will help you achieve your desired end.

If you compile your own mailing lists by initial prospecting via inquiry advertising—advertising designed to bring in inquiries that enable you to compile your own mailing lists—you must tailor your advertising to help you do the qualifying immediately, so that the resulting mailing lists will be reasonably close to the specifications. That, too, is possible. In both cases, mailing to a cold list and running inquiry advertisements to bring in response from qualified parties, you must decide what to say to readers, or what to offer them, that will persuade those meeting your specifications to respond, while discouraging those who do not meet your specifications.

If you fail to so structure your initial appeal, the base problem with inquiry advertising is that you get responses from the unqualified—the idly curious, competitors, children, and others who could never become clients—wasting your time and money. If you are working with names and addresses of businesses and/or advertising in business magazines, you probably do not encounter quite as much of this unqualified response as you would with a more general mailing and advertising in more general publications, but you still get some. Much of your direct mail and advertising will fall into the hands of children and others totally unsuitable as your prospects, no matter how it is addressed originally or where it appears. But a corollary problem, if you do not build suitable qualification controls into your prospecting, is that many of those who do meet your specifications—who are bona fide prospects—will fail to recognize that your appeal is addressed to them and their needs, and thus will not respond.

There is at least one complication in this. Any device you use to stimulate responses, such as a free calendar or other giveaway, tends to encourage that undesired response from the unqualified. Any device you use to control and minimize this, such as requiring the request to be made on a business letterhead or with a business card attached, tends to reduce the desired prospect response, as well as the undesired, unqualified one.

PROSPECTING COSTS

Both methods of prospecting—direct mail via rented lists and inquiry advertising followed by direct mail to respondents—are costly in money and time. As an independent consultant who must do your own marketing, you cannot afford to invest — at maximum — more than one-third of your time in marketing. The cost in dollars is also a major consideration for those who are not independently wealthy. Sending out mail will cost you $300 to $400 per 1,000 pieces, first class (more than one-half for postage alone). For your purposes, bulk mail is probably not a good alternative. Prospective clients are not likely to take you too seriously when your appeal arrives with the bulk-mail indicia or a precancelled stamp. Occasionally I get a piece of mail that says prominently on the front something such as "Personal," or even "Personal for Mr. Holtz." I might be flattered if it were not for the entirely ludicrous bulk-mail indicia printed on the envelope. I am amused, but sometimes I find myself quite annoyed, even offended by this shabby subterfuge. How likely is it that I will respond to this insult to my intelligence? In any case, even with bulk mail, your cost is going to be at least $200 to $300 per 1,000 pieces. And a mailing ought to be at least several thousand pieces as a rock-bottom minimum. Here is why: You can look to a response of as little as a fraction of one percent, and probably not more than four or five percent maximum, unless there is some unusual factor at work. Of responses, some small percentage may be expected to become clients — perhaps one percent or less and, quite conceivably, none at all. We do work with small figures in direct mail and advertising. The figures thrown out here are quite optimistic because conventional advertising is not very effective in winning consulting clients. The real work of winning clients depends on other means that we shall cover later. The figures here are significant when applied to certain special methods of prospecting for consulting clients through an indirect, but effective means in a two-step process, also to be explored later in more detail.

Print advertising is not cheap. For inquiries, you can use classified advertising, but even that can be costly. Most periodicals today charge by-the-word for classified notices, from $1 per word to well over $5 per word, depending primarily on the circulation of the periodical. That only brings in names for you to compile into mailing lists, further consuming your hours and dollars.

Despite all this bad news, there is some sunshine. It is possible to do much of this prospecting and marketing at little or no cost! By using PR — public relations — techniques and tactics you can defray much of your advertising cost, for example. You can also utilize affiliated activities that pay their own way and even produce profits—e.g., seminars and newsletters—as routes to prospecting for and winning clients for your more specialized consulting services. Ironically enough, these avenues that are the most economical and profitable ways to winning clients, are also the most effective means for doing so.

COMING FULL CIRCLE

Let us now return to our earlier observation that selling "pure" consulting services is not a one-call business; it requires the two-phase or two-stage process of first prospecting for leads and then converting those leads into sales. Even that is not the whole story of how to sell consulting services; there is an intermediate stage of selling a related service as one of several possible consulting services that may and do often act as preliminary or staging areas for selling consultation per se. Included are such consulting activities as seminars, newsletters, and similar presentations. They are important activities and they merit their own, independent discussions.

Seminars

Seminars may be regarded as a kind of group consultation, for they are just that if you operate them as such. There are many prospective clients who for one reason or another will not engage your services on the conventional full-time, one-on-one basis that most of us think of as the classic and true consulting service. Some may not be able to afford your full-time, direct services; others may believe that their need is rather simple and does not merit your full-time attention; and still others want to know more about you before venturing into a major consulting commitment. For all of these reasons, and perhaps others, many prospects who would not engage you in the classic consulting arrangement—or who are not yet prepared to venture into full-scale commitment with you—may attend your seminar.

Some of those who attend your seminar will ultimately become full-time, classic consulting clients if your seminar presentation inspires their confidence in you. I have presented few seminars that did not produce a consulting assignment or two, even when I did not actively seek such assignments. But you can seek them actively, for every one who attends your seminar is a good prospect and should be cultivated.

Actually, you get triple benefits from seminars.

1. The seminar itself is usually profitable, as it should be, for you are delivering a consulting service on a group basis, and you should be earning your fees.

2. Seminar attendees are excellent prospects for classic consulting services, and you ought to be able to win an assignment or two out of each seminar, especially if you make a selling effort.

3. The mailing of seminar literature, appealing to people to attend, is prospecting in general, as well as specifically, or can and should be made so. That is, your seminar mail-out should make it quite clear that you accept and seek direct consulting assignments, and are highly qualified for them.

In all, seminar production and presentation is itself a prospecting activity, as well as a consulting activity, and it is an aggressive, positive kind of prospecting.

Newsletters

Publishing a newsletter of your own is another way of proactive prospecting while offering another kind of consulting service that pays its own way—even producing a profit, as seminars usually do. Many organizations publish free newsletters as marketing tools because they are highly effective. Whether you produce your newsletter for marketing alone or for profit, it makes an excellent and self-liquidating vehicle for prospecting and generating sales leads.

There are other, related avenues of prospecting through public speaking and writing for publication. Through these kinds of presentations you can build your image as a true professional and engender in prospective clients the comfortable confidence in you that leads to consulting assignments. That confidence in you is essential; without it no prospect feels assured enough to move ahead. It does take courage: that prospect is being asked to undertake risk, perhaps of his or her career—or very own business perhaps—in entrusting you, your work, and your judgments, in some important matter. That explains why ordinary commercial advertising does not usually work very well for consultants. But these other, indirect, image-building methods do work very well when they are staged properly.

All Roads Lead to Rome

A key element in these discussions has been the philosophy that whatever works is right. But there is rarely only one "right way" to do something; there is almost always a multiplicity of ways to achieve a given result. We see this truth surface repeatedly when someone makes a breakthrough after long and Herculean effort. Later, sometimes shortly after, others begin to achieve the same result via other means. For example, Edison's incandescent lamp is still the most widely used artifical-lighting device, but there are several other kinds of devices used today to convert electricity into light. Each way usually has advantages and disadvantages, but that usually makes each choice the most suitable one for a given set of needs or circumstances. Fluorescent lamps cost more than incandescents and require special, more expensive fixtures, but they usually last longer, radiate less heat, and consume less power; halogen lamps are brighter; neon lamps are more suitable for making into signs and indicators, etc.

In Part III we are going to examine many ways to prospect for clients, methods that derive from the basic approaches described and discussed earlier. This does not suggest that any single technique is better than any other on an absolute basis, but only that it is one of many options open to you to achieve a result. You select the way that is best suited to your circumstances and/or needs.

THE METHODS FOR ACHIEVING CONSULTING SUCCESS

We are about to expand the discussions of basic approaches into detailed how-to explanations of and guidance in specific methods of prospecting and winning clients. In most cases the considerations that make one method advantageous over another for a given set of circumstances will be self-evident.

The discussions are divided, generally into proactive/aggressive and reactive/passive methods. This division is an arbitrary one, made to stress and remind you that there are such characteristics to consider when choosing a method for prospecting in quest of clients. The assignment of various methods to one or the other category is often equally arbitrary, since many methods fall into gray areas. In any case, the guiding principle is still: Whatever works is right.

PROACTIVE/AGGRESSIVE METHODS: SEMINARS, NEWSLETTERS, AND MORE

The decision as to how to characterize many of the methods is often difficult; so many fall on borderlines. But that is not important. What is important is knowing what your options are and how to exercise them.

AN EXPANDED DEFINITION

In early pages I defined my terms "proactive" and "reactive" by rather simple explanations. Proactive methods are those in which you seek out prospects aggressively — where, in effect, you go out in direct quest of the prospect. Reactive methods are those in which you attempt to persuade the prospect to come to you or the prospecting is an indirect and perhaps second-level result of some other activity — where, in fact, prospecting for clients may not even have been an objective. But there is a great deal more than that to be said about the differences because they are not often that black and white, and so a little more sophisticated explanation is in order. You will find, for example, that the presentation of seminars is listed both as a proactive and as a reactive method. Is that a paradox? No, because it is the basic purpose and intent of the seminar that makes the difference. A paid-attendance seminar does often produce new clients and direct consulting contracts, but that is a side-effect of the seminar; the seminar was intended as an income-producing, consulting activity—one of your services. So I regard it and present it to you as a reactive/passive marketing method. On the other hand, a free seminar, which normally produces a much larger number of attendees than a paid-attendance seminar, is conducted for the sole purpose of winning new clients and consulting contracts. I must therefore regard it as a proactive/aggressive method of pursuing business and present it to you as such.

None of this is to argue the case of one approach or method over another but simply to present and describe to you your many options so that you may select those most appropriate for your own needs. Try to bear two things in mind as we proceed:

1. Many of the methods described here are not truly suitable for marketing consulting services generally, although there are probably numerous exceptions, such as those of consultants whose practices include the provision (selling) of products to clients. (Security consultants, for example, often sell security equipment to clients.)

2. All the approaches and methods are proven ones that have worked in the past and continue to work in the present, but your own needs are the final arbiter of which are best for you.

PERSONAL CALLS

There are consultants who win most of their clients by making personal calls on prospects—almost literally knocking on doors and making sales presentations directly and in person. However, not all of these are cold calls—not all are calls, that is, made with no advance preparation and/or arrangements for the personal call.

The Problems with Cold Calls

There is more than one problem with simply walking into offices without preparation, although it can be effective in certain circumstances. Here are the basic problems in most cases:

1. It is usually inefficient in that you've no guarantee that the individual you want to see is in or, if in, is available or willing to see you without an appointment.

2. It is inefficient in that even if you do see the right individual(s) there is no assurance at all that this prospect is a true prospect, one who has the kind of needs you address and thus can use your services.

3. Consulting contracts are rarely sold in this manner or by a single call in any manner, so the best you can hope for is a lead to follow up in some way.

Some Exceptions: When Cold Calls Pay Off

There are exceptions, situations or circumstances in which personal, cold calls are a good approach. The following are some suggested circumstances that make the personal, cold call a reasonable approach to prospecting:

1. Calling on the large organization, where it is possible to visit a great many prospects within a single set of offices, so many that you can be reasonably sure that you will get to see a number of them.

2. The situation or circumstances in which you can be reasonably sure that your services and capabilities do match at least some of the needs of the organization or individual and thus every one you call on is, indeed, a true prospect.

3. When the services you provide are such that virtually every office or every business can make good use of them so that almost everyone is a true prospect.

Here are examples of how that can work for you when the circumstances are right:

Although I am not fond of making cold calls, I have, at times, found the practice a fruitful one. On one occasion I was inspired to visit the offices of the Occupational Safety and Health Administration (OSHA), a large organization within the U.S. Department of Labor, then occupying rented space in a downtown Washington commercial office building. (At the time I was interested in small government contracts and most of my clients were federal agencies.) I had decided that at least some of OSHA's needs fell in the areas of my own capabilities and services. In fact, I was following up what I thought to be a good lead suggested to me by an acquaintance in another government agency.

The lead proved to be a false one, well intentioned although my acquaintance had been. However, I found that I was in the midst of a large set of offices, each with its own set of responsibilities for OSHA functions. Reluctant to have made the trip for nothing, I decided to make calls on others in the organization. I asked my first contact about the makeup of the organization and sought his help in meeting others. I followed this pattern for two hours, meeting with five different individuals, each the head of an office. At the fifth call I struck pay dirt: A half-hour's conversation exploring problems and needs, and this executive invited me to submit a small, informal proposal. That, shortly after, led to a small contract directly and to others following.

The original call, in this case, was not a true cold call; I was following a lead. But the remaining calls in that organization, the calls that ultimately produced many thousands of dollars in consulting assignments, were cold calls.

On another, earlier occasion, I decided to call on the offices of the U.S. Postal Service Training and Development Institute in Bethesda, Maryland. I had learned that this organization had been reinforcing the ranks of its internal staff with a number of consultants who were kept busy every day at an acceptable, if not munificent, daily fee, and I knew myself to be qualified for much of the work being done there.

To my disappointment, I learned that the policy of hiring consultants to augment the regular staff had come to an end, and all consultants on board would soon be phased out. However, I was invited to submit an informal proposal for a need that existed at the moment. I did so, my proposal was found acceptable, and I was awarded a contract that kept me gainfully occupied for the next month and which was to prove only the first of many contracts with that organization.

Success Techniques for Cold Calls

Cold calls have the lowest expectation rate for producing business — for all the reasons cited. They should therefore normally have the lowest priority in your marketing scheme and activity options. Still, there are times when cold calls can pay off and may be the best alternative available. Here are some tactics and techniques that can raise the success probability or personal, cold calls:

1. Plan your cold calling in advance. Give serious thought to what kinds of organizations are best suited to your capabilities and services. Plan your basic presentation and the various slants you can give it to meet different situations and needs. Gather as much advance marketing intelligence as possible. Learn what you can about organizations you plan to call on. Consider who is most likely to be the right person for you to see—e.g., the purchasing agent, chief engineer, director of marketing, comptroller, publications manager, etc.

2. If your services are of more use to one type organization than another, improve your probabilities of success by seeking out situations where you can concentrate your calls. Most cities have office parks and office buildings and often entire neighborhoods where you can find concentrations of lawyers, medical practitioners, architects, high-technology firms, and others.

3. Ask prospects for recommendations to others, especially when you have had a pleasant session together but one that did not result in a sale or good possibility of an ultimate sale. Many prospects are willing, even eager to assist you in this way, sometimes feeling a little guilty for not being able to give you a sale. Try also to get the prospect to make an advance telephone call to the contact in your behalf or give you a note of introduction. The calls on these new prospects will, of course, then not be cold calls!

4. Remember always that the prospect is interested in his or her own concerns, not yours. Ask questions, learn what those problems and concerns are, and address them in your own presentation, demonstrating a capability and probability of solving the problem(s).

5. Show (and try earnestly to feel) a genuine and sincere interest in the prospect and his or her needs. That comes through clearly, and is hard to fake; it is important to try to develop that sincere interest, and it is the key to a successful approach.

6. Be sure to carry adequate literature with you to leave behind, such as calling cards, capability brochures, and other materials. Good capability brochures are especially important.

Un-Cold Personal Calls

If you follow these guidelines and recommendations at least some of your personal calls will not be entirely cold ones. You will still be prepared to make the most of the occasion. Perhaps more to the point, most of what has been listed in the foregoing six points applies to all calls, cold and "un-cold"—calls made as a result of appointments. They are good guidelines—and good advice—for all calls.

Obviously, personal calls go better with maximum advance preparation. That means personal calls in which you have done advance screening by some more efficient method than the trial and error of knocking on doors without more than minimal advance preparation—calls for which you have set up actual appointments. These are really sales leads at this point, for in most cases anyone willing to set aside time to see you when your mission is obviously to sell something is displaying enough interest to be qualified as a lead, at least. However, you must qualify the lead further to determine whether the individual simply has nothing better to do than spend time with you and, more importantly, has the money (authority) to do business with you. Even if he or she has not, all is not lost necessarily, as explained earlier. There is always the possibility that the contact who does not qualify as a true prospect—does not have the money or authority to retain you—can lead or direct you to someone who turns out to be interested and does qualify. A purchasing agent or, in the government, a contracting officer, does not ordinarily have a procurement budget of his or her own, for example, but usually knows those in the organization who do have budgets and authority and often knows what those individuals customarily buy or even what they may be seeking at the moment. Contracting officers in government agencies have often directed me to leads that resulted in consulting contracts.

There is another side to that: In organizations where, you have reason to believe, they do use consulting services such as yours that are purchased through a central purchasing agent—a not uncommon practice—you should have made yourself known to that purchasing agent and left some literature, especially capability brochures. Also "check in" periodically with that purchasing agent. Make an occasional telephone call or a visit, send on a fresh brochure, and distribute any advertising specialties you use, such as an imprinted memo pad or calendar. Make sure that the purchasing agent remembers you so that he or she solicits your bid or advises you of an impending procurement when the occasion arises. This is a conventional way of doing business with all government agencies — federal, state, and local — but it works with large private-sector organizations as well. In fact, purchasing agents are like government contracting officials in that they are delighted to have you do this. It adds to their resources for satisfying the needs of the organization and so makes life easier for them. You will usually find purchasing agents and contracting officers not only receptive but even eager to add your name to their lists of prospective contractors and suppliers.

PROSPECTING IN GOVERNMENT AGENCIES

The cases I cited of my success in making cold calls on federal government agencies were only two of many such success stories I could cite; the federal government is a rich source of business generally and consulting contracts especially, and no independent consultant who wants new business ought to overlook the opportunities. At present, the federal government spends well in excess of $200 billion (that is $200,000,000,000!) annually for goods and services supplied by and from the private sector. But that is only the federal government. By the best estimates available, the state and local governments in the aggregate — some nearly 80,000 "government entities," as the Census Bureau puts it — spend more than twice as much, so that annual government procurement amounts to probably about $650 billion.

How much of that is consulting? That's hard to determine because much consulting work is procured under various euphemisms, such as "R&D" (research and development), "training services," and "expert services." But it is a reasonably safe estimate that the procurement of such services accounts for at least $90 billion annually.

In general, government procurement offices encourage suppliers and potential suppliers to call personally on government procurement offices for the reasons cited — i.e., to meet the various contracting officers and buyers in those offices and make their services and availability known.

Government Procurement Methods

Most government procurement is based on buying via sealed bids — awards to the low bidder or competitive proposals — negotiations, based on proposals. Price is important but is not necessarily the decisive factor. (The adjudged technical quality of the proposed project or service is usually the most decisive consideration if the price is "within the competitive range.") This is true for both the federal government and state and local governments (county, city, town, and township), all of whom tend to pattern their procurement on the federal model. The basic philosophy in all public purchasing is a) maximum competition to keep the bidders honest and to assure governments of best prices, and b) equal opportunity to all who wish to compete, as befits a democratic society. (Admittedly, these goals are not always achieved, although they are the objectives of statutes governing public procurement by the various government entities.) But all also have certain defined exceptions, based on justified circumstances that include emergency purchases, small purchases, and special preference.

The federal government does a great deal of purchasing in Washington, DC, of course, but by no means is all of it done there. There are major federal centers in many large metropolitan areas such as Boston, New York, Philadelphia, Atlanta, Chicago, St. Louis, Dallas, Denver, Los Angeles, San Diego, San Francisco, and Seattle, but the federal government also has offices, military bases, laboratories, and many other facilities throughout the United States (and the world). Almost all do a great deal of their own buying independently through their own purchasing or contracting offices at each location. The state and local governments, on the other hand, tend to maintain centralized purchasing offices and do nearly all their buying in their own capitals, county seats, and town or city halls. However, all encourage those who wish to pursue government contracts to make personal visits to their respective purchasing offices to meet the purchasing officials and staffs of buyers.

Despite this tendency to concentrate and centralize purchasing, many of the state and local governments do allow their various agencies—which often number in the hundreds—to do certain purchasing independently, even if the paperwork must go through the central purchasing and supply office. Consulting figures prominently as a purchase usually decentralized because the user of the service—the real client—is the only one who can truly judge the need and select the best contractor, and the governments recognize that. So it is entirely practicable to prospect government agencies in much the same way you would prospect private-sector organizations.

Tools Needed for Prospecting in Government Offices

The federal government suggests that those wishing to do business with federal agencies make out and file a form called *Bidder's Mailing List Application*, Standard Form 129, although it is not a requirement. This simple form advises each contracting officer with whom you file a copy (you file one with each office where you hope to do business) what services or goods you offer and furnishes a little information about yourself. This is a request to the contracting officer to send you invitations to bid and requests for proposals, and is also one way of prospecting in government agencies. Most other governments require that you file a form similar to this with their central purchasing offices if you wish to bid or propose to them, but you need file only that single copy with each state and local government because each has only a single purchasing office, in most cases.

Be aware that filing these forms does not guarantee you will henceforth be sent a copy of every relevant solicitation, so you must pursue additional means to learn of the many opportunities to pursue government business.

A second necessary tool is the capability brochure, mentioned earlier and to be described in greater detail in Chapter 6. That should be supplemented with business cards and any other literature you normally use. The latter items are optional, but the capability brochure is a must — not a requirement of the governments, but a marketing need. All those who buy for governments keep files of such things so that they can select suppliers from whom to invite bids and proposals.

A third tool is, for federal agencies and offices, a subscription to the *Commerce Business Daily* (commonly referred to as the "CBD"), a federal publication that lists federal agencies' needs in synoptic form, while also listing the identification numbers of each solicitation package and the location where it may be picked up or ordered. (The CBD can be ordered from the Government Printing Office, which prints the publication in Chicago, or from the Department of Commerce, which publishes it. Ordering information is listed later in an appendix.) It is also possible to subscribe to a computer service — a public database, that is — which will transmit the CBD or any part of it you wish to your own computer via a modem and telephone line.

State and local governments have no equivalent publication but announce their needs and solicitation packages under a *Bids and Propos-*

als heading in the leading local daily newspaper. It is necessary to keep an eye on that source of information.

Government purchasing offices keep file copies of all solicitations extant, available for public scrutiny. In some cases they are all posted on a bulletin board, in others available in a bound volume. It is a good idea to visit any of the purchasing offices you can frequently – to keep abreast of any opportunities you missed earlier.

Many government offices have helpful literature, including lists of goods and services they buy, lists of agencies throughout their juris-diction (sometimes identifying the purchasing official in each such agency), explanations of procurement statutes and regulations, and other information of interest and utility. Many of these government offices have an actual bound manual supplied to anyone who wishes a copy, and ironically enough it is sometimes the smallest states and counties who supply the best literature.

Government Socioeconomic Programs

Many state governments have followed the example of the federal gov-ernment in establishing special programs to aid small business and minority entrepreneurs, with loans, loan guarantees, preference in contracting, and other such programs, and some give a slight prefer-ence to businesses located or headquartered within the state over those bidders from out of state. It is useful to inquire into these to see if any apply to you and may offer some advantage in prospecting and bid-ding.

TELEMARKETING

Telemarketing is still relatively new and yet it has been with us for a long time. It has gotten a great deal more visibility in recent years as the technicians have automated telemarketing so that a computer does the calling, reads a canned message, and records a response.

Obviously this is of no use to you. It would be extremely difficult, if not impossible, to sell consulting services this way. On the other hand, the telephone can be a useful asset in marketing, so that tele-marketing, in the most literal use of the word, does have a place in the scheme of things. But that use of the telephone is not as the prime prospecting tool. Rather, it is useful as a second step, for here is a prospecting method that works for many consultants:

Step 1.   This is the "telemarketing" phase, when you do call and try to persuade the prospect to see you by appointment. If that is agreeable, it is a good sign, and you may regard this as a bona fida sales lead.

FREE SEMINARS

There are two ways to use a free seminar for marketing, depending on the type of prospect you must pursue. That is, your service may be such that your clients are typically individuals, as in the case of the consultant who helps individuals stop smoking, overcome stress, learn how to start a business and make lots of money, etc. One entrepreneur who had made money in real estate ran many free two-hour seminars designed to persuade attendees to sign up for his $500 weekend seminar. By promising to teach the secrets of making money by buying real estate with no money down he had little difficulty in filling up a hall every time he offered the free seminar and, of course, he signed up many for his $500 seminar.

If you can legitimately promise something tempting enough, you can do the same. A small advertisement in the local newspapers, rental of a large room in a nearby hotel, and an ample supply of literature will place you on the dais, ready to make your presentation. Unfortunately, this is somewhat like the problem with inquiry advertising: You will get a large number of idle curiosity seekers who have no real interest in your services.

If your service is such that it is properly addressed to businesses, this is not going to be a viable approach; you will not lure many executives from their offices to attend a free, public seminar. Moreover, you will undoubtedly attract a great many of those idle curiosity seekers. So the plan is not truly viable in this situation. However, there is a way to adapt the idea gainfully to prospecting companies for your services. The idea is simplicity itself, and it is a refined and much more powerful version of the idea just discussed under the telemarketing title. There are two principal steps in this plan:

Design a brief seminar—one to two hours maximum—that presents useful information but is largely a skillful sales presentation for whatever service it is that you sell. Be sure to include a great deal of eye-opening teaser information. For example, when I make a sales presentation of my seminars in government marketing and proposal writing, I stress that I will teach attendees how to *appear* to be the low bidder, even when they are not, how to get paid promptly by the government, how to solve the seven most common problems in government marketing, and other such goodies. I will reveal one or two in a presentation, enough to whet appetites for more, while still keeping my promise to provide useful information in the free seminar.

Offer to present this mini-seminar free to organizations in their own conference rooms, to which they may invite any company staff they wish. (The more they invite, the better for you—the better the chance that some of them will get excited enough by your presentation to want the entire seminar.) You may do this by mailing out literature alone or by mailing out literature as a first step and then following up by telephone.

This free seminar is a sales presentation and free seminar rolled into one, and while the prospect is certainly smart enough to know that your purpose is marketing, you can easily make the free seminar attractive enough to persuade prospects to give you an hour or two. You are probably better off to propose only a one-hour seminar, for busy executives may balk at reserving two hours for you. Of course, if you get their attention fixed firmly enough in that hour, they are likely to keep you there for several hours, a consequence I have seen many times.

THE FREE NEWSLETTER

Publishing a free newsletter is also a useful way to market your services. As in the case of the free seminar, the free newsletter is always attractive to recipients, especially if you stage-manage the introduction of your newsletter so that it is not the newsletter but the subscription to it that is free! That is, the newsletter carries a printed subscription price, but you arrange things so that any likely prospect who wants it can get a complimentary subscription quite easily.

Advantages of the Newsletter

The newsletter offers many advantages over the seminar. There is no start-up cost and elaborate preparation for each issue, as there is for each seminar. The total audience you can reach with a single issue of a newsletter is much greater than that of a seminar. The number of prospects you can reach with a newsletter is really infinite, whereas it is quite limited with a seminar. You can reach each prospect at your initiative entirely, something you can't be sure of doing with a seminar, and the burden of labor is much smaller. The cost per prospect is much lower, and your control is much greater.

Start-Up

You need to control access to those subscribers who represent true prospects. Obvious controls are those mentioned earlier: Require, as a condition of the free subscription, that the request be made on a business letterhead or accompanied by a business card, which you can examine to satisfy yourself that the requestor is a genuine prospect. There are other controls, chief of which is the coverage in the newsletter: Presumably it will be of interest only to the types of organizations and individuals who are prospects for you.

Send out issues initially to organizations and individuals of your own choosing, enclosing or including in the copy a form for requesting a free subscription. The form may also invite the respondent to suggest the names of others who would like a free subscription. They may be other individuals in the same organization or in another organization. There are other ways to expand the number of prospects you reach. One is to include a routing box in the upper right or left corner of the front page of each issue, as shown in Figure 5-1. This adds to the number who will see your newsletter, and in large organizations there are many potential clients, hence many prospects. So, it is desirable to encourage the circulation of your newsletter as widely as possible in those large organizations and also to encourage many of those individuals to request their own free subscriptions. Some other methods of distribution, to be presented in paragraphs following, will also lead to subscriptions if you carry the invitation in every issue to make such a request. This need not be a lengthy piece; a simple form, requesting basic information, will suffice.

```
┌─────────────────────────────────────────────────────────┐
│                                                         │
│   [    ]  MKTG. MGR _____ │
│                                                         │
│   [    ]  PURCH. DEPT _____ │
│                                                         │
│   [    ]  _____ │
│                                                         │
│   [    ]  _____ │
│                                                         │
│   [    ]  _____ │
│                                                         │
└─────────────────────────────────────────────────────────┘
```

Figure 5-1.   Routing box for newsletter

Costs

Newsletters do not have to cost a great deal to publish. You have many options which enable you to control the costs. Later, we will explore and explain editorial work and production functions necessary to publish a simple newsletter and other literature you should have for your marketing. But there are certain, easy-to-understand principles that should be presented here:

- You do not have to publish the newsletter frequently. Bimonthly or even quarterly is adequate for the purposes of a free newsletter.
- You do not have to make it large or elaborate. A simple newsletter of two to four pages, if managed properly, will be effective.
- You do not have to use expensive composition. A good electric typewriter or, even better, a good computer printer will do an entirely satisfactory job of "typesetting."
- You do not have to pay for editorial material. You may write part or all of it yourself, but you can get free materials from many sources.

Publishing on a quarterly basis keeps costs down in several ways: One is the obvious saving in printing and binding four issues a year, instead of six or even more. Another is the obvious economy in mailing costs. Then, too, there is the lower per copy cost of printing enough for a three-month supply. Still another possible saving is in the difference between bulk-mail costs and regular mail costs. And if your circulation list grows large enough, you can send the copies out by bulk mail, cutting postage approximately one-half.

Perhaps publishing a newsletter appears to be too onerous. You can easily get professional help with your newsletter if you need it or simply don't want the burden of doing the work yourself. There are many free-lance writers, editorial consultants, and "letter shops" available in every metropolitan area, specializing in this kind of work.

Other Circulation Methods

While the primary circulation method is by individual free subscription, there are many other methods to circulate your free newsletter. Here are a few:

- Make them freely available at conventions, trade shows, seminars, etc., by leaving them on literature tables and in literature racks.
- Make them available as free handouts to organizations whose members are good prospects.
- Have a quantity folded to fit in an ordinary business-size envelope and enclose a copy in all your regular correspondence with individuals you believe suitable as prospects or who might pass the newsletter on to other prospects.
- Make complimentary subscriptions freely available to publishers of other newsletters and any periodical that you believe reaches an audience suitable as prospects. Give free permission to quote from and/or reprint/reproduce any portion of your newsletter with the proviso that the source (you) must be acknowledged. (In publishing this is referred to as "attribution.")
- Carry a supply with you at all times to hand out free. It's better than a brochure. (That's one reason for having a quantity folded, as suggested.)

Editorial Content

The free newsletter is a marketing tool, intended to sell your services—to help you find and win clients. Readers recognize and accept that. They will not accept a pure promotional brochure disguised as a newsletter. They will read and keep your publication only if it contains information worth reading and keeping. In short, it must be a legitimate newsletter, with a reasonable portion of it devoted to information of value to the reader. My suggestion is: Limit to about one-third of the newsletter the space given over to unabashed, admitted selling — advertising — of your services.

You can get direct marketing benefit out of the remaining two-thirds by making your byline prominent and by running features that work at building your image as a talented professional who can help your clients substantially. For example, you might run a column prominently titled, "Useful Tips from Jeffrey Martin" (your name). Develop features that give readers a reason to save each issue. Many newsletter publishers have their newsletters three-hole punched to suggest saving them in a binder.

Another excellent way to market your services indirectly while still presenting useful information is to describe case histories from your personal experience, making it clear that you were the problem-solving consultant. Present the case as a typical problem that anyone might have and explain how it may be solved by describing the actual case history. You should not identify the client without the client's permission. If you have that permission, make that clear with your thanks to the client for permitting you to tell the story and pass on the useful information to other readers. A thank you is the most gracious way to make attribution and also a way to assure readers that you have gotten the client's permission. Otherwise, the reader might fear that you would not respect confidentiality if he or she became a client.

You can also publish individual features about consulting that are useful to readers while selling your services indirectly. Here are a few ideas along that line:

WHAT CAN A CONSULTANT DO FOR YOU?
An Explanation of Consulting Services

WHEN YOU NEED A CONSULTANT
How to Seek Out the Right Consultant for Your Need

WHAT SHOULD A CONSULTANT COST YOU?
The Typical Rates for Different Types of Consultants

You might run features offering useful information about your special field. In my own case, I would offer tips on writing proposals, brochures, advertising copy, and writing in general, as well as tips on marketing to governments and marketing in general. You can do as much in your own field.

In the next chapter, we'll explore and explain some editorial and production matters that should be of interest to you.

ASSOCIATIONS, SHOWS, AND CONVENTIONS

There are probably more trade fairs, exhibitions, conferences, and conventions held in the United States than anywhere else in the world, possibly even more than in all other nations combined. Americans are joiners; most of us belong to various groups, including trade associations, professional societies, computer clubs, veterans groups, community organizations, and sundry others, numbering in the thousands. It would be hard to imagine a business, industry, profession, craft, hobby, or other particular interest that did not have some representative national or regional organization to which one might belong. Some people, in fact, belong to many organizations. Certainly, the choice is wide and abundant. (There are, reportedly, some 2,000 associations headquartered in the Washington, DC metropolitan area alone.) And a great many of these organizations hold annual conclaves at large hotels, convention halls, and other such facilities.

Such annual conclaves include a broad agenda of activities, including seminars, side meetings, hospitality suites, and—most important, in many cases—an exhibit hall where companies exhibit their wares, hold demonstrations, and meet potential customers and clients.

You can always rent space and set up a booth of your own, although this may be a bit expensive for the average independent consultant, unless you are trying earnestly to grow large rapidly and willing to invest heavily in the effort. It is helpful to belong to as many associations as possible and attend as many conventions and other such events as you can, to make many "contacts" there in order to get at least several good sales leads from each such event.

Hospitality suites—mini-conventions held in suites at the same hotel where the convention is staged—offer a good opportunity in this respect. Typically, those hosting such a suite distribute invitations to those in attendance (often by mail and advertising in advance to all who are likely to be in attendance). In the suite the sponsor demonstrates his or her wares, discusses needs with visitors, sometimes makes more-or-less formal presentations (so-called "dog and pony shows"), and offers refreshments. These sponsors may also have booths in the exhibit hall. The hospitality suite, however, is far more intimate an environment, and is often an excellent place to meet others and establish sales leads.

Such suites are excellent places to present mini-seminars that promote your services, and many entrepreneurs do so. You can easily arrange to have attendees register in some simple manner, such as signing a log or leaving a business card, although it is more helpful if you can manage to get them to provide more information than that. The idea, in this and your other activities at these annual mass meetings and exhibits, is to get specific leads to follow up. If you can persuade them to fill out a short and simple questionnaire, you will have a great deal better basis for evaluating the leads, rank-ordering them, and following them up with the greatest effectiveness.

DIRECT MAIL

Direct mail, referred to colloquially by those in the industry as "DM," is the mailing of packets of information to lists of addressees. It is like ordinary media advertising in that it, alone, won't produce clients and sales of your services. You would delude yourself to expect that. The prime purpose of turning to direct mail is to generate sales leads. So, if you choose to employ direct mail in your marketing, it should be used in some way that screens all the prospects—the addressees—and identifies those who give some evidence of enough interest to qualify as sales leads for your followup. Your direct mail must produce response from those who show enough interest to be considered sales leads.

A straight sales message may do; promising benefits may produce inquiries, but that is a passive approach. The aggressive approach attempts to stimulate the respondent and tries to provoke a reaction that indicates an active interest. Offering the free newsletter or the free mini-seminar discussed earlier is one way to do this. Another is offering a free report that bears somehow on the subject—e.g., "seven com-

mon problems in canning tuna fish and how others have solved them."
Still another is the offer of a free survey/evaluation of the prospect's
inventory-control system or quality-control procedures. Whatever you
choose, it must conform with certain principles to be useful:

1. It must be clearly stated as an *offer*, not a request.
2. What you offer must be absolutely explicit.
3. There is a clear *benefit* to the prospect; the offer will *do* some-
    thing for the prospect.
4. It must be clear that there is no obligation assumed in accepting
    the offer: it is *free*.
5. What the prospect is to *do* to accept and take advantage of your
    offer must be an explicit and entirely clear statement. (In fact,
    it should be expressed as an imperative, a directive—e.g., "Pick
    up the 'phone *now* and dial . . . .")

The Content of a DM Package

The DM industry has its own conventional wisdom, as do most industries and professions. The supposed mandatory items for a proper DM
package include these as a minimum:

1. A letter.
2. A brochure.
3. An order form.
4. A return envelope.

If you check your "junk mail" on any busy day you will find many
other items such as plastic cards designed to resemble credit cards,
circulars, plastic pocket calendars, copy all over the outside of the
oversize envelopes, contest entries, and a wide variety of other items,
including order forms designed to resemble valuable stock certificates
and bonds.

These serve very well for the average huckstering type of mail order, where the intent is to sell insurance, consumer merchandise, cor-
respondence-school courses, and other such things. They are not entirely appropriate for our purposes here. In fact, many of these items
would operate against your interests, convincing prospects that you

are not a serious and dignified professional. In direct mail, as in all your activities, you must be careful about maintaining a proper image. There should be a letter, a brochure, and some kind of form, preferably post-card size, for responding, if the respondent prefers that to telephoning. These all must be tasteful and not smack of huckstering.

Mailing Lists

Among the first problems to consider in contemplating a direct-mail campaign is the source of the mailing lists. Will you rent them from a commercial source or do you have practicable alternatives?

Source of Mailing Lists

There are dozens of mailing-list brokers. They often refer to themselves as "list managers." Both are correct designations, but the significance of the two is a matter of whether you have lists of your own that you wish to rent (as an income-producing asset) or wish to rent others' lists for your own use. The reason is that for the most part the lists you rent are not the property of those renting them (although they may have some lists of their own); most of the renters' lists are actually owned by others, and the list managers market those lists for the owners—that is, they act as *brokers* for the owners. But they do also manage the lists, in that they prepare them and take care of all the details attendant to marketing them for a percentage of the proceeds. So the lists may be presented to you in either of two ways: You can order lists sorted by such classifications as *engineers*, *bank presidents*, *home owners*, etc., or they may be offered in terms of whose lists they are, such as the Book-of-the-Month-Club membership lists, the customers of L. L. Bean, or subscribers to *Newsweek* magazine. This describes and classifies them. For some purposes, the latter classification is even more useful than the first one. A list of members of the Electronic Industries Association or the American Psychological Association would be exactly right for some consultants, while others might find a list of toy manufacturers or of training-program producers more tailored for their needs.

In practical terms, if you propose to make large or relatively large mailings—on the order of perhaps 25,000 or more—you probably have no alternative but to use commercial lists. Most alternatives are impractical for any mailing but that of a few thousand pieces, at most. On the other hand, there are other ways to approach the problem, if smaller mailings suit your purpose.

Alternative Sources of Mailing Lists

There are two types of mailing lists rented by list brokers. One is the list of customers, subscribers, students, or others described earlier. These are, in most cases, people who have bought something by mail and thus have a certain validity as mail order buyers, although lists of inquirers are sometimes rented too, albeit usually for a smaller price. However, *compiled* lists are also offered frequently, lists that were compiled from membership rolls, directories, and other sources. These are normally considered to be of less value, inasmuch as they are not lists of validated buyers or even interested inquirers.

It is possible to compile your own lists, if your mailings are not too great in size. I had difficulty in finding lists offered for rent that were suitable for my needs. I was looking for lists of companies who did or wanted to do business with the government. And I aimed especially to mail to those companies whose success in marketing to the government depended largely on their abilities to write effective proposals. I found that the way list brokers sorted their lists—that is, the ways in which I could have my lists sorted—were not truly suitable; they (the brokers) really had no way of knowing which were the companies that met this description and so could not use their computers to select them.

Had I been willing and/or able to make very large mailings—many thousands—this might not have mattered a great deal. While the percentage of response might have been rather low, I would have gathered enough responses for my needs. (This "shotgun" method is not very efficient, but then DM is not efficient in that it produces a low rate of response—typically one to three or four percent, sometimes even less.) In fact, I rather suspect that commercial lists are most suitable when the mailing is quite large. In any case, I decided to compile my own lists, and turned to several sources, such as the following:

1. Probably the best single source was the help-wanted advertisements in major newspapers, such as the *Washington Post*, the New York *Sunday Times*, the *Wall Street Journal*, and other such

newspapers. Knowing industry as I do, I found it easy enough to recognize on those pages most of the kinds of companies I wanted.

2. I found it possible to get some lists of contractors from government sources—from such agencies as the U.S. Navy, the Small Business Administration, the Commerce Department, and others.

3. I found it possible at the time (it is now no longer possible) to buy a copy of the list of subscribers to the *Commerce Business Daily*.

4. I was able to get membership lists from several associations whose members represented companies I wanted for my mailing lists.

I was making my mailings at a relatively slow pace, several hundred each week, so my mailing schedule and compilation were entirely compatible. In fact, I did not really want to make large mailings, for I wanted responses at a rate I could handle. Leads not followed up promptly become "stale" quickly and are soon worthless. It is wise to adjust your mailings to produce leads at a rate you can handle with prompt followup. A little experimentation should enable you to make the necessary adjustments.

SOME PRACTICAL CONSIDERATIONS

In Chapter 6 we will be discussing many practical matters of writing copy, testing, and other aspects of marketing. But before leaving this chapter there are some other practical matters that must be discussed.

In marketing consulting services you must usually make at least two sales: You must first sell prospects the notion of responding in some manner—arouse their interests sufficiently to evoke a substantial indication of that interest. You must somehow persuade the prospect to request a free subscription, invite you to make that mini-seminar sales presentation, send that free report you offered, or otherwise identify themselves as being interested enough for you to label them as sales leads. Then you must sell them your consulting service—somehow close the sale. And often there are additional sales to be made between these two, such as persuading a prospect to seek authority to do business with you, agreeing to a second meeting, accepting your minimum terms, and others.

If you remain in the consulting profession, you will have all of these experiences and many more. Even when someone calls you out of the blue and invites you to agree to an assignment and accept a purchase order, that's a second sale. You sold yourself somewhere, somehow at an earlier time or you would not have gotten that easy order. On the other hand, events and signals are sometimes deceptive.

A Few Danger Signals

Sometimes the easy sale seems too good to be true—and it very well may be exactly that. It should be helpful to be aware of and recognize these danger signs:

ASKS ONLY THE PRICE. Some prospective clients launch the question, "How much?" almost immediately. It seems to be the only question they have, and it is not a promising sign.

DOESN'T ASK THE PRICE. The client that does not ask the price at any time is sending a signal too. It's also not a good sign.

MONEY NO OBJECT. In some cases a prospective client indicates or even plainly states that cost is no object. This may mean that the client is absolutely desperate or really doesn't care about money. The first possibility, desperation, is real enough; the second is highly unlikely. Even desperate clients care about money. If a client *appears* to be indifferent to cost, that should be enough to arouse suspicions and cause you to proceed with caution. If the client actually *says* that money is no object, it is time to get *highly* suspicious.

TOO AGREEABLE. Sometimes a client asks virtually no questions, agrees without a murmur to everything you suggest, is ready to give you a go-ahead immediately without discussion. This is an equally dangerous sign.

What Such "Good News" Signs Really Can Mean

The individual whose first question is "How much?" is rarely worth spending time with. He or she is simply shopping, will probably select the cheapest consultant available, and then will give that unfortunate soul a great deal of trouble because with the bargain price the client will be convinced that the services are no good, the consultant not competent, etc.

On the other hand, whenever a prospective client does not ask what my services will cost it is because he or she does not expect to pay for my services. Sometimes the prospect assumes that I will work on a commission or contingency basis: If they win a contract, I get paid; if not, *I* am to bite the bullet! Sometimes they think I will enter into partnership: If I win the contract, we will do it together. And sometimes they are simply trying to use me with no intention of compensating me no matter how my efforts turn out or what they produce.

How to Handle Such Situations

In the earlier years I was "taken" more than once by such clients. After a while I learned how to handle such situations. But first a relevant tip about sales technique:

It is generally considered by sales experts to be a mistake to volunteer the price to a prospect. You enjoy an advantage when you can induce the *prospect* to ask the price. The idea is to sell the prospect performance—quality, dependability, results. When the prospect asks the price it is an indication of interest, an indication that the prospect is sold, except for settling the price. The approved technique is to close and close again, until the prospect *does* ask the price.

Despite this, some clients do not ask the price, and it is necessary to determine whether that indicates problems of some sort. In any case, it is necessary to move forward and there are two ways to do this. One is to introduce the subject of cost yourself, and the subject of cost yourself, and the other is to introduce the subject of a retainer—partial payment in advance.

This is, in fact, a simple qualification of the prospect and results in clearing up the situation rather quickly. In almost every case I have experienced that was the end of the discussion.

Obviously, if you have a signed contract with or a purchase order from General Mills, IBM, or U.S. Steel, the risk of not being paid is relatively slight. On the other hand, getting a retainer—I recommend asking for about one-third of the total estimated cost up front—does not assure that you will collect the rest of your bill. It does show intent and invariably is a reliable qualifier. I have never lost a nickel with clients who agreed to a substantial retainer.

You do not need to get advance retainers from major corporations, simply because it is contrary to their normal practices. Where and when you do insist upon a retainer is a matter of judgment, but I recommend it as something to ask for and get whenever possible. It means fewer problems. Don't be afraid of offending a prospective client, either. Any prospect who is offended by a businesslike approach is a prospective client to be most wary of. I would not be concerned about losing such a prospect.

CHAPTER 6

PROACTIVE/AGGRESSIVE METHODS: DIRECT MAIL AND OTHER TECHNIQUES

Proactive/aggressive is a state of mind, a philosophy, a policy. But it must be implemented to be effective.

THE DIRECT MAIL PACKAGE

Direct mail is by its very nature a proactive and aggressive means of marketing—seeking out prospects by mail in their homes and offices. You have probably received your own ration of "junk" mail, as many refer to it, and know what it looks like. It comes in all size envelopes, from ordinary number 10 white business to 9- ×12-inch envelopes, and a variety of sizes and shapes between. The envelopes are of as many colors as Jacob's coat, with a number of shapes seeming to match the number of colors. They come with plastic windows, boldly printed messages on the outside, and with an astonishing variety of contents, besides the obligatory sales letter, brochure, order form, and return envelope.

Models to Be Avoided

Most are worthless as models for you; you can't sell consulting services the way you sell correspondence school courses or life insurance. For one thing, you are appealing to a different kind of prospect
entirely. Unless your consulting field is rather novel, you are prospecting business executives in their executive capacities, not as individuals and private citizens or average consumers. Buying as average
consumers usually means risking money, but little else. Buying in an
executive capacity for the organization means *career* risks and tends
to make the prospect a more cautious buyer. In any case, the direct-
mail package you use must not huckster and sacrifice dignity to be
persuasive. Your letter—and there should be a letter as the centerpiece—should not have those marking-pen bold marginal notations,
underlines, encircled words, and "bangs" (exclamation marks) that ty-
pify the huckstering type of direct-mail salesletter. Nor should the envelope carrying your package be of an unusual color, size or shape or
be covered with bold messages imploring the reader to open the envelope and discover the marvelous opportunity offered inside.

For Instance . . .

Despite the caveats listed, your letter must be persuasive, somehow
inducing the reader to want to know more. It should appeal to the
reader's desires, offering the promise of achieving goals most to be
desired, and yet doing so in a manner that is credible. One of my own
most successful salesletters had a modest headline as follows:

MAYBE I AM JUST LUCKY . . .

. . . OR MAYBE I KNOW SOMETHING
THAT YOU SHOULD KNOW

The letter then went on to say that if it is luck, then it seems to rub
off on my clients, for they begin to win government contracts after
they have become my clients. The letter went on to explain—briefly—
my own background of success in winning government contracts for
former employers, for clients, and even for my own account as a small,
independent government contractor.

There was, of course, much more to this letter and the entire package, but before exploring all that let's analyze this opening and see what it did and how it did it:

Why and How the Headline Works

This headline, first, does several things:

1. It arouses a bit of curiosity. Remember that this letter went out to people who were in the business of contracting with the government, and it was on a letterhead that said *Government Marketing News*. The respondent understood the connection immediately.
2. It suggests, in teasing terms, the promise of a benefit of special information that produces success of some kind connected with marketing to the government.
3. It lays an immediate basis for claiming credentials on the part of the writer, and makes the message a personal one — notice it said quite plainly *I* and *you*. *You* is always a most important word in any message, and the use of *I* is a good idea when expert services are involved in the offer.
4. It virtually demands that the reader scan at least the first few sentences following if for no better reason than curiosity, but it also furnishes the basis of appeal to self-interests.

The Followup

No headline can do the job alone. The purpose of a headline is twofold: to get the reader's attention and to persuade the reader to read on. Thus the text that follows the headline must be followup text: It must be text that continues the message of the headline, rolling out of it, reinforcing it, expanding on it, and acting as a bridge to the body of the letter. In this case the followup reinforced the promise of success or greater success in winning government contracts, while it also expanded on and began to validate the claim to credentials as an expert.

THE INGREDIENTS OF SUCCESS IN SALES AND ADVERTISING

The foregoing are necessary steps in a salesletter, as they are necessary steps in any sales presentation or advertising. In general, to achieve success in advertising or sales (which respond to the same truths), it is necessary to do three things:

1. Furnish a promise of something the prospect will desire greatly.
2. Explain how to achieve that desire—what you ask the prospect to do.
3. Furnish proof or evidence that doing what you ask will produce the result you promise.

In the case cited, the promised benefit is success in winning government contracts or, in the case of those already successful—greater success. The prospect is asked to retain me to help them write proposals and/or train their staffs in proposal writing. The evidence is my record of success in doing this, which is also the basis for my credentials as an expert. I would have a difficult time convincing a client of my ability to make good on my promise if I could not point to a record of having done so in the past—to a suitable set of personal credentials.

The Promise

What you promise the prospect is most important. Here are a few guidelines to consider when formulating the promise:

1. The promise should not be trivial, such as a more handsome appearance or a more efficient format for the prospect's proposals. It must be a promise of something important enough to the prospect to justify retaining you and motivating the prospect to do so. It must be concrete—e.g., *Win more government contracts*—not vague and general—e.g., *Enjoy more marketing success*. Vague promises are an absolute no-no because they elicit skepticism at worst and fail to arouse enthusiasm at best.

2. Don't go to the opposite extreme and offer some extravagant promise that begs skepticism as a response – e.g., *You will triple your volume*. The promise ought to be believable on its face. Even if you sincerely believe that you can do something that justifies a startlingly radical promise or a string of superlatives in describing it, resist the temptation to go to extremes and temper your language and the promise. Despite the fact that some advertisers succeed with such advertising, you are dealing with level-headed executives who need some convincing evidence for even modest promises before they will talk further to you.

3. Headline and focus on the main promise (preferably a sole promise). Do not dilute and weaken it by distracting the prospect's attention with other promises. Such "polypharmacal" approaches – the hope that if you include enough promises, at least one of them will work – are not effective at all. They weaken your whole presentation because they appear to be acts of desperation, reflecting small credibility in your own arguments. You are always better off to keep the prospect's attention fully focused on important matters.

What You Want the Prospect to Do

Many sales and advertising efforts fail or produce far sparser results than they should because the prospect has not been told what to do. Incredibly, even successful and decisive executives waver uncertainly or fail to act in response to appeals when they have not been told precisely what to do next. That is the heart of closing in direct mail, since you can't carry on an actual dialog and ask questions, as you would in a face-to-face closing. That is why you see well-written sales appeals use such directives as *Call this number today!*, *Just drop this card in the mail*, and other such imperatives. Usually these directives are preceded and introduced by such "payoff" statements as *For fast results*, *To get us started solving your problems immediately*, or similar words.

Evidence

Evidence is extremely important, and must be in proportion to the promise: The "bigger" the promise, the more convincing the evidence must be. (That is one reason for avoiding extremes in promises: Even when an extreme is justified technically, the increased problems in furnishing satisfactory evidence may prove insurmountable.)

Bear in mind that we are not talking about evidence in the same sense that police departments and courts use the term. Evidence and proof are whatever the prospect will accept as evidence or proof. If you can claim to have written successful proposals for many millions of dollars and you cite a few for-instances, most prospects will accept that. That is, they will usually accept that if you are entirely specific and as precise as possible — if you cite exact figures and name names, especially if some are names they recognize, such as IBM, RCA, General Motors, and others equally well known.

When we speak of evidence here we are also speaking of credibility, for they are so closely related in this context as to be almost the same. When I cite specific contracts, companies, dates, and specific figures, that is generally accepted by prospects, where vague generalizations would not be. If the number is $93 million, don't refer to it as "approximately $100 million," "nearly $100 million," or even as "over $90 million." Even when you are estimating, use the most exact figures possible. And when you are citing other clients as examples, use their names, if possible: Not "a well-known maker of steel products," but "U.S. Steel." (Of course, this assumes you have permission to cite them as a client.) This is equally the case for lesser-known companies. Even if few prospects are likely to recognize the name, use such citations as "Paducah Furniture Fabricators, of Paducah, Kentucky," rather than a vague reference to "a furniture manufacturer." Readers know that you would not make up those names and places, so they generally accept them without further question.

Credentials and Credibility

If credibility is almost the same as evidence, so are credentials. I speak here of the credentials of achievement, not of academic preparation. A college degree is a credential, and advanced degrees are additional credentials. Past employment represents credentials, too, especially if some positions you held in the past relate to what you promise to do for the prospect. In some cases, where physical facilities and resources are essential to your doing what you promise, evidence that you have these are credentials too. But as in the case of a resume when you are out trying to sell yourself for a new position, none of these kinds of credentials are quite as important — as convincing and persuasive — as are specific achievements that give evidence of your being able to do for the prospect what you promise to do.

Decide in advance, in planning your literature package, which are your most important credentials — what is your most important and convincing evidence — and be sure to focus attention on that, not on the distractions of your academic achievements. A Ph.D. is a fine credential, but suffocating the evidence of noteworthy achievements in favor of stressing that advanced degree (because you are so impressed with your own doctorate!) can easily prove fatal. I recall one vice-president of marketing who discovered that it was best to make absolutely no reference to his doctoral status because so many of his prospective clients appeared to believe that anyone with a doctorate belonged on a college staff and not in business and industry. And I have worked with managers who were guilty of reverse discrimination and snobbery, tending to contempt for anyone who had "wasted his or her time in going to college at all, let alone compounding the offense by enrolling for advanced studies!

You may be just starting out in a career (although most consultants are people who have had a few years of working experience) and have nothing but academic achievements to point to. In such a case you have no choice, at least not until you have acquired other credentials. But you must try to judge what the prospects are likely to find most impressive about you, and you must try to get outside yourself to do that successfully; it is not easy.

Blurbs and Getting Attention

Bear in mind in writing salesletters — and all copy, for that matter — that the people you address are busy executives (for the most part) who are probably besieged by myriad demands for their attention. If you can't capture their interest quickly, you may never do it at all.

The headline is the primary device for getting attention. However, a solid, unbroken body of text is somewhat forbidding to someone who is busy and wants to grasp the essence of the message quickly. Even an effective headline may lose much of its effectiveness when it is followed by a large body of text set solid. That argues for text that

MAYBE I AM JUST LUCKY . . .

. . . OR MAYBE I KNOW SOMETHING

THAT YOU SHOULD KNOW

If it's just luck, it seems to rub off on my clients;
they start getting lucky and winning contracts too!

Figure 6-1. Headline and blurb

has many short paragraphs and short lines—lines that end far short of the right margin—and has an "open" look, appearing easy to read. There is another device you can use to achieve that same objective of appearing to be easy to read, at least in its opening presentation. That is a device known as a "blurb."

A blurb is a brief sentence or two, following the headline, that expands on the message of the headline and summarizes the overall message or—preferably—expands on the headline in such a way as to further provoke and stimulate the reader's interest to induce him or her to tackle the main body of the text.

For an example, see Figure 6-1. It's the headline I mentioned in Chapter 5, from a successful salesletter of my own. Instead of using the opening lines of the body copy to expand and explain the message in the headline, I use a blurb to do so, and build further with the body copy, as shown in Figure 6-2, where the body copy begins to expand on the headline and blurb and explain the services offered.

The Body of the Letter

In a manner somewhat reminiscent of the "inverted pyramid" taught to journalism students, the letter expands into more detail as it proceeds. In the original the letter ran two pages and was accompanied by a brochure, an order form, and other material intended to accentuate the prospect's need for help. There was a paper with a series of questions, with a heading, "What Is Your Proposal IQ?" Answers to the questions were not supplied. They were not exactly rhetorical questions but were designed to help the reader perceive the superior knowledge of important details that would be placed in his or her service upon retaining the consultant. Here are a few of the questions that were posed:

How can you *appear* to be the low bidder? (Even if you aren't!)
Where do one-third of all proposals fail immediately?
How can you avoid the danger of later contract disputes?
How can you maximize your technical rating?

The questions were enclosed on a separate sheet, along with observations that these represented only a small sampling of the extensive knowledge that could be put to work on behalf of the prospect and his or her staff. There are other ways to incorporate these questions effectively into the letter, especially when they are linked so closely to the

MAYBE I AM JUST LUCKY . . .

. . . OR MAYBE I KNOW SOMETHING

THAT YOU SHOULD KNOW

If it's just luck, it seems to rub off on my clients;
they start getting lucky and winning contracts too!

$360 MILLION WORTH OF SUCCESS

It has been my good fortune to write proposals that have won over $360 million in government contracts for my former employers and for my clients. But of course it is not luck that is responsible, for luck is not that consistent. It is a combination of knowledge and hard work that accounts for that kind of year-in and year-out success.

CAN I DO THE SAME FOR YOU?

Among past employers and clients have been IBM, Philco-Ford, GE, RCA, U.S. Industries, Control Data Corporation, Dun & Bradstreet, and many others, and among those agencies who have awarded contracts on the basis of my proposals have been the Department of the Navy, the Office of Education, the Labor Department, the Department of Commerce, the General Services Administration, the Department of Energy, the Job Corps, the Federal Aviation Administration, the U.S. Postal Service, and others.

A RANGE OF SERVICES

As an independent consultant I *tailor* my services to your needs, so there is no set pattern. We talk first--no obligation on your part for this, of course --and agree on your needs and how I can best help you. I then tailor my services for you, furnishing you a proposal, written or verbal. The typical services I am called on for range from front-end assistance to help organize your proposal team and get them started to actual participation in writing, leading your team, assuming total responsibility for your proposal--or anything between the extremes.

Figure 6-2. The beginning of the body copy

headline. Figure 6-3 illustrates this. Note the format used is designed to make those introductory questions stand out. But note also that a blurb is used to make very sure that the reader knows what the promise is—winning contracts, in this case. For that is what the prospect wants; everything else is secondary, perhaps the means to the end but not the end itself.

That is the critical thing to understand: you must be sure to parade the prize before the prospect. Better proposals mean more contracts— logically, at least—but the prospect does not care to make the translation. Explain later, as evidence of *how* you help your clients win contracts, all the details and the chain of logic, the rationale. But be absolutely sure to first *dangle the prize*. Unless the prospect is truly

MAYBE I AM JUST LUCKY . . .

. . . OR MAYBE I KNOW SOMETHING

THAT YOU SHOULD KNOW

. . . *some things that will help you write the kinds*

of proposals that win the contracts

Do you know three ways in which you can *appear* to be the low bidder, even when you are not?

Or the most common cause of proposal failures, a factor that causes fully one-third of all proposals to be rejected on first reading?

Or one cardinal principle of proposal writing that reduces the risk of disputes to almost zero by putting you in a win-win position in the event of disputes?

Or one simple method to maximize the technical rating awarded your proposals?

The answers to these and many other equally important questions are what make the difference between the winning proposal and the rest of the proposals. And I can bring you and your staff all those answers and help you win contracts from now on.

HOW AND WHY I CAN HELP YOU

Pardon me if I appear to be bragging a bit here, but you are entitled to know what makes me think I can help you, and I can't explain that without listing the important things I have accomplished in this field and the organizations with whom and for whom I have accomplished them:

Figure 6-3. Another approach to the body copy

interested in the prize—wants it enough to ask you to present your evidence and help him or her decide to buy from you, all will be in vain. Yes, prospects do want your help in this; they want to be sold—once they have become eager for the prize you promise. No matter how much they want to believe you, they need to be sold.

That is where the reason enters the picture. The desire and the decision to buy are emotion-based, but they must be reinforced by whatever will pass for evidence before the prospect will commit fully and give you the order. Even those who exploit the gullible people who want badly to believe that there are easy ways to get rich must offer some kind of rationale, specious although it may be, to help the prospect go from desire to firm commitment.

Form and Format Matters

Note that this letter has no salutation. If you have a list of individual names and think it important to address each one you can do so with any computer and suitable software or easily arrange to have a mailing service handle this for you. However, it is an unnecessary expense for most applications because you will (presumably) be making the mailout to develop leads—that is, to offer sample copies of a free newsletter and/or to draw a response of some sort, not to establish a communication with a given individual. In fact, there is an advantage to be gained in not addressing any individual:

First, people do change jobs, either through promotion or through moving on to another organization. There is an excellent chance that many of those you address by name will no longer be with the organization or in the same position. So there is an advantage in addressing the envelope to a suitable functional title—*Director of Marketing, Comptroller, Chief Executive Officer*, or other such designation. It is not necessary to address the letter, itself. Although you may receive such mail, with letters addressed "Dear Executive" or "Dear Friend," it is neither necessary nor desirable to do this. It makes no difference in the respondent's reaction to it, and it hampers your freedom to design the letter in the most effective way possible. Use your regular letterhead, date it, and sign it, so it is obviously a letter, but do not even think about addressing it, unless you are going to go out to a select list of people you know or know of and wish to address personally.

You can also gain an important advantage by using a routing box, such as that of Figure 5-1, in one of the upper corners of the first page of the letter. (I like to use the upper right-hand corner for this.) Fill in the first line or two to get the letter started to whomever you think would be the most likely prospect. It is also most useful to guide whoever opens the mail in routing it. You do not then have to address even the envelope.

Notice too (in Figure 6-3) that the copy is simple typewriter-like copy from an ordinary computer printer. No effort has been made to dress it up. With almost any modern computer, printer, and readily accessible software, it is easily possible to right-justify the copy, use boldface and other fonts, and even to use proportional spacing, which would make it resemble formal typeset copy. However, there are sound arguments against doing that. The letter should look like a letter and not like an artfully designed circular or brochure.

On the other hand, if you enclose a brochure, feel free to turn to formal typesetting, more expensive paper to print it on, and other refinements. These are entirely acceptable for a brochure, but they are out of place in a letter. At the same time, be aware that the cosmetic characteristics of a brochure, beyond the point of clean, professional appearance, have little result on its effectiveness as a marketing tool. An overly fancied-up brochure may be harmful to your objectives because there are those who regard such a brochure with distaste as being ostentatious and indicative of a lack of cost-consciousness. The brochure need only be cleanly printed on a reasonably good grade of paper to appear businesslike and professional. Ironically enough, it is sometimes the less costly papers and processes that appear most expensive. A number of years ago, while working on an Air Force publications project in the offices of a large defense contractor, there occurred one of the inevitable periodic attacks on wastefulness and excessive costs. As a result, the customer requested that we cooperate and eschew all frills. Under Air Force direction we actually selected a more costly paper for printing because it looked like cheaper paper!

The Rest of the Package

I have experimented with various combinations of materials in making up direct mail packages, including the obligatory ones—letter, brochure or circular, order form, and return envelope. Among other lessons, I learned that the return envelope was rarely used: My respondents were all executives with secretaries, and used their own envelopes to enclose their responses. But I also learned that there were few advantages and some disadvantages in the obligatory ensemble of direct mail elements. For one thing, I wanted to encourage circulating my appeal to a number of executives in each organization. But the ensemble of different pieces made that awkward and tended to defeat the purpose of my routing box. A single sheaf of printed pages, all the same size, was much more practical, and I could not find any lessening of response resulting from my gross violation of DM "rules." I finally settled on five sheets of 8½- × 11-inch paper, with all body copy typed, with suitable headlines, printed on both sides, with the bottom one-third of the fifth sheet used as an order blank. The first two sheets (four pages) were given over to the letter; the remaining sheets included various items, including the questions mentioned, the order form, and miscellaneous related information.

Why five sheets? Because five sheets of ordinary typewriter paper—20-pound sulfite bond or 60-pound offset paper (which are really two designations of the same thing)—will travel at the first-class postage rate for a single ounce. I had long decided that from the marketing viewpont it was worthwhile to use first-class postage since I did not mail in large enough quantities necessary to take advantage of bulk mail rates. Five sheets printed front and back allow you up to 5,000 words or their equivalent in copy, and that is usually ample for your purposes.

There is a moral buried in this, and not very deeply: It is the truism that nothing makes up for a lack of substance—not any brochures, response envelopes, forms, advertising giveaways, or other distractors. Prospects do not buy those things, nor are they swayed very much by them. They buy—or do not buy—what you offer, if it is attractive enough to them, is well presented, and is sold properly. Perhaps window dressing helps reinforce a sound presentation of an attractive offer—but certainly it cannot and will not sell an offer that is all wrong nor can it compensate for a poor presentation.

Unfortunately, some individuals have allowed themselves to be seduced by the frills and fancies available for direct mail, spending large sums of money on elaborate brochures, expensive advertising novelties, and many other items that have not promoted marketing success. In this, sadly, they have forgotten—or perhaps never learned—this important truth. The true need is to concentrate your creative effort on the offer—what your service will *do* for the prospect—and on selling it with clearly expressed rationales, evidence, and guidance in what steps to take. Until you are completely satisfied with that, don't even think about the materials for your DM package.

THE CAPABILITY BROCHURE

The need for a capability brochure is particularly evident in connection with marketing to governments. This is a rather specialized kind of presentation, used almost exclusively to market custom services, such as consulting. It is also a necessary marketing-to-governments item. If there is ever an occasion when you can make a virtue of necessity, this is surely it. The capability brochure can be used much more widely than most consultants have used theirs.

Why a Capability Brochure?

Government agencies and executives who buy from the private sector with any regularity usually like to maintain files of catalogs and/or brochures from the suppliers appropriate for their needs. These serve as a resource for compiling bidders lists when they wish to solicit bids and proposals, especially when they have sudden and unexpected needs. Consequently, they will often ask you specifically for such a brochure.

If you make it your business to read the *Commerce Business Daily* to search out leads for contract opportunities, you will run across many formal requests for capability brochures to establish preliminary qualifications for contemplated future procurements. For example, the U.S. Air Force may announce that they are planning to install a new system, described synoptically, and will need certain specialized services, also synopsized. The announcement invites interested parties to submit capability brochures to qualify as bidders. Only those so qualifying will be invited to bid or propose for the work.

For these purposes, the capability brochure usually needs to be slanted—specifically oriented—to the requirement or intended requirement. Therefore, it is a common practice to assemble brochures on an individual basis, from a store of standard pages, supplemented by special pages as required. So capability brochures, at least those intended for the purposes discussed here so far, tend to be unique or to be at least custom-tailored to the individual need and application.

Some Practical Considerations

For example, you would have preprinted pages that describe your own credentials and those of any associates. You would have pages describing your resources, facilities, past projects, and other relevant items — perhaps already assembled as standard capability brochures, especially if you are so highly specialized in what you do that most of your projects are similar. But if you undertake many different kinds of projects you may find that no single model of your capability brochure is truly suitable for all cases. So, you will tend to use some standard pages but also prepare many pages especially to customize your brochure.

With a word processor, all those preprinted pages need not be literally preprinted. Instead, they may reside in your computer files, ready to be modified, adapted, and otherwise tailored to the requirement and then printed out — an almost ideal situation.

Thus those who market exclusively or almost so to government agencies usually print or copy capability brochures on a rather limited basis. They print each one (on a computer printer, that is) individually, after customizing it for the intended usage.

Capability Brochure Versus Proposal

In many ways the capability brochure resembles the proposal, in a most general fashion. In a proposal you describe the requestor's needs, as you see them, discuss them analytically, propose your solution to satisfy the needs, explain your qualifications for doing so, and present a price. This is for a specific need and project, described by the customer. In a capability brochure you do not have a specific project to address, although you may be addressing fairly specific contemplated needs, but you are describing your capabilities in a specialized arena which may encompass a variety of projects. It is an exercise in skillful writing, requiring that you demonstrate specialized expertise and capabilities, and yet show a general range of application of those talents.

One final point: Do not use a flimsy, unbound brochure for the purpose. That will almost inevitably wind up in the "circular file" (the wastebasket). To avoid this, be sure that your capability brochure is of 8-½ × 11-inch physical size and bound in some kind of substantial covers.

PROPOSALS

The capability brochure addresses general and prospective needs. The proposal addresses absolute or specific, identified needs. The capability brochure says, "These are the things I am capable of doing and can do for you." The proposal says, "Here is what I propose to do specifically about your current problem." The capability brochure may or may not be tailored for the prospect, but is more likely to be general. The proposal is always tailored specifically for a project.

Unfortunately, the one thing the two have in common is that they are rarely offered voluntarily by the consultant, but are usually produced only as requested. That is a grave mistake.

Aggressive marketing dictates that you must provide—*of your own volition*—both capability brochures and proposals at every opportunity; do not wait to be asked. Carry a supply of your standard capability brochures with you everywhere and distribute them freely. When and if you run into the special case that requires the special capability brochure, get the name of the individual who should have it, prepare the one you need promptly, and send it to that contact without delay.

The same principle applies to proposals. When you encounter someone with a specific need and you believe that he or she represents a legitimate sales lead, don't wait for a formal request. Write the proposal voluntarily as soon as you have enough information to do so and submit it. You may get an exclusive this way. You will have already done the prospective client a service in several ways, certainly these three:

1. You will probably give the prospect a clearer insight into and definition of his or her need than he or she had before. That is a result of the study you did to write the proposal.

2. You will make it possible for the prospect to avoid the labor of writing a request for proposals and all the work that attends making a procurement that way.

3. You will have given the prospect a formal presentation that he or she can study at leisure and circulate to others in the organization.

A Hazard

Many consultants note a hazard in submitting proposals: They fear that prospective clients may make their proposals or the essence of them available to competitors directly or indirectly through using their proposals as the basis for an RFP (Request for Proposals). It is a real enough hazard in the commercial marketplace, although less so in marketing to government agencies. To counter this do at least two things:

1. *Copyright the Proposal.* All that is necessary to do this – to gain a common law copyright – is to place the copyright notice prominently, usually on the title page, as follows: *Copyright* (month and year) *by* (your name). *All rights reserved.*

2. *Do not reveal all.* Tell only enough about your plan to explain it generally, but not enough to enable another to put it to use. This may be a bit tricky to achieve, but most consultants are able to judge the strategic breakpoints in what they should and should not reveal. However, make it clear to the reader [i.e., the prospective client] that there is far more to the plan than the brief summary presented in your proposal.

Formal Versus Informal Proposals

Formal proposals are required usually for large contracts, which I would define in today's world as those running substantially above $25,000. Thus, by default, those below that figure become small contracts. Of course, the division can never be that precise – although the federal government permits the expenditure of up to $25,000 as a small purchase, which can be made under a purchase order, rather than by formal contract – but must be approximate.

A formal proposal should be a bound document, running to about

20 or more pages, and—unless otherwise stipulated—containing the following categories of information:

- Introduction of yourself.
- Your statement expressing your understanding and view of the need or problem.
- A discussion of the need or problem, exploring the problem and approaches to solution.
- A proposed approach.
- The specific details of the proposed project to provide a solution.
- A description of what you will do and what you will deliver.
- Proposed schedules.
- Your qualifications.

In my normal approach to preparing proposals, I divide these items up among four chapters or sections, sometimes with appended material, organized along the following general lines with the content of each generally as follows:

1. Introduction
   Short introduction of yourself.
   Brief—but cogent—appraisal of the need or problem, in essence.
2. Discussion
   Exploration of the need/problem, alternative approaches, pros and cons of each, selection/adoption of one and reasons for your choice.
3. Proposed program
   Specifics of proposed work: organization of tasks, description of end-items, schedules, other details.
4. Experience and other qualifications
   Resume, facilities, other resources, past projects, testimonials, other relevant information.
5. Appendix (if and when needed)
   Material that may or may not be of direct interest to reader(s) but is helpful in supporting proposal—for example, complete text of report cited in proposal, list of clients, other such items.

NEWSLETTER FORMS AND FORMATS

Among the thousands of newsletters published in the United States there is a wide variety of forms and formats. Some are more or less de facto standards — found to be in common use — and so by their very appearance imediately identify the newsletter as such. Figure 6-4 illustrates a rather typical such newsletter, *The Direct Response Specialist,* written and edited by direct-mail consultant Galen Stilson and published by Galen and Jean Stilson, Editor and Associate Editor, respectively.

The rectangle enclosing the name and other data at the top of the first page is known in the newsletter trade as the *nameplate.* In this case the nameplate also encloses the bulk mail permit indicia, the copyright notice, and a list of contents.

The copy including headlines, is set in typewriter-quality type and run ragged right, rather than right justified. This newsletter is three-hole punched also to facilitate saving and filing the copies.

This is not a free newsletter although it definitely serves to help market Galen Stilson's services as a direct-mail consultant. It is also not as much of a burden to write as it would be if Stilson had not recruited the assistance of five other outstanding and well-known specialists in the field to serve as consulting editors. (Each issue carries articles by one or more of these individuals.) It is usually possible to find such individuals who will take the time to write for you, partly as a kind of *noblesse oblige* and partly for the added PR exposure it affords them. The notice listing the ownership, consulting editors (known also in the trade as *contributing editors*), place and frequency of publication, subscription rates, and other such information is known as the *masthead.* In a newspaper the masthead is generally on the editorial page, running from top to bottom; in a newsletter it is generally on one of the interior pages. In this case the publishers opted to place the masthead on the back page of the 8-page newsletter. (See Figure 6-5.) Note that the masthead also grants permission to quote freely from the content as long as attribution is made.

Again, a modern computer, equipped with one of the desktop publishing programs, is a great asset in newsletter publishing. In fact, several of the desktop publishing programs are designed especially for newsletter work. A listing is supplied at the end of this chapter.

DIRECT *the* RESPONSE
Specialist

Published by: STILSON & STILSON, P.O. Box 1075, Tarpon Springs, FL 34286

(formerly MAIL ORDER CONNECTION)

Written/Edited by... *Galen Stilson*

INSIDE ...

20 ways to improve your catalog sales ...
Write effective salutations ... Cute ads
may work ... To tease or not to tease ...
One of the top teasers ever ... and more.

EXPANDING FEATURES
INTO SELLING POINTS ...

The following examples are presented to
illustrate how to take a product feature
and turn it into a selling point. They
are excerpted from John Caples' book, HOW
TO MAKE YOUR ADVERTISING MAKE MONEY.

The first sentence tells only what the
product feature is. The second sentence
expands upon that feature in order to
make it a legitimate sales point.

To get the most out of this little exercise, you should pause after reading each
"Sentence #1" and visualize how you would
expand it. Then read Sentence #2.

Ad for Stainless Steel Cookware:

#1: The cover fits snugly.
#2: The cover fits snugly to seal in
    moisture and health-building vitamins
    and minerals.

#1: These utensils have a hard surface of
    stainless steel.
#2: These utensils have a hard surface of
    stainless steel for easy cleaning and
    lasting beauty.

#1: These utensils have molded, heat-
    resistant handles.
#2: These utensils have molded, heat-
    resistant handles that won't turn or

loosen or burn the hands of the user.

Ad for a Folding Cot:

#1: This cot has a rigidly braced,
    tubular aluminum frame.
#2: This cot has a rigidly braced, tubu-
    lar aluminum frame that provides
    strength without weight...can't rust.

Ad for a Traveling Bag:

#1: This bag has a cover of grained vinyl
    laminated to cotton.
#2: This bag has a cover of grained vinyl
    laminated to cotton that is easy to
    care for...just wipe clean.

Ad for a Book on Memory Training:

#1: This magic key opens up the memory-
    storage cells of your mind.
#2: This magic key opens up the memory-
    storage cells of your mind and
    enables you to perform amazing feats
    of memory.

Are these the best possible sales sen-
tances one could create from the features
given? No, of course not. But they show
you how simple it is to take a feature
and expand on it to make it more salable.

[Source: HOW TO MAKE YOUR ADVERTISING
MAKE MONEY by John Caples. 383 pages.
$6.95 from Prentice-Hall.]

Figure 6-4. *The Direct Response Specialist,* Issue #2, March 1987 (courtesy of
Galen and Jean Stilson)

THE DIRECT RESPONSE SPECIALIST is published 12 times per year by Stilson & Stilson, P.O. Box 1075, Tarpon Springs, FL 34286. Telephone: (813) 937-3480. **Quotations** with complete attribution are permitted. Otherwise, material may not be reproduced in whole or part in any form whatsoever, except with written permission.

Subscription prices: One year (12 issues) US $77. Two years (24 issues) US $130. Subscribers outside North America, add US $25 per year.

EDITOR: Galen Stilson. **ASSOCIATE EDITOR:** Jean Stilson.
CONSULTING EDITORS:
Rene Gnam, President, Rene Gnam Consultation Corp.;
Luther Brock, Ph.D., "The Letter Doctor";
Ed Burnett, President, Ed Burnett Consultants, Inc.;
Andrew Linick, President, L.K. Advertising;
William Cohen, Ph.D., Professor of Marketing, Calif. State Univ. at L.A.

Figure 6-5. Masthead of *The Direct Response Specialist* (courtesy of Galen and Jean Stilson)

SUMMARY: RULES AND EDUCATION

If there is a single most important truth that should have emerged in this chapter it is this: Rules in all the activities discussed here are for other people, not for you. That is, they are for the people who formulated them, for they are expressions of what those people have found to be true *for them* and have decided ought to be true for you. But are they? In that same edition of *The Direct Response Specialist* (Figure 6-4) Galen Stilson presents a portion of the outstanding copy used in a successful salesletter. And then Stilson "discovers" that the copy writer failed to include a postscript to the letter, thereby violating a copywriting rule. And his letter was successful nevertheless! How can one account for that?

Once again, let me invoke the wisdom of the U.S. Army Infantry training school at Fort Benning, Georgia: "Whatever works is right." Do read *The Direct Response Specialist,* the *DM News,* and other periodicals of the trade, and learn the rules of others. They may work for you. But remember that they are others' rules. Test them. Try out your own ideas and test them on a small scale so that you make $50 mistakes, not $5,000 mistakes—for you will make mistakes; that is how you will learn. In fact, they aren't really mistakes; they are education, and you may as well gain the experience as cheaply as possible. You can't do that without trying out ideas. So regard all rules and all conventional ways of doing things as tentative and experimental, to be accepted only after being proven in practice.

That is the way to become an expert. It is the only way.

A FEW USEFUL REFERENCES

There are many computer programs devoted to what is now called *desktop publishing* (and the number is growing rapidly). Many are specifically designed for newsletter publication. They enable you to actually make up the newsletter on-screen by electronic cut-and-paste operations, and they even furnish clip art electronically. There are other related programs that enable you to set type, including headlines, and make up charts, graphs, and other illustrative material. Several such programs are listed here, along with other bibliographic references.

DESKTOP PUBLISHING SOFTWARE

The Newsroom Pro
Springboard Software, Inc.
7808 Creekridge Circle, Inc.
Minneapolis, MN 55435

ClickArt Personal Publisher
Software Publishing Corporation
P.O. Box 7210
1901 Landings Drive
Mountain View, CA 94039

Fontasy
Prosoft
7248 Bellaire Ave
P.O. Box 560
N. Hollywood, CA 91603

FormWorx
Analytx International, Inc.
1365 Massachusetts Ave.
Arlington, MA 02174

The Office Publisher®
930 Bernicia Ave.
Sunnyvale, CA 94086

RELEVANT PERIODICALS

Desktop Graphics
6000 N. Forest Park Drive
Peoria, IL 61614

Publish!
PCW Communications
501 Second Street
San Francisco, CA 94107

Desktop Publishing™
PCW Communications, Inc.
501 Second Street
San Francisco, CA 94107

CHAPTER 7

REACTIVE/PASSIVE METHODS: BUILDING YOUR PROFESSIONAL IMAGE

There are both tigers and pussycats in marketing, and sometimes the pussycats get better results than the tigers do.

IF THE SHOE FITS . . .

You may or may not be comfortable with the aggressive marketing methods we have been discussing. Many shrink from marketing, especially aggressive marketing. Still, marketing is an absolute essential to your survival as a consultant. Even physicians and other medical specialists for whom commercial advertising and other overt marketing are forbidden find discreet, permissible ways to market. If such is the case for you, I offer a variety of other far less aggressive ways to win clients. They can be used as an alternative to the more aggressive methods, or together with them. They have many virtues of their own. Despite the stress laid here on proactive, aggressive marketing, those marketing methods that I have chosen to designate as passive methods play an important and necessary role also in the marketing of your services. They should certainly not be neglected.

The lines of distinction between the methods are not clear cut, of course. By even the most basic definition, the aggressive methods are those that go out after the client, pursuing relentlessly, while the passive method is to wait for the client to come to you—or to persuade the client to come to you. More specifically, the passive methods are those designed primarily to build your professional image and give you greater visibility. They are methods that make many others, including but not restricted to prospective clients, aware of your existence and the services you offer, as distinct from methods that are designed especially to pursue prospects and sales leads individually.

There are many points of similarity between the methods. Involved are many of the same media and activities—writing, speaking, PR, and others already discussed—but there is at least this distinguishing feature of these passive methods: The primary objective of the activity is not to generate individual sales leads to pursue directly, nor is the activity necessarily addressed directly to people identified as good prospects. Neither is directly relevant to the overall goal of gaining increased visibility and building a professional image.

In a large sense this sounds very much as though it is a PR effort, and in a sense that is so, but certainly you will be alert for sales leads resulting from any of these activities, whether or not that was your primary goal. In all these marketing activities you are demonstrating your professionalism and competence, but you will also be letting your respondents and audiences know what your capabilities are and what you can *do* for clients.

THE METHODS IN GENERAL

The underlying strategy of proactive marketing is to find prospects and screen them to uncover sales leads to pursue individually. The underlying strategy of passive marketing, as applied here, is to gain publicity while presenting the desired image in that public exposure to the view of those who are likely to become clients. A simple enough idea. And the basic media and means, which are conventional enough, are also simple enough, including the following:

- Writing.
- Speaking.
- Participating.
- Achieving.

Let's look at each of these to see how each can be employed to achieve the end-goals.

WRITING

I chose to begin with writing, rather than with speaking, because I believe writing to be less traumatic than speaking for those who shrink from both—and far too many do just that. While a great many have a distaste for writing, many have an absolute *fear* of speaking publicly. They would sooner face an angry polar bear.

In speaking of writing, we are speaking of writing for publication, because publicity and image-building are the objectives. But we are also suggesting writing for publication in media that are likely to be read by the class of readers who also happen to be suitable prospects for your services; there is little point in writing to a different audience than that, except a general audience that will include prospects. For example, it would certainly serve your purposes to be published in the *New York Times* or *Wall Street Journal*, despite the probability that 95 percent of the readers would never be good prospects for you. But that remaining five percent—! That is a large audience for your purposes, well worth reaching.

Let us not deceive ourselves. Like most independent consultants, you are not going to write for publication in the *New York Times* or *Wall Street Journal*. Your targets must be considerably more modest than that.

Writing for Trade Publications

Every profession, trade, and industry has its own trade periodicals—newsletters, tabloids, and magazines. In some cases there are a great many such periodicals covering the field; in others, surprisingly few. There is no apparent connection between the number of newsletters covering the field and the size of the industry or the number of people employed therein.

In any case, just as consultant/publisher Galen Stilson welcomes editorial contributions by other professionals in his field, so other editors and publishers will be gratified to receive your contributions. Some will pay modest sums of money for your writing—three to ten cents a word, typically, or perhaps $5 an item—but like others in your position you do not write for the money, if any, but for the PR benefit of being published—to have your byline appear as often as possible—in the pages of all publications in your field.

You may not think that there is a great deal of glory in appearing in most of these modest little journals, and to tell the truth there is not. However, in addition to the progress you make toward becoming a recognizable figure in your field, you are also beginning a collection of clippings of your own intellectual achievements: your published articles. These become assets in your resume, in your capability brochure, and—especially—in your proposals.

Many people starting out to write in this manner for the first time tend to ask the inevitable question, "What will I write about?" Here are a few ideas for things to write about:

- Technical discussions in re your field and the industry or profession you address in seeking clients.
- Your position or theory on any relevant controversial issue of the moment.
- Articles on consulting generally and/or vis-a-vis the field or industry to which you offer your services—for example:

    What *is* consulting?

    What can consulting do for you?

    Consulting case histories.

    How to choose a consultant.

- Analysis and explanation of relevant technical matters.

Appearing in a Letters to the Editor column can also be helpful. I have known of cases where such an appearance was most beneficial to the writer in surprising ways. In one case, someone in a major book publishing house was sufficiently impressed by such a letter to write the author and ask if he would be interested in writing a book on the subject of his letter.

Writing for Your Own Newsletter

If you publish your own newsletter you have even wider opportunities. You *own* the medium. Here are just a few suggestions for materials you can write (or have some contributor write) for publication in your own journal:

- News of the industry—that industry which you serve or hope to serve as a consultant: mergers, acquisitions, divestitures, personnel changes, new products, other items.
- Features about your specialty vis-a-vis the industry.
- Reviews of current books, magazine articles in re the industry.
- Editorials.
- Questions (from readers) and your answers.

Papers and Proceedings

Many professionals who never write for commercial publication, not even in trade periodicals, do write papers to be presented before conferences and other such events (generally annual conclaves) of the professional societies to which they belong. This is publication, too, albeit of a special kind, when the society publishes the proceedings of the event at which your paper was read. The proceedings are normally a bound volume of all the papers read, often divided into classes and categories.

Such professional papers and publication in the official proceedings are generally more prestigious than are articles in commercial periodicals. They tend to be regarded more seriously as "professional" writings. And they are at least as useful as citations in and exhibits or appendices to proposals, brochures, resumes, and any other literature you may prepare for marketing purposes. The opportunity to write and present these papers is one of the several benefits of membership in such organizations. (Of course, you are not supposed to join such organizations for marketing purposes, but you *can* gain marketing advantages from such membership.)

Writing a Book

The writing that normally brings you the greatest amount of prestige as a serious and distinguished professional is the writing and publication of a book. Probably the most prestigious type of book is the scholarly work, replete with footnotes, references, bibliographic listings, and other evidences of careful scholarship and painstaking research. That is the type of book that comes ultimately to be cited by others, even sometimes to be adopted as a text by a college or university. But, on the other hand, that is also the type of book that is usually circulated (sold, that is) and read in quite limited quantity and sometimes remains in obscurity forever. And for this reason it is often the type of book most difficult to get published. Still, having a book published is probably far less difficult than most people imagine, especially in these times when some 40-50,000 books are published each year, more than one-half nonfiction works of various kinds. Nor does your book have to be large. On the contrary, with costs as high as they are in these times, many book publishers tend to favor modestly-sized books, and many relatively small books are published today.

Self-Publishing Your Book

Many books are published today by their authors, either because the author has not found a commercial publisher willing to publish his or her book or because the author wishes to be his or her own publisher for business reasons. The fact that the author has not found a commercial publisher is not necessarily a reflection of the quality of the book; many highly successful books were self-published, at least in their initial editions, and more than a few talented and famous writers— Edgar Allan Poe, for example— self-published their early work. Despite that, self-publishing is generally interpreted by others as meaning that your book was not worthy of publication by the established book publishers. Moreover, part of the prestige of having your book published derives from the prominence and reputation of the publisher, from the evidence that your book was accepted by such a publisher. It is therefore highly desirable, if you wish to gain prestige from having a book published, that you do try earnestly to find an established commercial publisher for your book. And the "secret" of doing so—assuming, of course, that your manuscript is a publishable one—lies in doing two things right: One, do careful research to find the *right kind* of publishers—those who publish books of the same general type—and into the accepted practices of preparing manuscripts and seeking publishers. Two, be persevering in your quest, which is at least as important as the other injunctions and caveats because many rejections have nothing to do with the quality or publishability of your book but reflect publisher's problems that are totally unrelated to that, such as having a book on the same subject already in production.

One thing to note, in passing, is that even if you succeed in having one or more books published, you should still work at having papers, articles, and letters published. Being the author of one or more books tends to be prestigious, probably even more than being the author of professional papers. But authoring many articles and letters—especially articles—usually brings you more visibility than being the author of books and papers; many more people in the industry or profession you address become aware of your existence when your name graces the pages of the periodicals they read regularly.

PUBLIC SPEAKING

Addressing groups in public is probably as effective as writing is in conferring visibility on you, and if you handle the platform well it can be even more productive simply because the audience can see what you look like and how you handle yourself. They can—and will—judge you in a way that they cannot do just from your writing. Judging you from your writing means, principally, judging you by *what* you say in your writing (although you usually get a tiny bionote for identification). An audience judges you differently. They evaluate your physical appearance, even how you dress. (One critic who did not approve of my choice of clothes suggested rather caustically that I needed a clothing consultant, although he was asked to comment on my presentation, not my appearance. That undoubtedly colored his opinion of my presentation, however.) They measure your apparent self-confidence. They judge your charisma. They assay your manner of responding to questions and comments—even your willingness to accept and respond freely. They audit your fluency. But probably most of all, they judge your persona. If you are a likable personality, they work hard at thinking the best of you. If they find you offensive or abrasive in some way, they will look for things to criticize and condemn; they react as humans, of course.

Now that does not mean that you should be a Bob Hope. You don't have to be a comedian or a "hail-fellow-well-met" to be likable. But you do need these things for a winning platform personality:

A pleasant manner.   You must make it obvious that you are most pleased to be there on the platform talking to (not at) these fine people, and you thoroughly enjoy it. That's hard to fake; audiences have a talent for sensing phoniness of any kind. Try to truly feel that pleasure.

Enthusiasm, open and obvious.   Nothing is more offensive or insulting to an audience than a speaker who appears to be bored to death. (Many in the audience will interpret that as contempt for the audience.) *Show* your enthusiasm. Be uninhibited in raising your voice, gesturing, stomping excitedly about the platform, invading the audience space by coming down the aisle, making faces, pausing for effect, and otherwise acting and reacting *naturally*, as you would at an exciting ball game. No, you will not make a fool or a spectacle of yourself, nor will you damage your image; quite the contrary, you will present honest emotion and your audience will love it because nothing in that room is as contagious as honest enthusiasm. It must be honest. If you are not enthusiastic about the subject, don't lecture on it. Find another one, one that you can get enthusiastic about.

A relaxed appearance.   You must appear to be at your ease with your audience if you expect your audience to be at ease with you. (Do not confuse this with a *bored* appearance, which is to be shunned.)

An obvious graciousness.   Offer an open and sincere invitation to ask questions, make comments, challenge your statements. Respond good-naturedly, showing a ready willingness to admit the possibility that you are in error or that the topic is a subjective one—a matter of opinion. Don't "prove" the challenger or questioner wrong, even if he or she is. Be courteous to everyone, even the occasional (and seemingly inevitable) heckler who seems to show up at such events and/or other objectionable characters. (Even if the rest of your audience is offended by such guests they will judge you by the tact and patience you exhibit in dealing with them.)

Speaking Opportunities

The opportunities to speak publicly are as ample as you wish them to be. You can arrange to speak at any or all of the following occasions and events, a few of which I have already mentioned:

Meetings of associations, societies, other organizations. It doesn't matter whether you belong to these or not. I have lectured to many, many organizations, few of which I have belonged to, sometimes for fees but often out of a kind of *noblesse oblige*. For example, these have included local small-business associations, public-interest/community groups, congressional-coalition groups, local clubs—computer clubs, consultant societies, writers' clubs, and others devoted to such special interests. I have spoken to them on the subject of government marketing, consulting, writing, and whatever else I have been involved in with enough success to have a little credibility as an expert of sorts. When I spoke to the local chapter of the National Speakers Association, for example, I was favored with a small but gratifying consulting contract shortly thereafter from one of the audience, who called me in again on a later occasion for another assignment. And a luncheon presentation to a local group of editorial-business owners produced, ultimately, a profitable in-house seminar assignment. Many times a free speech, given with no thought of reward, resulted in an assignment that paid a substantial fee.

Guest speaking at others' seminars. You can get yourself invited to be a guest speaker at many seminars, as I have been, sometimes for an honorarium (a modest fee), often for the privilege of serving society at large and dropping a supply of my brochures and business cards on a literature table in the back of the room. Sometimes these appearances have resulted in new clients and assignments, often not. But I regret none of them. They were all worth doing.

Your own, paid-attendance (public) seminars. Although you stage attendance-paid seminars as a for-profit enterprise primarily, rather than as a marketing effort in pursuit of consulting clients, assignments often result from good presentations at any event and on any occasion.

On Getting Invited

Being invited to speak at the various occasions may come about spontaneously and often does. But that is an unreliable way to generate the opportunities to make these appearances; that is depending on chance, which means that you are not in even limited control of the situation, as you should be. You have to manage the creation of these opportunities, and you can do so with a little ordinary marketing activity.

It is not difficult in fact, to market yourself as a speaker, especially if you are willing to speak on any basis offered — for a regular speaker's fee, for a nominal honorarium, or entirely without compensation. Many organizations and many seminar producers want speakers but have most modest — or zero — budgets for guest speakers. A suitable announcement — I suggest a news release, as suggested in Figure 7-1 — circulated to local groups, clubs, associations, seminar producers, and others will soon bring you offers. I believe the news release to be more useful than a letter because it confers greater freedom and flexibility, while it also serves as a medium for soliciting publicity from the local press and other media.

This type of announcement has multiple uses, although its ostensible primary use is as a PR — public relations — device. It is intended for the news media, but in practice it is sent out to *all* possible public relations media — newspapers, newsletters, trade journals, and TV and radio news rooms — and used as an insert in direct-mail campaigns. You can also send it, alone and without embellishment, to associations of all kinds as a general announcement.

It is possible to write this information in the first person, as a letter requires, and say everything gracefully, but a great many individuals find this difficult and have a much easier time when writing a news release because of its third-person style. Of course, you can do this as a letter, if you prefer, but I suggest that you prepare a news release of this type first, and use it as an enclosure with a brief letter if you believe that a letter is a necessity.

A letter might be necessary in making your availability as a guest speaker at seminars and as a member of panels known to producers of

WINDFALL ASSOCIATES, CONSULTANTS
3201 Serendipity Lane
Happenstance Falls, OH 45555

NEWS RELEASE

June 20, 1989

Contact: J. Silver, 555-0001

LOCAL CONSULTANT AVAILABLE AS SPEAKER

Harrison Eloquent, a Happenstance Falls marketing consultant and
president of Windfall Associates, announced today his availability as a public
speaker on several subjects in which his experience lies and in which he
renders services. His special field is direct-response marketing, known to
some people as "mail order," and he speaks most often on the application to
direct-response marketing methods to the solution of civic problems. The
topics involved include explanations and discussions of graphic arts, copy
writing, packaging, and other other related matters.

Eloquent is active in civic affairs and has spoken before a number of our
civic groups and associations, including our local Rotary, Lions Club, Small
Business Association (of which he is a member), and Manufacturers Association.
He invites all to call him at the number given above to make necessary
arrangements.

###

Figure 7-1. Announcement of availability as a speaker

seminars, program managers of associations, and others responsible
for putting together programs. A brief letter explaining such availability, enclosing a copy of the news release would serve the purpose
nicely.

The suggested release makes no mention of fees, unless you wish
to make it a policy that you accept no fees or honoraria for speaking
before groups. It is permissible to state that—you may wish to call it a
civic duty, for example—but do not state fees. Readers will probably
infer that you charge a fee, but most will call you to inquire about it.

You can then decide what you wish to do. (My own practice is to charge normal fees, except in cases where I believe it to be civic duty or *noblesse oblige* to speak without fee, as in the case of a civic group, a small club, or a fledgling association.)

Annual conventions often include entire schedules of association seminars. For example, the well-known trade magazine, *Training*, stages several conventions (with an accompanying substantial trade show) each year, the main one during the first week of December in New York, another in Chicago, and another in San Francisco. Each of these week-long events includes a lengthy program of 3-hour seminars every morning and afternoon. The seminars are presented by volunteer specialists, many of them consultants, on a no-fee basis. However, the presenter is paid for travel and subsistence, gets publicity, and has a pass to "mingle" at all events for the week. Most who participate do so for the PR and marketing benefits they achieve.

Community College Courses

You may wish to offer your speaking services to local community colleges in adult-education programs, sometimes at a single session of a couple of hours. These colleges normally pay small honoraria, but they do attract people who can become clients. (I have gained clients from such speaking engagements, and in one case it was a major client who called a number of years later!) The way to investigate this is to inquire into the programs at any local or nearby community colleges. Typically, the programs are divided into a number of categories, and the college is always seeking good instructors. In fact, the usual origin of a class is a proposal from an individual who offers to conduct the class or lecture. In many cases the colleges are actively seeking lecturers for certain kinds of courses, and it is only the lack of a suitable lecturer that delays the announcement of the course.

PR AND THE BROADCAST MEDIA

PR—public relations—offers an excellent avenue for gaining visibility and building your image. Most of what we have been discussing in this chapter has been PR—the seizing of every opportunity to speak publicly, appear on panels, appear in print, and become visible elsewhere. One avenue we have not so far discussed is appearing on radio and TV.

Why the Broadcast Media?

The broadcast media are equivalent to the daily press in PR importance. In fact, they are analogous to the press in that they include news programs, documentaries, and special features in their programming, just as newspapers do. However, probably the best targets for your purposes are the many talk shows, both local and national, on radio and TV.

Getting Yourself on the Air

As Dr. Jeffrey Lant points out in his new book, *Money Talks* (JLA Associates, Cambridge, MA, 1987), being successful in print is so helpful in getting yourself invited to go on the air that it is virtually a requirement. He (Lant) observes that media people tend to be far more impressed with credentials thus established—in print—than with licenses and degrees. It is true enough that many talk show guests are authors, noteworthy in some way. But happily, while the observation about print credentials is true for the general case, there are many exceptions. An individual is invited to a talk show because the producer believes that the individual will make an interesting or entertaining guest, whatever the basis for that assessment. In my own case, for example, before I became the author of many books—of any books published by a commercial book publisher, in fact—I appeared on such shows as an authority on marketing to the federal government, with an interesting profession—consulting to those who needed help in winning government contracts. Perhaps more important than that, however, were some novel and interesting facts I could reveal about government procurement, such as being paid about $6,000 to answer the government's mail and contracts in which the government rented mules and handlers. Add to that my willingness and ability to answer call-in questions spontaneously and chat with callers while we were on the air, as another inducement. (Later, to be sure, interviewers did focus on questioning me about my books.)

What Is Interesting About You?

Before you attempt to get on the broadcast media try to put yourself in the place of the producer (not the host) who makes the decisions and to whom you must communicate your request and answer the question: Why should you be invited to appear and be interviewed? What is it that is interesting about you and/or what you have to say? Or what have you done? To answer those questions you must train yourself to think in terms of the nonexpert general public. What is interesting to you, as a professional and expert at something is not at issue here.

As someone with a knowledge of electronics, I might find the new "surface mounting" or some new "sputtering" technique fascinating, but the average individual would be bored to tears with it, even if I were to explain it carefully in the simplest lay terms. The average viewer would be more likely to be entranced by some of the things that applications of these might help bring about, such as an entire computer in a package that fits into a shirt pocket or an automobile radar that prevents collisions. Other than the celebrated — the famous and the infamous — it is the kinds of people and things that audiences find interesting that producers want to put on the air: That which is likely to have a direct effect on their lives and/or that which is new, novel, outré, gigantic, minuscule, and otherwise completely out of the ordinary. What do you have to offer that meets any of these specifications?

Aside from failing to offer something interesting to the producer, one of the most basic mistakes many individuals make in trying to get on the air is the same error that beginning free lance writers usually commit about the publications they are addressing: They make no effort to study the program and determine its format and policy — the kinds of guests normally invited to appear, the topics discussed, the taboos, and other characteristics of the show. To the untrained eye and ear such shows probably often appear to have no set format or policy, but invite and interview almost anybody. That is never true, of course. Some shows change their formats and policies, if and when it seems necessary and wise to do so, but there are always specific formats and policies, and you must take the time to study and understand them if you want to be invited on to be interviewed.

Who to Contact and How

There is one other common mistake that many individuals make in trying to get themselves booked on broadcast shows: They write and call the host of the show. Understand here and now that the "boss" of the show is the producer. The producer is responsible for everything — including the programming, which is what you are trying to become a part of. The producer will book you on the show or no one will. You write, call, besiege, harass, and otherwise make life miserable for the producer, not the host (except in those cases where the producer and host are the same individual, as is sometimes the case. But even then you address the individual as the producer, not as the host!)

Ordinarily, it is not easy to get a *yes* from the producer. In fact, producers normally like to find the subjects *they* want to use, not have the subject come after them; they prefer to be the pursuers and not the pursued. Perhaps they are like most of us and do not appreciate anything that comes to them too easily. They may be even suspicious of anything offered too freely or perhaps it is simply the typical experience of producers that most volunteers are not what they are looking for, and they are reasonably sure that interviewing such prospects will almost always be unrewarding. Whichever the case, you are swimming upstream immediately, against the current and against the tide. Nevertheless, it is the only way; otherwise, you must leave it to chance, which means it will almost surely never happen.

Before I had my chance to appear on the rather highly-rated Washington, DC show *Panorama* (only recently deceased after about a score of years on the air), I did in fact virtually besiege the producer with telephone calls and letters as reminders that I was available and on short notice. That quick availability is most important. Since Washington is the kind of place it is and *Panorama* was a rather "big time" kind of show, the producer never lacked for interesting — or, at least, important — guests, most of them far more important and far more interesting than I. Still, I harassed that poor woman until she not only knew my name, what I did for a living, and what I wanted to be interviewed about, but she also almost knew what I liked for lunch! So she had no problem at all in remembering my name when she suddenly got stuck for a guest one afternoon because her scheduled guest canceled out or failed to appear. Panicky for a replacement, she called and was suitably grateful when I promised to be there in a few minutes. (She obviously had underestimated the appeal of what I had to offer, for she and I were besieged with telephone calls and letters for weeks afterward from viewers who wanted to know more.)

There is something to be learned here, and it applies in many places and in many situations: Emergencies—last minute disasters, sudden changes, and unforeseen needs—do occur with distressing regularity (distressing for the victims) in radio and TV shows, as they do in your world. They are others' problems—producers' problems—but like all problems, represent opportunities for you, if you are prepared to take advantage of these situations. To capitalize on these inevitabilities you must do two things:

1. Be persistent in keeping after producers so that they not only know of your eagerness to get on their shows and what you have to offer that their audiences will find interesting, but also that they learn your name so well that they are unable to forget it. Only repetition and unrelenting persistence, to use Jeffrey Lant's words, will achieve this reliably.

2. Make it abundantly clear, over and over so that, again, the producer is completely unable to ever forget it, that you are a dynamic individual who is ready to drop what you are doing and fill in as a last-minute rescuer when there is trouble. Instead of a *plea* to be allowed on, make it an *offer* of rescue when the emergency arises.

The idea is to make the producers so aware of your name and readiness—your *offer* of availability on an emergency basis—that they cannot help but think of you almost automatically in an emergency situation. (It is equally important that producers know what your own special expertise is because sometimes they need someone with special qualifications to act as a counterpoint to another guest or to serve on a panel.)

There is a downside to this and you should know it. Some producers, especially the producers of those top-rated national talk shows, build a safety factor into their programming by overbooking deliverately, as commercial airlines have been doing of late. Shows that feature guests usually have a kind of "green room" or "ready room," where guests waiting to go on sit around staring at each other or watching the monitor. But on many of those shows there is usually a larger reservoir of guests in the ready room than the show can accommodate, insurance against last-minute emergencies and panic. Those of lowest priority, some of them even guests of considerable reputation and highly recognizable names and faces—often never get to go on at all, unless someone of higher priority is taken ill or for some other reason cannot appear.

That may seem a rather cynical and cruel approach for producers to take, one that is hard on guests. But the producers' world is a harsh world, and they firmly believe that such draconian measures are not only necessary but completely justified. So you may find yourself in that situation: a guest—perhaps even a frequent guest—in the green room and never in the studio before the cameras and microphones. That's a hazard you must accept, unfortunately. But persist, nevertheless; eventually you will succeed, and it will get just a bit easier the next time and each succeeding time, as you gain experience and demonstrate that you are a desirable guest to interview.

OTHER PR ACTIVITY

Appearing in print as the subject of the writing, rather than as an author, is the classic use of PR, one that Hollywood has often depicted in extravagant and even dramatic terms. In Hollywood PR people are always wild-eyed zealots with ingenious ideas, a carload of brass, and nerves of tempered steel, who achieve stunningly brilliant and spectacular successes. In life, PR is only rarely dramatic; for the most part it is a dull and unrelenting attack with a lengthy stream of tiny successes, and hardly ever a single monumental victory. Public figures have a somewhat easier time of it. They can more easily "plant" items; the newspapers, tabloids, and magazines are eager to accept such items. For you, print publicity is much more difficult. But it is not impossible, although it does require persevering effort and perhaps more than a little bit of *chutzpah*—probably the most important and most effective element! Certainly, PR success does not come to shrinking violets.

How Different Must You Be?

At one point in *Money Talks*, Jeffrey Lant relates that following the publication of one of his earlier books, *The Unabashed Self-Promoter's Guide*, he had the opportunity to speak with many people who were seeking publicity unsuccessfully or failing to seek it at all. Among the excuses he heard were laments such as these:

"Promotion isn't for me. What I do isn't unique or special in any way."
"Other people do what I do."

This is reminiscent of a story about a Milwaukee brewer who retained a well-known New York advertising professional. The brewer's clear view was that there are no truly significant differences between or among most brands of beer so the marketing problem is one of achieving the most effective advertising. In his quest for an angle or lead for a campaign, the advertising executive was struck by the fact that the beer bottles were sterilized with live steam immediately prior to being filled. He proposed to build the campaign around that fact. The brewer protested that this method of sterilizing the bottles was a common industry practice. "Everybody does it," he explained. The advertising executive was unmoved. "That's irrelevant," he responded, "because no one else *says* so!"

The public had no way of knowing that this was not a unique feature practiced for their safety, and so it was possible to build a successful campaign around it.

This is a truism in PR also because winning the PR battle is as much a marketing job as is the selling of anything else. It is the customer's *perception* that matters. And for that word *customer* you can substitute *reader, producer, editor*, or the identification of anyone else you must persuade; it is always that other individual's perception, not yours, that counts. Marketing involves shaping that other individual's perception, and success or failure in PR, as in marketing, is an excellent indicator of how well you have done that.

The Release

The chief PR tool for many people is the news release, such as the example in Figure 7-1. It should be double-spaced, carry a date, and a "contact"—someone to call for more information, should the editor want more or perhaps want a photo. If it runs more than a page, it should say *more* at the bottom and should be on one side of the paper only. The end of the item should be indicated. The common indicators used are these: *END*, *###*, *(30)*.

Figure 7-1 was designed to do double duty as a release and as a kind of salesletter. In fact, it's use as a release was secondary; the main recipients were to be respondents, rather than media. Using a release for publicity, as in the case under discussion, means that the media—print primarily—are the main targets. The release should therefore be designed for that purpose. And that means putting a "hook" of some sort into it. Open with an attention getter that will arouse curiosity and provoke interest immediately. But first recognize two relevant facts:

1. The release was designed to stress your availability as a speaker, and so focused on that fact.

2. the term *news release* is a euphemism; in many, if not most cases, the purpose is publicity, not news, and some even refer to these documents as *publicity releases*, rather than as news releases.

The significance of this latter item is this: A "news" release does not have to carry news at all; it can as easily be a *feature* story of some sort. Editors are glad to get feature stories too. In fact, a good feature story is certainly better than a poor news story; what editor would not agree?

Interest is therefore the more important consideration. Capture attention with a good hook, and then make good on the promise of the hook.

Finding a Hook

Admittedly, it is not easy to come up with good hooks, as a rule, but it can be done. If that release shown in Figure 7-1 were to be recast as a news or publicity release, it might appear along the lines of Figure 7-2. Here, the hook is the use of mail order to solve a few community problems (Hopefully a novel enough idea to arouse interest), and the term *mail order* is used instead of *direct response marketing* because it is probably far more familiar and understandable to most people.

With a little imagination and a lot of energy and determination, you can find many interesting ideas upon which to base releases. The energy can be expended in the public library, in research. Here are just a few starter ideas for you:

- The history of your own special field: How did it come about? What were its beginnings? Whose are the great names in it? What were their own beginnings?

WINDFALL ASSOCIATES, CONSULTANTS
3201 Serendipity Lane
Happenstance Falls, OH 45555

NEWS RELEASE

June 20, 1989

Contact: J. Silver, 555-0001

USING MAIL ORDER TO SOLVE CIVIC PROBLEMS?

Harrison Eloquent, a Happenstance Falls marketing consultant who specializes in what he calls "direct response" marketing (which others often refer to as "mail order"), believes that the application of direct-response marketing techniques can be effective in solving many of our civic problems. For example, he points out, direct-response methodology offers a less abrasive method of collecting delinquent taxes than the methods now used. He believes that whenever the civic authorities are seeking the willing cooperation of the citizens of our community they should use direct mail to persuade citizens to comply and cooperate.

Eloquent is president of Windfall Associates, a local small business. He is active in civic affairs, and is a member of and has spoken before a number of our civic groups and associations, including our local Rotary, Lions Club, Small Business Association (of which he is a member), and Manufacturers Association.

###

Figure 7-2. Publicity release

- The same as the above for things related to your field. If you are a marketing consultant, what is the history and prehistory of advertising? What about the same for packaging and industrial design?
- Do you have some novel ideas, as in Figure 7-1 and 7-2? What are they? How would they affect the average person?

CHAPTER 8

REACTIVE/PASSIVE METHODS: SPEAKING AND WRITING

Speaking and writing are probably the most prestigious income-producing activities you can engage in to build and support the professional image you need.

HAVING IT BOTH WAYS

One of the major problems of the independent consulting practice is the cost of marketing, and that cost is primarily in your time. You can engage in all the PR and many other marketing activities described earlier at relatively little out-of-pocket cost in dollars, but the cost in your time can easily become prohibitive. The time you dedicate to such activities is overhead. It must be paid for, so it becomes an operating cost calculated in dollars, and you must set your rates accordingly. But there are, of course, limits to how high your rates can go before they cause you to lose clients.

Fortunately, there is a solution: You can combine at least some of your PR and other marketing activity with income-producing activity. You can undertake activities that produce income but have PR and other marketing benefits as side-effects. The two principal and most important such activities are speaking and writing.

SPEAKING AND WRITING FOR PROFIT

Not everyone who speaks publicly does so for PR or other marketing purposes. Nor is every speaker a consultant, although the combination of speaking, writing, and consulting is a common one. Many consultants undertake public speaking out of a conviction that it is a rational and proper activity of their professions and should produce income for them. That is a perfectly valid and defensible position. (In fact, some consultants discover that speaking is their favorite activity, and so they make it their primary one.) At the same time, there is no good reason for not gaining whatever PR and other marketing benefits derive normally from speaking before groups, whether to win clients for consulting assignments or for additional speaking engagements. You can do both—earn a significant income from speaking as a major element in your consulting practice, while also gaining useful marketing PR from your speaking engagements.

Exactly the same things can be said for writing. Writing can become a major income-producing element while it serves also to bring you effective PR to promote your consulting practice generally. Writing "seriously"—articles and books on subjects in or related to your professional field—is probably an even greater image enhancer than is public speaking, especially in the case of authoring books. Certainly, you normally reach a much larger and wider audience through your books than through speaking if your books do well at all. Add to that the factor that many people are much more impressed—even awed— by your ability to have your book or books published than by your appearance on the platform. Having one or more books published is, in our society, considered by many to be an admirable act of scholarship and substantial evidence of your competence. And a book that sells well can contribute substantially to your income. Finally, you may find so many rewards in writing and/or speaking that you devote a major portion of your time to writing or speaking, or to both.

In terms of profitability, writing books is likely to pay better than writing articles, but speaking is probably a more consistent and reliable source of income than writing is. Free lance writing is high on the list of ventures with uncertain and erratic success, is a notoriously underpaid profession for probably 95 percent of those who practice it. (Who can predict the reactions of the public to a new offering of any kind?) On the other hand, should the lighting strike—unexpected and almost always totally unpredictable great success with a book—the financial rewards of writing can be quite great.

FISH OR FOWL?

Many individuals combine and integrate the three professions so completely that it is difficult to say whether the individual is a consultant who also speaks and writes, a writer who also speaks and consults, or a speaker who also writes and consults. (And some even become entertainment personalities, as Art Linkletter did.) For example, the pages of Dottie Walters' bimonthly journal, *Sharing Ideas*, written for professional public speakers, are full of stories of such diverse activities by the readers, many of whom are also members of the National Speakers Association. Several articles in those pages advise readers on effective methods for combining consulting and, especially, writing with their speaking activities. Well-known consultant and consultant-trainer Howard Shenson often appears in the pages of *Sharing Ideas*, as do the distinguished speaker/consultant/author Nido Qubein and many others of great repute in one or more of the three professions.

There is a large population of men and women who practice public speaking as a profession, some as a part-time activity but many on a full-time basis. Many of these individuals, including those who consider themselves full-time professional speakers, write extensively and more than a few are also consultants. They speak at colleges, conventions, business meetings, professional conferences, on cruise ships, at luncheons, banquets, seminars, and at sundry other occasions. They travel extensively to do this, sometimes for individual engagements, sometimes on extended speaking tours. Most have come out of other professions. Many are still practicing their original professions but are better known as speakers or writers, a la Norman Vincent Peale, a clergyman well known as a spellbinding speaker, but best known—famous, in fact—for his book, *The Power of Positive Thinking*. (In fact, that classic book has been the model for hordes of imitators, among whom probably no one has covered the subject nearly so well or so successfully as its author.)

THE SPEAKING BUSINESS

In the speaking business there are speakers, agents, and lecture bureaus. Their roles, as well as the distinctions between and among their roles, appear to be greatly misunderstood. This leads many neophytes in the speaking business to send their resumes, letters, and brochures to lecture bureaus and fume indignantly when the bureaus do not respond with offers. (I plead guilty to having once been precisely one of these ingenuous beginners!)

Lecture bureaus do not present the speaker at all; they represent and perform a service for the client, the organization who retains and pays the fees for the speaker. The lecture bureau may list your resume — you may just be exactly what some client is looking for today or next week — but will not go out and seek speaking dates for you. Quite the contrary, the lecture bureau goes out and seeks the speaker the client wishes to engage, acting in behalf of the client — as a booking agent, in fact.

In some cases the client wishes a specific speaker, perhaps Henny Youngman or some other well-known name, perhaps a speaker of a given type (e.g., "a Henny Youngman-type"), or perhaps one who speaks on a given subject. The lecture bureau will try to find just what the client wants, and may send the client resumes, brochures, and/or audition tapes of several candidates for the client to review. The client may invite more than one lecture bureau to submit candidates to meet the requirement, just as companies in need of help often list their needs with a number of the "job shops" of the defense and related high-tech industries. (These are companies who supply technical-professional consultants as temporaries to a high-tech employers.)

Some lecture bureaus will tackle and handle any and all requirements; others may specialize. Some, for example, specialize in celebrity speakers. They book the famous and the infamous, but not the unfamous. Many will approach even a temporary celebrity by virtue of being involved in the headlines in some manner, a la Gordon Liddy, of Watergate infamy, for example.

Speakers do not sign exclusives with lecture bureaus. You may, in fact, register with any number of lecture bureaus, very much as technical-professional consultants may register with — and submit resumes to — a large number of job shops. You may encounter a similar situation in being offered the same speaking date by more than one lecture bureau, as some consultants are offered the same temporary assignment by more than one job shop. Both are brokers and, as all brokers do, earn commissions, usually from the sellers. Job shops, however, earn their commissions and satisfy the client's requirement by actually hiring the consultants, placing them on their own payrolls and reselling them at a higher hourly rate to the clients. Lecture bureaus, on the other hand, charge the speaker a flat commission, which ranges widely, from about 25 to 40 percent of the speaker's fee (or as low as 10 to 15 percent, in the case of celebrity speakers, who can dictate terms). There are exceptions with lecture bureaus sometimes simply adding a flat sum to the speaker's normal fee, thereby gaining their profit via markup, rather than commission. The entire speaking industry is characterized by the lack of any true standards.

Agents, on the other hand, represent the speakers and negotiate for them with clients directly or with a lecture bureau. An agent is usually in the picture when the speaker is a celebrity, someone who is in heavy demand or someone, such as an author, who already has an agent willing to handle the individual's speaking engagements. The agent may be the celebrity's manager, acting as agent also. Agents are paid by the speaker, of course, usually on a commission basis.

Speakers' fees vary as widely, from purely nominal sums to many thousands of dollars, with top-rated speakers earning as much as $25,000 (Bob Hope is reputed to draw $40,000) for an engagement, and most professional but noncelebrity speakers drawing from about $1,000 to $5,000. A number of lecture bureaus report that they would not consider booking a speaker who could not earn a rock-bottom minimum of $500.

The fact is that, with the exception of a few who are so well-known that they are in great demand, almost all speakers arrange a great many—probably much more than one-half—of their own bookings. Moreover, many of the lecture bureaus are those operated by a speaker who is his or her own best client—perhaps only client!

KINDS OF SPEAKERS

Speakers are of almost any type and description. They can be classified in a number of ways, most of which lend themselves to numerous subclassifications. One is by the type of material. Many speakers are, for example, also comedians. (Do you wonder whatever happened to old so-and-so, whom you used to see on the tube? He or she may be playing Vegas, but is more likely to be found speaking for fees at numerous banquets, dinners, and meetings.) Less well-known publicly as comedians, but no less talented, are many others, such as Will Jordan, who does remarkable impersonations or "impressions" of well-known public figures. (General George Patton is one he specializes in frequently.) Still others less well-known as public figures are humorists, rather than comedians, a la the late Will Rogers, who became famous indeed.

There are inspirational speakers, those who stir an audience as Norman Vincent Peale does, or trainers who can instruct and inspire sales professionals, as Nido Qubein can. Or those who specialize in the how-to instruction of some subject (as I do). There are others who have had great adventures and speak of them, or those who have been involved in world affairs and tell interesting stories. A relative of mine, for example, always used his vacations (he was a Postoffice employee) for hunting expeditions to the most remote corners of the world. When he retired he devoted much of his time to speaking engagements, in which he described his most hair-raising adventures and displayed some of his trophies.

Many are purely after-dinner or luncheon speakers and some are seminar presenters. Some will speak for an hour; others all day. Some are true orators with such masterful delivery and a voice of such marvelous timbre that he or she can recite *Mary Had a Little Lamb* and hold an audience, while others have dreadful speaking voices—even speech defects—but have interesting material.

It is therefore almost impossible to generalize about speakers, other than to say that you do not necessarily need to be a practiced orator or comedian, have an especially good speaking voice, be a world figure or a great adventurer, have some "natural" gift or "be born with" some talent for speaking publicly, or conform to any specific standard or model to be successful on the platform. Neither do you have to be completely at ease on the platform; many successful speakers never get over their stage fright. If there are any immutable rules for success on the platform, they have so many exceptions that they outnumber conformances with, the rules. Probably the best advice is to keep trying—speak as often and in as many places as possible—until you discover your niche: what you do best on the platform.

WHAT KIND OF SPEAKER WILL YOU BE?

Presumably you will speak on whatever your consulting specialty happens to be. Beyond that, you will have a style all your own or you will develop one. You may be a natural humorist, as some people are. Or perhaps a natural instructor or simplifier, as writer Isaac Asimov reports he considers himself to be. Perhaps you favor the brief address of a half-hour or so. Or you may be comfortable presenting an all-day seminar. Those are matters you will resolve, probably over time, as you experiment and experience different situations. A style will evolve from these. In all probability you will wind up a different speaker than you at first envisioned.

GETTING BOOKINGS

The universal advice offered those who wish to break into the speaking business is: Speak as often and in as many places as possible, with or without payment, at least in the beginning. This has a twofold purpose: One is to enable you to gain experience and feel comfortable on the platform—to get over platform nerves and develop a presence, a platform personality. The other is to help you become known as widely as possible as a speaker, for the obvious reasons that this is the most direct marketing approach possible and probably the most effective. However, it is certainly not enough all by itself; there are other assets you need to become a full-fledged speaker earning substantial fees.

You need to market yourself as a speaker, just as you must market yourself as a writer, consultant, or anything else in which you wish to venture. Only rarely do the good things—paid speaking engagements, in this case—happen all by themselves, even when they appear to be happenstance. In no profession is this more true than in public speaking. There is ample competition for these paid speaking engagements, and you must be able to hold your own in the competition. Aside from and in addition to what I have suggested earlier in this chapter, you must have certain specific marketing materials.

Marketing Materials

To market yourself as a speaker, whether or not you also register with lecture bureaus, you need materials that represent a first-class written presentation, the next best thing to making the presentation in person. For this you need a letter and a brochure as an absolute minimum, but an audition tape—an audiocassette tape, that is—is an asset that many professionals in this field believe to be indispensable. Many professional speakers today go beyond that and use a videocassette tape. In either case the tape must be such as to present the client with an idea of how you come off in a presentation. The videocassette gives an idea of how you look, as well as how you sound. Lacking that, it's a good idea to have a glossy black-and-white photo of yourself, preferably one taken while you are on the platform, included in the brochure. (You can use a color print, if you wish, but it is not truly necessary. For promotional reproduction, black-and-white is preferred.)

How Much Is Enough?

Many professional speakers use a quite elaborate (and correspondingly costly) brochure. Many go overboard in this respect, and they resort to overkill in doing so. This does not increase their salability as speakers or the power of their sales arguments. In fact, some of the brochures I have seen are so elaborate that they may have an effect that is the reverse of what is desired: I often find such brochures to be overly ostentatious—gaudy, even—rather than in good taste. That is not the effect you want to achieve. Your brochure must not be shoddy; both it and your letter ought to be tastefully done, printed on a good quality paper, and your audition tape should be of professional quality. Anything less—anything that looks amateurish, homemade, or otherwise like corner-cutting to save a dollar—will harm your image and your marketing effort. It is not necessary to go beyond good taste and professional appearance. If you do, it tends sometimes to come off as protesting too much, making a prospective client wonder why you find it necessary to press so hard.

Brochure Content

This same philosophy must apply to the content of your brochure and letter. Obvious "hype"—hyperbole—has a negative effect. Flat statements, using nouns and verbs principally, with an absolute minimum of adjectives and adverbs and no superlatives at all have the ring of sincerity and truth. They come across as quiet statements of fact whereas hype comes across as loud, huckstering claims. Don't represent yourself as a "gripping speaker." Use modest understatement, even slightly self-deprecating, such as "I am usually able to keep an audience awake, even interested, and sometimes amused" to get attention and reflect a quiet self-confidence that fosters others' confidence in you.

Instead of claiming "many, many" audiences or "hundreds of engagements," report an estimated number, such as "about 240 speaking engagements over the past four years," etc. It is helpful also to list at least a few clients and occasions on which you have spoken.

Actual testimonials from clients are extremely helpful. Occasionally, a client may offer written endorsement of your services, but more often you must ask for it, as in asking attendees of a seminar to complete a questionnaire. But you must also get formal—*written*—permission (a *release*) before you can reproduce the testimonial in writing.

Of course, the brochure must describe what you speak about, listing each main topic, if there is more than one, with descriptions of each, length of presentation, and anything you may wish to offer about customizing your presentations and/or editing them to fit into the time allotted in the client's program and schedule. That is the primary essence of the brochure and should be written with great care.

Your brochure ought to have a brief bio of yourself—a summary, not a complete resume—highlighting your special qualifications and mentioning prominently that you are a consultant. If you have written a few things, list the vital statistics of your writing—bibliographic data. If you have written articles that are relevant to you as a speaker or had articles written about you that are relevant, include reprints in your package of literature.

The Letter

The letter—and there should be one—simply introduces you, describes briefly why you are writing, and introduces the other materials enclosed. It need not be long, but should enclose your business card and suggest keeping all the materials on file for future reference, as well as for immediate use. Some sales argument ought to be included here: the main reason for having you serve as a speaker. In closing, invite the client to call or write for any additional information required and express your eager readiness to accommodate the client in that or any other respect.

Dress

Apply the same reasoning to your personal appearance. Be careful about wearing casual clothes. It is safer to dress conservatively, with a white shirt and conventional necktie. Be doubly sure that you are photographed—*professionally*—wearing quiet, businesslike clothing.

WHO HIRES SPEAKERS?

The market for speakers is broad and diverse. I have contracted directly with numerous associations—the Land Improvement Contractors of America and the Association of Automobile Parts and Accessories, for example—and with many government agencies—the Office of Personnel Management (then the Civil Service Commission) and the Department of Commerce, to name two—as well as with private companies and others who hire speakers. I have never found a standard approach to selling myself as a speaker—probably the very diversity of the market for speakers precludes that—but here are a few suggested avenues and approaches to put your feet on the path to at least a few of the many markets.

Every association appoints or elects a program director (not necessarily known by that title), a member responsible for planning and arranging programs for meetings and for national conventions and conferences. In the case of major conventions, the association may have its own staff meeting planner or may hire as a convention manager one of the many companies that specialize in handling all arrangements for such conclaves and often handle the booking of speakers and otherwise help arrange the program itself, as well as the physical details.

On the other hand, speakers are sometimes booked through theatrical agencies, as well as through lecture bureaus. This is especially the case when the speaker is someone already established primarily as an entertainer of some sort.

In selling yourself to private companies it may be an executive responsible for training who will hire you or any other executive. The director of marketing, for example, may wish to have someone train the sales force and may contract directly with a speaker or may act through the company's training manager or purchasing agent, or may use a lecture bureau.

Not all speakers are hired strictly for training or other solely business purposes. Some organizations—associations, labor unions, and even companies—have social affairs and hire speakers who are entertaining, as well as interesting. This does not necessarily mean that they are not consultants or do not speak on business or technical subjects. There are often amusing aspects to those subjects, and there are many speakers who are also talented humorists, discussing the foibles and fumbles in and about their own business or professional fields. There are, for example, many stories about government purchasing and procurement—about the federal bureaucracy, in general—that are both interesting and amusing, some of which I relate in my own seminars. Quite likely, you can find such material in your own field, especially if you are inclined to humor as a speaker. (But even if not, an occasional amusing tale about your field adds greatly to any speech or presentation you make, and is far better than introducing irrelevant humor, as many inexperienced speakers do.)

YOU CAN OFTEN *MAKE* IT HAPPEN

Although there are many well-defined markets for speaking, if you are serious about making speaking a regular income-producing activity as well as a source of good leads for consulting projects, you cannot rely on organizations or individuals searching for you specifically. You must help Dame Chance a bit. Many speaking engagements come about because the speaker *suggested* a seminar or other speaking engagement to a prospect. Many of the seminars I have presented as custom, in-house orientation and/or training sessions were not the result of anyone in the organization perceiving a need for such a session and going in search of a speaker. Rather, they were the result of someone in the organization learning that I made such presentations and approaching me to discuss the possibility. They may also have arisen from casual contacts at conventions or elsewhere, as a result of word-of-mouth publicity, or other such chance exposure. But the result, a speaking engagement or contract to present a seminar, was not accidental. It came from my recognition of a new prospect or sales lead and my direct and agressive follow-up.

You must be alert for all such opportunities, but you must also help your luck a bit. (Fortune really *does* favor the prepared mind, as some sage has observed.) Here are some things you can do in that respect:

- Mention seminars, training, lecturing on your business card, letterheads, general literature. Make sure that everyone knows that you do these things.
- Be sure to promote it verbally when the subject of what you do comes up, no matter the occasion, and/or when any conversational gambit creates the *opportunity*.
- Create a special brochure — a specialized capability statement — covering these activities and circulate it as freely as possible.
- Never miss an opportunity to submit a proposal to anyone who appears to be interested.
- Always follow up proposals with a call or two, trying to stimulate action.

THE WRITING BUSINESS

Writing is or can be as much a business, income source and activity leading to good leads for consulting projects as is speaking — if you are serious enough about it. As in speaking, but to a somewhat lesser degree, your name becomes recognizable in time and makes your marketing easier. Despite that, there are probably more differences than similarities between the two, once you are past the superficial aspects and considerations. For example, each piece of writing, whether it is an article, a book, or other, is judged on its *own* merits and must stand or fall on those regardless of your reputation and reader reaction to your previous work. The advantage of an established reputation as a writer lies far more in getting your work considered seriously for purchase and publication than in getting accepted. That alone — getting serious consideration — can be a serious obstacle for the beginning writer, at least until he or she learns some of the fundamentals of writing and selling the written work.

Getting Started

The chief mistake the beginning writer makes is trying to start at the top or most prestigious periodical, although sometimes that merely reflects naivaté as to what constitutes "the top" in writing for commercial (and paid) publication. But even that varies, according to the field of writing. Here, we are concerned with technical/professional/business writing of books and articles for the journals relevant to the respective fields. But those fields of writing and publication must be subdivided into classes also. Some of the trade journals are addressed only to professionals in the field and are highly technical, even dealing more in abstract theory than in practical application, while others are the opposite and address application-oriented readers. Still others may deal in administrative, marketing, and/or management matters in some given field. But there are also periodicals that deal with management or marketing generally, without regard to industry or field. So the diversity here is quite complete in itself. Here is a brief sampling of *types* of trade publications, in terms of their industries, professional fields, or kinds of readers addressed:

Accounting	Energy
Art	Finance
Automotive	Government
Aviation	Health services
Building interiors	Hotels
Business management	Law
Data processing	Printing
Drugs	Transportation

Books have a similar diversity. Some publishers undertake to publish almost all kinds of books. (Usually, these are large publishers with numerous divisions and imprimaturs.) Many others specialize. The broad division among the 40,000 to 50,000 books published annually is between fiction and nonfiction. Even then there are many subcategories, the most basic one in nonfiction recognizing the difference between the general-interest and the special-interest books.

As a consultant, undertaking to write a book, you might write for either of those latter two categories, depending on your special field, but it is more likely that you will be writing for the special-interest reader, just as you address your consulting services to the prospect with special problems and needs. Let's proceed on that assumption, but most of what I will say will apply in any case.

Other Common Mistakes of Beginners

Change is probably even more inevitable than death and taxes, and things have changed in the publishing business over recent years. Many individuals who have only a nodding acquaintance with publishing still believe in ancient and now obsolete practices. Often this well-meant but erroneous information is passed on as good advice to inexperienced writers—who are still sending bulky manuscripts to periodical and book publishers in the belief that they will be read, evaluated, and acted upon.

Unfortunately, most publishers of periodicals and books, but especially of books, have been compelled to cut back on overhead costs, among them the reading of unsolicited manuscripts. The percentage of usable material that can be culled from the "slush pile"—those unsolicited manuscripts—is too small to justify the high cost of first readers, editors who sole duty is to read those manuscripts that have come in "over the transom" (unsolicited). So most publishers today have a simple policy of returning unsolicited manuscripts—if return postage was enclosed—without reading them. The sole occasional exception to this is the very short article manuscript.

That does not mean that they have closed the doors. Far from it, they welcome new writers, but they find it necessary to do some screening in advance. Hence, they ask the writer to submit a query letter—a proposal—as a first step.

The Query Letter of Proposal

There is a tendency to use the term *query letter*, especially in connection with articles for periodicals, so it is necessary to recognize that term and know what it refers to. I much prefer the term *proposal*, whether it is used with reference to an article or to a book, for a simple reason. *Query letter* suggests an inquiry or, even worse, a kind of hat-in-hand plea, and some of the suggested models have reinforced that idea, which has a pronounced negative tone to it, in my opinion. *Pro-*

posal, however, has a positive note to it implying an offer, rather than a plea. In any case, I use the term *proposal*, and I believe that there is a pronounced psychological benefit deriving from the use of that more positive term.

The proposal is used to suggest an article or book to an editor, offering a good summary of what it is to be about, to whom addressed, why readers will want to read it, the author's qualifications, and other pertinent data to help the editor decide whether to consider the offer and encourage the author to go ahead or invite the author to submit some or all of the material. (Sometimes the author has a manuscript ready; in other cases the author is asking for encouragement to go ahead and begin writing.)

As in all cases, the proposal may be an informal letter of a page or two—where it concerns the writing or proposed writing of a brief article—but in the case of a book it must be somewhat longer, if it is to give the editor enough information to make a reasoned judgment. Some book editors have written small books on the subject and declared that book proposals must be 25 pages or longer. I have usually managed successfully with proposals that were well under 10 pages. I think that *what* you say in a proposal, not how much you say, is what counts. My experience appears to support that theory.

The editor will usually respond, especially if the response is a favorable one, with an offer and a query as to when you can have the manuscript on his or her desk. Frequently, the busy editor prefers to telephone; it's much faster than writing. Be sure to furnish your telephone number!

Description of Manuscript (or Proposed Manuscript)

Describe the book or article in objective terms. Skip the adjectives and adverbs; stick to nouns and verbs. Furnish an outline, as detailed as possible. If you are proposing a book, furnish a list of chapters and description of the content of each. The editor must have enough information—and the right information—to envision the finished product and pass judgment on the practicality of encouraging you.

Your Credentials

You need two kinds of credentials: credentials as an authority on the subject and credentials as a writer. The editor must judge the probability that you will produce an acceptable final product. Explain your own credentials as an expert (if most of the material will depend on your own knowledge) or the source, if that is to be the basis. If you have no credentials as a writer, the editor will have to judge your writing capability by the writing abilities you exhibit in your proposal. (He or she will be influenced by that in any case, so do try to write the most coherent, lucid, and persuasive proposal possible.)

Fees and Profitability

Typically, fees for articles in trade publications are rarely what might be described as "generous." Quite the contrary, they tend to be what might be described mercifully as "conservative." Some journals pay by the published word, some by the published page, some on flat fees for different types of articles, and some on the basis of whatever the editor judges the article is worth. (That fee may be subject to negotiation with the editor.) Some pay on acceptance, some on publication, and some well after publication. Sad to add, some pay only after you complain that you were never paid at all.

In most cases book publishers pay authors royalties, usually twice a year. Typical royalties are approximately 10 percent of actual dollars recevied by the publisher, but the percentage is usually increased to 12.5 and finally to 15 percent if sales are large enough to merit the increase—to enable the publisher to afford the increase. In some cases the publisher pays an advance against royalties. The established writer may get that advance or a part of it before submitting a manuscript, but the beginning writer will probably not get an advance, if he or she gets any at all, before the manuscript has been received and accepted.

A typical first printing for a book is 3,000 to 5,000 copies, unless the publisher expects the book to do very well and start selling briskly immediately, as in the case of new books by certain well-known and popular authors. That does not necessarily mean that that number of copies are on the shelves. The economics of book publishing are such that it may pay to print 5,000 copies but bind only 1,000, keeping the rest of the copies as "flats," printed sheets that can be bound and made into books quickly if and as necessary.

Publishers provide editing services, and all manuscripts are edited. Publishers' editors will perform normal editorial functions to shore up faltering grammar and rhetoric and correct absolute errors in spelling and punctuation, but they will not rewrite bad copy. They may offer suggestions for rewriting, however, if they think the manuscript is salvageable.

There are publications that report what various publishers say their policies and practices are. (These publications are listed in appendices.) These statements by publishers may or may not be precise truth. Sometimes they describe only the typical or average cases, and sometimes they are pure fiction. My experience with many publishers has often been considerably at variance with what is reported as their claimed policies and practices. That does not mean that my experience has always been less rewarding than reported policies and practices promise; sometimes the opposite has been true, and I have been pleasantly surprised. Remember that the established author has considerably more bargaining power than does the newcomer who is as yet of unknown potential as an author. So use these reports as general guidelines only.

Subjects

Beginners sometimes worry about where they will get ideas for things to write about. Probably every writer has had that worry in the beginning. However, and oddly enough, it is that very concern that itself tends to solve the problem: Consciously or unconsciously, as you worry about this, you condition yourself to a state of near-constant alertness and vigilance for new ideas and before long it is not new ideas you seek but time to work on all of them. However, here are a few starter ideas, all concerning your own special field, of course:

- New developments—technical, legislative, or otherwise.
- Reports on special events, such as conventions, conferences, trade shows.
- Simplified explanations of complicated matters.
- How-to guidance and instruction.
- Explanations of consulting and how consultants work.
- Pro and/or con arguments on controversial matters.

A Few Ideas on How to Get Ideas

There are several ways to stimulate your own idea-generation by specific, deliberate actions. Here are a few suggestions along that line:

- Examine books in your field to find chapters on subjects that merit complete books of their own. (Many of my own books were born in this manner, some by examining chapters in my own early books and deciding that they needed to be the seeds of new books.)

- Read the current trade journals. What do they mention briefly that could constitute entire books? What ought readers to know about consulting—what it is and what it can do for them?

- Read the daily press. What should the lay public know about your field? How might it affect the public generally?

- Join relevant associations and go to meetings and conventions. Listen to others. Mingle and talk. Be deliberately alert for ideas. Try to sense what others feel a need for.

- Listen to/watch radio and TV talk shows to learn what topics appear to be interesting to producers of the shows, not only for what questions are raised, but also for those that are largely unanswered.

A FEW OBSERVATIONS AND IDEAS ABOUT PR IN GENERAL

Hollywood movies to the contrary, effective PR does not work by a "big bang" effect of one or two major PR coups. Such PR has a transient effect, perhaps a large one, but only temporarily. Effective PR is a slow, evolutionary process, like the sea making sand and pebbles out of rocks over many millennia. PR, for you and me, is a daily process of very small coups in dozens—even hundreds—of publicity byways. It is hundreds of press releases, letters to the editor, articles in obscure publications, brief interviews on local radio stations, and sundry other minor exposures repeated many times. It is also not the rifle shot reaching the exactly right target—the ideal prospects; it is the scatter-gun reaching a broad population, of which perhaps 10 or 20 percent, at best, are reasonably close to being the right targets. Bear this in mind to understand the significance of the following few paragraphs.

Personal Correspondence

One characteristic of busy people that I find distressingly more common is failing to answer personal mail. I have been outraged again and again by those who appear to think it unimportant to answer mail or who use uninformative and impersonal form letters, which are only slightly less offensive. Aside from the fact that it is rude to make no direct response to personal letters, it is also unwise. Not only is it poor PR, tending strongly to estrange well-intentioned people, but it also ignores and misses the opportunity for good PR.

I do not get sacks full of mail every day, but I do get a fair quantity of mail from readers of my books, making comments and asking questions. I make it a practice to respond, usually the same day, partially out of fear that if I lay it aside I will overlook and neglect it, but largely because I am eager to respond for two reasons:

First, it is an appeal to ego to get letters from strangers who are readers of my books, who usually have nice things to say. (Fortunately, few readers appear to find my writing offensive.) I am truly grateful for these letters and delighted to thank the writers for their kind words. But I am also pleased to add one more small drop of PR to the pool, since it can only help me in the long term.

In that vein, I also correspond with several people, some on a long-term and continuous basis, others on an occasional basis. As the years go on, more people become aware of and are reminded of my existence, and my name is mentioned more frequently.

The Small Presses

You don't have to be a writer of books to get letters from strangers, nor do I mean to suggest that. I have been getting such mail and corresponding with strangers for years, in many cases since long before I turned to writing books. Many activities can spark this kind of correspondence, including initiating it yourself.

There are thousands of small periodicals, for example, most of them of limited distribution but reaching a great many people in the aggregate. Over the years many small publication publishers have written or mentioned my name, books, and work, and I write many brief articles for these publishers on a "complimentary" basis — without cash payment, that is. There is John Hall, who publishes a little periodical for writers, *Writers' Journal*. There is Rohn Engh, with his periodical for free lance photographers and photo journalists, *PhotoLetter*. There is Chet Lambert, with his journal for hams and computer enthusiasts, *CTM*. There is Galen Stilson, mentioned earlier, with his newsletter for those in mail order, *Direct Response Specialist*. And there is Dottie Walters, also mentioned earlier, with her periodical for speakers and consultants, *Sharing Ideas*. There is also Jeffrey Lant, a consultant who is a prolific writer of books (mentioned earlier), with whom I maintain correspondence and exchange small PR favors. Nor are these all, but just those who come to mind immediately.

I write for and about these people, their periodicals, their books, and their work, and we all benefit. They get materials without cost, they get the publicity I am able to give them, and they give me the exposure and publicity they can confer. I learn many things from them in their writings and in our correspondence, and I hope that I contribute an occasional tidbit of knowledge in return. It's a mutual support system, and anyone can join the circle and benefit as you contribute. Use some of the information appended as a starting point, for example, by writing to some of these publishers and asking for a sample copy.

FOLLOWING UP

If prospecting is the pick-and-shovel work of marketing—digging the foundation—following up is the masonry and roofing—creating the structure.

WHY "FOLLOWING UP?" WHAT DOES IT MEAN?

The premises upon which this book is based (stemming from personal experience and largely substantiated by responses from readers of *How to Succeed as an Independent Consultant* and other indicators) are that the typical independent consultant needs help and guidance in marketing—finding and winning clients—more than anything else, and that the major need in that effort is for effective prospecting—finding those prospects most likely to become clients. To put that another way, the major need is for effective means of developing sales leads.

The corollary to that, implicit if not explicit, is that the typical independent consultant will not need major assistance in closing leads—in following up and converting sales leads into clients and contracts. I believe that to be true in a comparative sense, in the sense that the consultant's need for guidance in following up is far less important than the need for guidance in developing those sales leads. That does not mean that following up properly is less important than prospecting effectively, or that consultants would not benefit from some guidance in this also. This book would be glaringly incomplete without the latter coverage. Hence, and without apologies, I offer in this chapter whatever words of wisdom I can summon from my own experience over several decades of persuading prospects to become clients and award contracts and purchase orders for my services and those of others I led. There are a few other points to be made before going on to probe the subject of this chapter.

Following up is not a new subject even in these pages, for I have necessarily been compelled to touch on it, from time to time, in discussing marketing. At times you have seen the term *closing* used, most often in the general, layperson's sense of getting the order. Still, as I explained earlier, the term has a very special meaning to the sales professional as *asking* for the order to determine whether it was time to shut up and write the order or to continue the selling effort. We will review all of that again because following up means that you have entered that final phase of the marketing effort, the *sales* phase, that specific effort to win the individual sale. So following up is *selling*, pure and simple, and *closing* is a necessary and important tactic in selling. I also mentioned the term *qualifying* and discussed it only briefly, for it is on the borderline, part of selling only in the sense of validating an apparent sales lead or, in some cases, assessing its potential as an indirect avenue to a sale, making it also an important marketing tool.

IDENTIFICATION/CLASSIFICATION OF SALES LEADS

There are many ways to prospect and generate sales leads. But we have not addressed closely what a sales lead is—its form—how it makes its appearance. A prospect becomes a sales lead when there is some reason to believe that the prospect is seriously interested in what you offer—when there appears to be a good possibility that the prospect might become a client. But how do you perceive this show of serious interest? Is it an inquiry by mail, telephone, or in person? Is it a request for general information, specific information? For a direct quotation of some sort? For a proposal? For face-to-face discussion?

Each of these is a possibility, and each has a different implication. They might be rank-ordered in importance—in probability of proving to be serious sales leads—as follows, highest priority first:

1. Request for proposal or for quotation on specific requirement.
2. Request for face-to-face discussion (possibly for verbal quote/proposal).
3. Request for specific information—e.g., details of your services, current availability, capabilities, qualifications, or other.
4. Request for general information about any of above.

If the first numbered item is the case the prospect has a specific immediate need and intends to retain somebody to satisfy it. The second case suggests serious interest, may even mean that the prospect's need is so great that he or she cannot wait for a formal cycle of written quotes and proposals, but wants to select someone and get started immediately. The third case suggests a serious interest, but either no existing need or no urgency about an existing need. Possibly, it suggests anticipation of a future need or an organization that has periodic needs and wants to keep track of all available services. And the fourth category suggests some interest, but possibly only idle interest.

Why is it important to make such an analysis? Simply because there are sometimes conditions under which it is necessary to rank-order your sales leads or *apparent sales leads*. Sometimes, for example, your marketing and PR suddenly produce a large number of leads, and you are hard-pressed to follow up. Because you cannot follow up on all at once, it becomes important to decide which leads have the highest priority—the greatest potential for realization as contracts and projects—and thus should be attended to first. Or you may be quite busy with current projects and need to decide how much time you can spare for follow up—sales activity. To do this you must evaluate the likelihood that the leads will materialize in something other than a waste of time.

The possibility/probability of realization as a sale is not the sole criterion of worth, nor is it possible to reduce the valuation to anything resembling a set of absolute rules. An almost sure sale of a very small project may have far less value than a less-certain sale of a large project. Only you can make that valuation.

There is also the consideration of when a sale is likely to result, if at all. That may have a large influence on your valuation of the lead. If you are idle and in need of work as soon as possible, the small project within easy grasp becomes much more attractive, for example. On the other hand, if you are overly busy at the moment, you may have to pass up opportunities for immediate projects and deliberately seek projects that will not materialize for many months. Or you may prefer one type of project to another. Or one kind of client to another.

There are many things that may influence you, so it is not possible to reduce the decision-making to an absolute methodology. But you do have to have some methodology — at least enough to evaluate the possibility/probability of the sale. Hence the suggested first-level indicators of possible/probable validity of the lead as a true sales lead and at least rough gauges to help you decide on following up the leads.

PROACTIVE VERSUS REACTIVE FOLLOWUP

Followup can be proactive or reactive, just as prospecting can be. You can wait for a prospect to ask you to supply a proposal to make an appointment to discuss your services, or you can act without waiting to be asked. Some consultants wait to be asked to furnish a quotation or proposal because they are not yet sure that the prospect is seriously considering contracting for a project; they are fearful of wasting their time and energies in writing a proposal that could not possibly succeed because the prospect is by no means firmly established as a solid sales lead.

That caution is entirely understandable, but it reflects a passive approach to the problem. It means, in truth, that you have not yet qualified the prospect, itself a manifestation of reactive marketing. Sometimes the prospect will do the qualifying for you; I have had some prospects whom I had approached on my own initiative simply request that I furnish a written bid or proposal, assuring me that a purchase order would then be issued to me. But more often the prospect will not do the job for you; you will have to do the qualifying, on your own initiative.

Qualifying Prospects

Although there are important secondary considerations that ought to be considered as a proper part of qualifying a prospect, the qualifying has a single and immediate primary purpose: to determine whether you should invest your time, money, and effort in trying to sell your services to that prospect. To do that you need first to get answers to these two questions:

1. Does the prospect have money and/or authority to retain you — to issue or have issued a purchase order or contract?
2. Does the prospect appear serious about buying consulting services?

There are secondary questions too. If the answers to the first two questions are affirmative, the next questions concern how soon the prospect is likely to move and how large the contract is likely to be. You need to know these answers too so you don't waste time on trivial requirements at the expense of neglecting the pursuit of much larger and more important prospective contracts.

On the other hand, if the answer to the first question is negative, you do not necessarily give up the pursuit immediately, but you investigate whether there is a good future prospect or an alternative to which the prospect is the key. In some cases the budget is not available at the moment, but is likely to become available sometime in the future, making this a "back burner" sales lead, one to keep an eye on for future followup. In other cases the individual may be able to get his or her superior to approve and authorize a contract or can guide you to someone who can do so. So while you should not waste your time on those who are merely idly curious, you also should not give up on a prospect without serious efforts at qualification. But do remember that you must usually exercise initiative to get these answers.

Common Mistakes

The most common mistake some consultants make with respect to qualifying prospects is to guess at the answers. It is easy to be deceived by appearances: The prospect occupies a large, handsomely furnished office, is a mature individual, and appears quite at ease and confident, so you take it for granted that the prospect is a senior executive and therefore obviously qualified. On the other hand, the prospect appears to be quite young, occupies a nondescript office, and is so quiet as to appear meek, so you find him or her "obviously" not a senior person and therefore not qualified as a bona fide sales lead.

The opposite may be true. The multimillionaire head of one of the major computer software firms is so boyish looking (and is quite a young man, at that) that it would be quite understandable if a stranger assumed that he was the mail clerk. And that mature gentleman in the well-appointed office may be a humble and junior functionary.

Another mistake is to be misled by vague generalizations. A prospect may tell you that he or she intends to get going "soon" with the project. What does "soon" mean? Next month? Next year? In two years? A prospect may tell you that he or she expects the work to be funded in the next budget. When will the next budget be approved, and how confident is the prospect that the work will be budgeted at that time?

The problem is that the consultant is fearful of pressing too hard and so risking giving offense and destroying any chance of making a sale. But what that means, if you suffer from this, is that you need a little guidance in approaching the problem so that you get specific answers without giving offense. You do this through a combination of the right euphemisms and reading between the lines.

When you want to ask the prospect whether he or she has the money for the job, a euphemistic question generally fetches the answer you want. No prospect ought to become offended by the casual and totally impersonal question uttered at the right moment, "Are there funds available yet for this project?" (Of course, there are many variants of this phrasing you can use, but the form has always worked well for me.) Finding out what kind of authority the individual has may be ferreted out by another euphemistic and impersonal question, such as, "How much of a signoff procedure is required here to authorize this work?"

Even that is fairly direct, and there are even more subtle ways of phrasing your feelers. I have found sometimes that a grin and a casual, even more indirect question—for example, "Is this now an approved project or is it still in the talking stage?"—brings me the answer I want.

If the other party is coy and fends off such casual and indirect probes, deliberately avoiding a direct response, that, itself, sends a message that you must construe as the answer. When you are totally unable to confirm that the prospect qualifies, reason compels you to assume that he or she does not qualify and that you are wasting time if you linger longer. Incidentally, don't be surprised when you find that individuals in large organizations, even in privately held companies, may occupy well-appointed offices and yet be relatively junior, devoid of real influence in the organization, and idle, in the bargain. I have found that many large corporations, both for-profit and nonprofit, can become and often are as bureaucratic as are governments and their agencies.

Of course, if you are talking to a purchasing agent or contracting official you can be more "up front" with questions because purchasing agents and contracting officers only administer the purchase of consulting services, as a service to the real buyers, normally. They are therefore not at all offended by direct questions as to whether funding exists, who could or would authorize a contract, and similar probing questions because those questions do not bear on that individual's position, prestige, or influence in the organization. Quite the contrary, if you take the time to become truly friendly with such officials the rewards can be great. They can be very helpful in telling you who is who and what is what in the organization. It is a potential resource well worth exploring thoroughly. You begin by ascertaining whether there is such an individual in the organization and then calling on him or her.

The first case is one in which the prospect is ready to award the contract, but must first write the contract or purchase-order request. That means describing the need, the work, the costs, and other details. If you must wait for the busy executive to do that it may never happen. Writing a proposal that covers all these details—per your discussions—is actually writing the contract or purchase-order details for the prospect and greatly increasing the probability that the contract or purchase order will be issued promptly—to you.

The second and third cases are situations where your prospect wants or needs to sell you and your services to others in the organization. A well-thought-out, well-written proposal is an excellent means for doing so.

In some cases, especially where the prospect agrees that he or she needs the help of your proposal to sell the project to others, it is wise to suggest writing a draft proposal, submitted off the record for the prospect's review and comment, before writing and submitting the "official" proposal. Unsolicited proposals to government agencies are often developed in this manner. In fact, they sometimes even go through an earlier stage as a "white paper," which serves as a basis for discussion and is followed by a draft proposal and, finally, the formal or official proposal.

There are other alternatives to a proposal as the next step. The principal alternative is a more or less formal presentation (a "dog and pony show," to the initiated in formal contracting) to or at least a meeting with others, usually with arrangements made by your prospect. This is likely to be an intermediate step with a written proposal following (although, as you will soon see, the reverse may be true). Unless there are competitors who have also been invited to make presentations and submit proposals, your chances for swift acceptance in this case are quite excellent.

PROPOSAL CONTENT

The proposal is probably the most important tool available to most independent consultants, and its direct cousin, the capability brochure, is only slightly less important. A generalized proposal outline is offered here, with suggestions for coverage and brief discussions, as necessary. The outline presupposes a document of four or more sections or chapters, with front matter and appendices. For small projects, and often enough for sizable projects, a full-blown, multisection proposal is not required, but an informal, letter proposal will serve the need adequately. The coverage suggested here is a continuity that may be adapted easily to the short form of a letter proposal.

1. INTRODUCTION
   a) Brief statement of who/what the offerer is, general qualifications.
   b) A concise statement of understanding, to demonstrate that you truly comprehend the need/problem. You must state this in your own words, and not as an echo of the client's words.

2. DISCUSSION
   a) Extended discussions of the requirement, bridging from and expanding on statement of understanding in previous section.
   b) Analysis of requirement from all angles, identifying problems, exploring and reviewing alternatives, with pros and cons of

each. (This is key section in which you explain the benefits and superiority of what you propose to demonstrate the validity of your arguments and grasp of the problem.)

c) Identify your approach, sell it, lay foundation for proposal proper — your specific plan — which is to follow.

3. PROPOSED PROJECT

a) Describe and specify staffing and organization.

b) Identify key person (you) and others, if there are to be others.

c) List major phases, tasks, functions, anticipated outcomes.

d) Describe end-item(s) to be delivered.

e) Provide schedule.

f) List resume(s).

4. PROPOSER'S QUALIFICATIONS

a) Description of proposer — organization, facilities, resources.

b) List, describe past/recent/current projects, especially those similar to the one under discussion.

c) List/describe special items — awards, testimonials.

5. APPENDICES (If needed)

Closing

To the sales professional, closing means asking the prospect for the order. But there is a special technique to closing effectively, and it is literally not *asking* for the order but *assuming* it by asking questions that indicate you have the order.

The ostensible purpose in doing this is to press the prospect gently to a buying decision, and it does achieve this in many cases, when the prospect is sold but still hesitant to make the buying commitment. However, it has the deeper purpose also of serving to provide feedback about the prospect's state of mind with regard to a buying decision, and so guides you, as the seller, in the proper next move. That is, suppose you close by asking the prospect how soon he or she wants you to start the project. The answer tells you quite quickly what the prospect's state of mind is and also tells you what your next move must be.

There is another consideration in closing: The alternative is to stop and wait for the prospect to act or to literally ask for the order. In either case, if you do this you lose the initiative and pass it to the prospect. Closing enables you to keep the initiative, and that alone is an important element in selling; losing the initiative too often means losing the sale.

Selling consulting services is quite different from selling vacuum cleaners or home improvements, and closing must also be different. The suggestion of submitting a written proposal or making a formal presentation is a kind of closing that is appropriate. It enables you to keep the initiative. But you must be prepared to react to and handle rejection by having alternatives in mind. If, for example, your prospect says that a written proposal would be premature, inquire as to why and have an alternative to suggest, such as the presentation referred to or perhaps a general meeting with your prospect and others of the organization. Begin with the suggestion of a written proposal and reserve that of a presentation or formal meeting as a fallback position so that you do not lose the initiative if it proves unfeasible to submit a written proposal.

On the other hand, the prospective client may request a formal presentation and/or meeting after the proposal has been submitted and reviewed. This normally signifies that your proposal is regarded favorably and you are at least under serious consideration for award. It may even suggest a negotiating session. However, if there are several competitors who have been invited also to submit proposals, all may have also been invited to make presentations and/or meet to discuss their proposals, as a process of elimination and selection of a winner.

This is a common practice with government agencies, but is certainly not an unusual practice in procurement by organizations in the private sector, especially by organizations who are government contractors and so are quite familiar with government purchasing and contracting practices. If the project you are discussing with a prospect is actually a subcontract on a government project for which your prospect is the prime contractor, your prospect may be required by contract to employ competitive bids or proposals for subcontracting; that provision in a prime government contract is not at all unusual.

BEST AND FINAL OFFERS

Frequently, the prospect who has requested a proposal, and especially the prospect who has used competitive procurement by inviting several consultants to submit proposals, asks proposers to submit "best and final offers." That is, or course, the prospect's final effort to get the best possible price.

That request can be made in several ways. I have had a telegram wired to my office requesting that I submit my best and final price. That means that I either confirm my previously quoted price (in my proposal) or submit a lower figure as my best and final price. Such requests have also arrived by letter and telephone call. And, quite commonly, the post-proposal presentation, meeting/discussion, and/ or negotiation proves actually to be a request for a best and final offer. After a presentation by you, discussion of a number of points in your proposal, and possibly negotiation of certain items, you are asked to submit an amendment to your proposal, documenting in writing those changes to which you have agreed. Almost as an afterthought (as though it were not a prime objective of the meeting), you are also "invited" to "take another look" at your "numbers" and amend them if you wish to.

Thereby hangs a dilemma: Should you or should you not amend your price? Will it make the difference between winning and not winning? Are your competitors being subjected to the same pressures?

It's a stressful situation, and there are no easy answers to the questions; each is a unique case. You can only use your own best judgment. Even after having been through this precise situation and seeking answers to these same questions on more than a few occasions—and having made at least my share of mistakes, too—I can offer only the following advice:

1. Greed—fear of "leaving money on the table"—is self-defeating. It will cause you to lose contracts you should have won.

2. If you can afford to reduce your price without undue risk, do so.

3. Seek in the discussions and negotiations, if there are such, to find refinements and embellishments that can be eliminated (that

the prospect indicates are not of great value to him or her), and remove them as a cost-reduction measure.

The Continuing Followup

You may or may not have noticed that the entire process is one of progressive phases. First there is the prospecting, to generate sales leads. Then there is the beginning of the followup, to gather the general description of the prospect's needs. Then the qualification to determine the wisdom of continuing the followup. And now, after you have satisfied yourself that you are not totally wasting your time—that there is a real potential for a sale of your services here—you must go on to determine those other factors we mentioned: at least the general scale of the potential project and the probable start date. You cannot plan the next step properly without knowing these two details.

Again, a common mistake is to enter this phase too early, wasting time in gathering details before determining that there is a true potential for a sale and that you are dealing with the right party. But, once you have done that, what next? Will you wait for your prospect to say, "You're hired! When can you start?" Probably not; sales simply do not come that easily. It is up to you to make the next move. But you must also propose that next move to the prospect. And I stress *propose*, not *ask*. Moreover, be highly specific in proposing. Don't say, "I'll get back to you," or "When can I expect to hear from you?" Those are direct invitations to indecision and procrastination. You must keep the initiative, and you must have a definite plan of continuing followup—keeping the ball in the air—if you are serious about winning the contract.

The purpose of gathering information beyond the basic qualification of the prospect is simple enough in principle: It is to get what you need—enough detailed information about the prospect's needs—for the next step in following up.

The Next Move

Ideally, the next step is to furnish the prospect a proposal. If conditions are right, getting the prospect to agree to accepting a proposal is an excellent move. But only if conditions are right; otherwise, the agreement to accept a proposal may only mask a device to stall off decision. Following are some circumstances that usually make the submittal of a proposal a good next move:

1. The prospect has the authority and funds to issue the contract or purchase order and appears committed to moving on with the award without delay.

2. The prospect wants to get on with the project and the organization is committed to it, but the prospect needs approval of others in the organization.

3. The prospect wants to get on with the project but needs to sell the idea in his or her own organization first.

CHAPTER 10

KEEPING THE CLIENTS YOU HAVE

One of the important decisions you must make in planning your marketing is whether you wish to create sales or clients.

SALES OR CLIENTS?

There is nothing frivolous in the question of whether you are or should be in pursuit of sales or clients. It is quite possible to make sales of your services and earn profits, even large profits, but rarely, if ever, get repeat patronage. It is also possible to win clients who will remain clients and call on you repeatedly to furnish your expert services, as well as recommending you to others. The advantages of this approach to marketing are obvious enough: Over time you build a practice and while you probably will always have the need to win new clients, as your practice grows, the need for new clients lessens. That enables you eventually to reduce your marketing effort and expense.

There are some definite difficulties in marketing in such a way as to create clients from whom you can expect continued patronage. Admittedly, some of these difficulties represent disadvantages—the downside of pursuing clients, rather than sales. It is quite possible that the very nature of the services you offer militates against repeat contracts and assignments from clients. However, here are some specific points which make the pros and cons clear:

- The services you offer must be such or must be so structured that your typical client has need of your services more than once — from time to time, that is.
- Where and when there is a problem in your relations with a client — i.e., a dispute — you must be conciliatory in whatever way is necessary.
- You must be sure that every client is *completely* satisfied with you and your service.
- You must maintain contact with every client after the initial contact or assignment is completed.

The Services You Offer

My own is a case that illustrates the difficulty in pursuing repeat business — trying to create clients, rather than sales — when the very nature of your services is such that clients are likely never to need your services again or to believe that they do not, which is the same thing in marketing, where the prospect's perception is the only truth that really matters.

My original consulting service was to assist clients in developing winning proposals for federal government contracts by actually writing them and/or leading their writing teams. I succeeded in helping many achieve that success. But there were factors in opposition to repeat contracts:

1. In a number of cases a large contract resulted, representing so much work for the client that the client did not wish to pursue another contract for some time to come.
2. In some cases the client retained me only for a proposal the client thought exceptionally difficult to write, handling other proposals internally as a routine.
3. In some cases the client did not win the contract, for any of many possible reasons, and decided therefore that my services were of little value.

4. In many cases—probably in the majority of cases where I did not win additional, subsequent assignments—the client decided that he or she and the staff had learned from the experience what they needed to handle future proposals on their own.

Despite the fact that the nature of my services does not encourage subsequent assignments from established clients, I have enjoyed at least some repeat patronage. Probably I could have enjoyed more by being somewhat less generous in training clients who had hired me to do (analyze, develop strategies, and write), rather than train them, but I have always chosen to give clients a "baker's dozen"—somewhat more than the minimum required. However, once I began to diversify my services to offer training seminars in several related subjects, I began to enjoy a great deal more repeat patronage and more assignments via referrals.

Probably most consultants can do likewise. Even if your basic service is not what your typical client can use repeatedly, with some analysis and introspection you can probably find some variant service that does lend itself to this. Certainly, it is worth spending a little thought on. Consider additional or alternate services—seminars and other training programs, perhaps—additional or alternate media for delivery of your services, and other possibilities, perhaps the development and sales of relevant products.

Consider also some inducement to clients that will encourage repeat sales. An annual retainer might be one such device. But you might also sell clients subscriptions to a newsletter or series of reports, and provide special discounts or other inducements to subscribers who use your consulting services. Or, vice versa, you may offer consulting clients special deals on other services or products you have to offer.

Client Relations

An old platitude is that you can't win an argument with a client. That means that if you win (the argument) you lose (the client). Differences of opinion between you and a client inevitably arise occasionally. The sensible thing to do is to be sure that differences are not permitted to deteriorate into serious disputes if you wish to maintain good relations with the clients and pave the way for additional business.

One of the differences that may arise most easily is over your bill. Many situations can lead to client shock and protest over your statement of charges. The client may have had a different understanding than you did, expecting you to guarantee to do the job in 30 billable days, whereas you found it necessary to use 40 days and thought there was no problem about it. Perhaps you may have explained a need for extra days before putting them in and run into strenuous objections from the client. Or the client may believe that you quoted a firm fixed price when you meant your quote as a ballpark estimate only.

Usually, if you hold your position and firmly insist that you are right and the client is wrong, the client will pay the bill but determine never to retain you again. Yet, it is easily possible to avoid these situations or, at least, to minimize both their occurrence and the destructive effects of such differences of opinion about fair billing. First, here are some general practices that will help achieve these objectives:

1. Always document the basic agreement with the client in written form. This does not have to be a formal contract. It may be a letter proposal, a quotation, or simply an informal letter of agreement. But it should state the basis for the billing—an estimate, an agreed-upon firm price, or other, and should state exactly what you are to deliver for that price. Be sure that the client has a copy with your signature and, if possible, have the client sign a copy for your files. Just be sure that the letter is completely explicit.

2. No matter what the agreement says, always clear any overruns—expenses beyond the original estimates—with the client along the way before you incur the costs.

3. If it happens that you have overruns or incurred extra costs without discussing them first with the client, avoid the unpleasant surprise of a bill larger than expected by discussing the extra costs with the client first.

4. If at all possible, do not bill the client at all for minor overruns or other small and unanticipated costs, even though they were incurred through no fault of your own.

My own practice is to charge a daily rate large enough to "eat" small overruns, such as a few extra hours. (Billing by the day, I have no fixed standard as to what constitutes a "day" except the calendar, so I simply do not count hours when the client agrees to my standard day rate.) Even on large overruns I have found these practices usually head off disputes and help me maintain excellent relations with my clients. On many occasions I have volunteered to "eat" even fairly substantial overruns of my time, but in almost every case the client insists that I am entitled to be paid for all of my time. In one case a client gave me a $1,000 bonus for putting in an around-the-clock effort to meet a deadline that we could not have otherwise met. On balance, I believe that doing the honorable thing and being generous with clients pays worthwhile dividends. But there is another, highly practical consideration, and it concerns these three highly pertinent questions:

1. How much does it cost to *create* a client?
2. How much does it cost to *replace* a client?
3. How much does it cost to *keep* a client?

How much does it cost to create a client? It does cost money and effort—your time—even if you cannot identify precisely how much money and effort. If you spend $3,000 out-of-pocket and 120 hours of your time on a marketing campaign, and the campaign produces 10 clients, each client costs you $300 and 24 hours of your time. That may amount to a lot of money when you add the dollar value of your time to the $300. You may value the cost of creating a client at perhaps $1,500 or more. Many mail-order firms lose money on first sales to new customers, and must rely on repeat sales—on creating customers—to earn eventual profits.)

If you lose that client for some reason, you must find another client. That is the cost of replacement, that hypothetical $1,500, perhaps, which you might also consider to be a $1,500 loss. Losing clients *is* losing money.

Now consider what it costs to keep a client. If you had a dispute about your billing, with perhaps a few hundred dollars at stake, is it not good business to write it off and keep the client?

Every difference with a client should be analyzed in this manner, with the question of what it would cost to replace a lost client versus what it would cost to keep that client.

Aside from that, client relations depend on establishing an amicable working relationship and that means with all of those on the client's

staff with whom you must work. I often find myself working with a
half-dozen or more of the staff, since I do much of my work on the
client's premises and proposals of size are by necessity team efforts.

This, then, becomes a question of interpersonal relationships. Be
quite careful that you do not give anyone offense. Do not criticize the
employer, even if members of the staff do. It is far better to smile and/
or nod understandingly, and make no comment. Be pleasant, but avoid
controversy even in just making small talk or personal chatting. You
are inevitably and unavoidably an "outsider" in the minds of the staff,
while they are "family." Still, problems can arise that make it difficult
to avoid having differences, as an anecdote you will soon read illustrates quite well.

Client Satisfaction

The question of client satisfaction is closely related to that of client
relations and indeed includes client relations. But the principal concern here is that of satisfaction with both the work you have done and
the manner in which you have done it. When it comes to this question
of client satisfaction with your work—with the result you achieved and
with the smoothness of your working relationships with the staff, as
well as such other matters as cost and schedule conformance—you
must consider who, precisely, is your true client.

That may appear to be an anomalous question. Is not the organization—the payer of your fees—the client? Yes, in a sense that is so, but
the true client is an individual, that individual who brought you on the
job and to whom you are responsible directly for what you do. Con-
fusion about this can bring trouble, as it did for me on an early-years
assignment with a large and prominent computer corporation which
had hired me as one of several consultants to prepare the series of
manuals for a large Air Force system the corporation had designed
and built.

The general manager who had interviewed me and appointed me for
the assignment had made a point of specifying that he had handpicked
me to write the introductory manual, which he quite rightly considered to be the most difficult and most critical one of the entire set. He
thought my personal qualifications, particularly my newspaper and
general writing background, added to my technical background, suited
me best for this assignment. And so I reported for work on the client's

premises, where all of us could have access to the engineering staff, drawings, and other necessary resources.

I was supplied a broad and most general outline of the overall project and asked to first prepare an outline of the manual I was to write. I did so. It did not meet with the approval of the supervisor appointed to manage that portion of the project. He interpreted the manager's broad, overall outline much differently than I did and so insisted, over my objections, on an entirely different approach to the organization and treatment of the introductory manual. Reluctantly, I rewrote the outline to match his concepts and, getting approval now from him, proceeded to draft the manual.

Weeks later, having by now submitted a first, rough draft, I was asked by the general manager of the program (who had handpicked me) to confer with him. He proceeded to express his disapproval of my entire approach to the subject and his total disappointment with me. I then explained the problem and produced my original outline. At that, the manager looked at me sadly and said that he was more disappointed in me than ever. And when he amplified that latter remark, I could do nothing but agree totally with him. For he said that while he agreed that my original outline was the correct one, he thought I should have had the integrity to refuse to do what I thought wrong and brought the issue to him, instead.

He was right. Much as I wanted to get along with the staff and avoid friction, *he* was my true client—he had interviewed and retained me for the lengthy and profitable assignment—and I had failed him. I had violated my agreement to do the job he believed me capable of and had hired me to do.

Was this perhaps an exception to that rule about getting along amicably with everyone? Had I gone overboard with that rule and allowed myself to be compromised in my eagerness to get along with everyone? Yes and no. Yes, I had gone overboard in compromising my integrity, but no, I did not have to violate my rule about getting along with everyone. I had simply not been wise in how I handled the situation. Capitulation to an unreasonable demand was not the right answer. Confrontation was not the appropriate way to handle the matter. Were I to face such a situation today, I might approach the general manager quietly and explain the problem, also explaining carefully that I did not wish to cause a conflict of any kind or to embarrass the other individual. But, that too would be a mistake that could do nothing but cause additional problems. The wise thing here would be to have an approach to suggest to the manager so that the problem could be resolved without appearing to be a "whistle blower" or a chronic complainer. (That would make an active enemy of the supervisor, which would be in no one's interest.) My suggestion for this case, incidentally, would be to have the manger review all outlines personally, as a routine procedure, which would then enable him to "suggest" a rewrite.

Fortunately, in this case I was able to salvage the situation and retain the goodwill of my client for the future, but I never forgot the lesson learned there.

As a consultant, you must be true to the objective and to your own professional integrity. It is hazardous to compromise these in the interest of expediency. Consider who is your true client and what you owe him or her in the way of a result of your work. Be watchful that you do nothing to embarrass or cause problems for the client, however.

Marketing Followup

It is probably characterisic of consulting that even when clients have repeated needs for your services those needs generally occur at irregular and relatively infrequent periods. (In my own case it is often as long as two or three years between calls from a given client, and has sometimes been even longer.) Under those circumstances and remembering that changes are taking place in organizations as the organizations and the individuals grow, it is quite easy for clients to forget you when the need for such services as yours arises again.

Obviously, you must do something to help clients remember you and your services. There are many reminders you can employ, including at least sending clients and their staffs such items as the following, always inscribed with your name and even signed by you, when appropriate:

Calendars.
Scratch pads.
Desk pads.
Pens, pencils, key chains, rulers, etc.
Brochures.

Most of these advertising novelties are pretty standard items, easily obtainable, inexpensive, and used quite commonly to help clients remember you. The point is to send out such items regularly. You should send these to everyone you met on the project, for any of them may be the key to another contract with the organization. Moreover, people you worked with get promoted, start their own ventures, or leave and go to other organizations. So often they prove to be keys for bringing you into another organization as a consultant. I recall one staff person whom I grew to dislike thoroughly on two projects I carried out for one organization. I controlled myself and tried to work as amicably as possible with that gentleman. He later left the organization to join a larger one, and brought me into the second organization for several projects. I have often won new projects and new clients exactly in this manner, as people move around from job-to-job and from company-to-company these days. This is true for government agencies too, as clients change agencies and bring me into their newer agency.

There are many somewhat more expensive advertising novelties—cigarette lighters, pocket calculators, and others—and you may wish to be a bit more conservative in dispensing these because of their higher cost. The hazard is in giving one contact a calculator while giving someone else in the same office a ball-point pen. This can easily be construed as unfair discrimination and arouse resentment. It is probably best not to risk this. If you can't give all parties the more costly gift, give all the inexpensive one or even brochures. But do remind them of your existence and readiness to help again.

The salesperson from whom I most recently bought a new automobile has sent me (and my wife) thank you notes, calendars, birthday cards, and similar personal messages and thanks for our patronage, and the organization overall has done a fine job of after-the-sale care and followup. I can't imagine that we will go anywhere else for our next car. That highly personalized followup is quite a bit of trouble, but is the best kind of followup. Do take the trouble to learn the birthdays—executives' secretaries generally know them or can find them out for you—and send birthday cards. Don't imprint them; that's too commercial. Scrawl a brief message, sign the card, and enclose your business card.

An occasional "touching bases" letter helps. It need not be elaborate, but just the expressed wish that all is going well with the client, thanks for the opportunity to serve, and the assurance of readiness to serve again.

Finally, telephone and/or personal calls help greatly. Don't drop in unannounced; that can be inconvenient for the client. But do call and arrange to visit, or perhaps invite the client to lunch.

In any case, do not allow the client to simply forget that you exist.

A Followup Gambit

Having only one service — consulting per se — to sell is a handicap because clients may have many needs, but only an infrequent need for that basic consulting service. You may remind them of your availability many times, but until they do need consulting services, you will not hear from them.

For that and related reasons I continuously urge readers to diversify — to offer additional services to clients. However, there is a problem here too:

It is an all-too-human habit to hang a tag on everyone and to characterize everyone by one function or one specialty. Perhaps that is partly the belief that everyone must have a specialty of some sort — that no one does more than one thing really well (a rather foolish notion, of course) or perhaps tagging one somehow — "the consultant," "the computer guy," "the quality control guy," etc. — is necessary to help us remember the individuals. I have found this to be something of a problem, especially when I wish to offer a variety of services. When I present seminars, attendees are often somehow unaware that I am a consultant in my most basic calling, despite all efforts to make that fact known. Repeatedly, they will approach me privately and inquire, almost timidly, "Do you consult privately?" And the inverse is true: Clients who have retained me to help them produce a proposal appear to be surprised when they learn that I also offer training seminars in the subject and help write various kinds of marketing copy, despite all my literature that attempts to make that clear.

That can be a problem, costing business because clients had these misconceptions. On more than one occasion I found that I had not been invited to submit a quotation or proposal for a requirement because the client did not understand that I offered the appropriate service and would be interested in competing. That kind of problem is partially my own fault because I have failed to do what I am recommending here. However, I believe that every problem is an opportunity turned inside out—that you can turn a problem around and convert it into an opportunity. Here, the opportunity is to convert that human quirk into an asset as a followup gambit—a reason for the followup letter or brochure. And that "reason" is to offer the client some additional, perhaps even "new" services, such as seminars or other training sessions, newsletters, or others. Certainly you do not want them to seek out your competitors to avail themselves of services you provide. But to do this you must work vigorously at advising your clients of *all* the services you provide and equally vigorously at reminding them of these services frequently.

CHAPTER 11

CLOSE-UP ON PR

There is more to PR—public relations—than meets the eye. Here is more—much more—on how to use PR effectively.

THE TRUE NATURE AND VALUE OF PR

Several chapters ago you were introduced to PR in a brief orientation in and explanation of some of the most basic PR practices and strategies. The subject merits far more extensive and intensive coverage, for it can be your most powerful marketing tool if you learn to master and use it well. If what you learned earlier about PR was the undergraduate course, this chapter is the graduate course. It is devoted exclusively to PR on a more advanced level and is intended to serve you as both a much more definitive guide to the important details of publicity and as a general reference for everyday use in prospecting via PR—and thus building your practice. First, let us review the fundamentals and get a more intimate understanding of what PR really means.

Those two letters, PR, stand for *public relations*, and the two letters are used far more commonly than are the words they stand for. However, the term those two words stand for, "public relations," is a euphemism; the real meaning of "public relations"—the true goal of PR—is *publicity*—free advertising, that is. And the value of publicity is not so much that it is free or nearly so (it does cost something); it is that good publicity is usually far more powerful than is paid advertising. For one thing, readers find publicity more credible because it is editorial matter—news and/or features—and so it is not immediately suspect as hype, whereas paid advertising is so suspect. For another thing, publicity often gives you far more widespread and more penetrating coverage than you could afford if you had to pay for the same space as commercial advertising.

THE TOOLS OF PUBLICITY

In the earlier, brief introduction to PR you saw examples of news releases—Figures 7-1 and 7-2. Releases are among the most basic tools of the PR industry. And it is an industry, as well as a profession, peopled largely by individuals who are experienced journalists or advertising specialists. Public speaking and public appearances, as both speaker and writer, are other basic tools to which you were introduced. But they are the rudimentary tools; more sophisticated spin-offs are available and used by the professionals in the game.

The Press Kit

The release is only one element in a full press kit, which you should have prepared for full-dress media events, such as being a keynote speaker or honoree at a major convention. A "media event" does not often happen by itself, not even when a celebrity of some sort is involved. They are orchestrated—arranged and caused to happen. Major celebrities, and even some minor ones, hire PR professionals and pay them to arrange media events; you and I, unfortunately, cannot normally afford PR professionals, but must do this for ourselves, being our own PR experts.

The release—releases actually, for usually there are several releases in a press kit—are the centerpiece; they explain the event, introduce and identify you, present the text of your speech, and otherwise present the press with a complete package of information. Other elements in the kit may include photographs—usually black and white and either 8×10 inches or 4×5 inches, a fact sheet (usually about you, your background, personal details, etc.), your brochures, and any other information about you, your practice, others who may be contacted for information, and the event that you find appropriate to the occasion. The photographs are of you and also of products you may offer—books or tape sets, for example. The brochures are likewise descriptive of you and your practice. Many press kits include reprints of articles written about the individuals and their activities, their business cards, details of their formal education, honors and awards bestowed, and whatever else will help the press perceive and report on the whole person.

In arranging the media event you will have notified the press—newspapers, radio, TV, and perhaps magazine and newsletter editors—of the event and furnished information explaining the newsworthiness of the event—why it ought to be covered by the press. You may use a "tip sheet" for this, as Jeffrey Lant recommends in his *The Unabashed Self Promoter's Guide* (JLA Publications, 1983), or you can furnish all of this information in one of your news releases, which you would have sent out earlier, but a copy of which should also be in the press kit.

NEWS RELEASES

News releases may be on a preprinted form labeled NEWS RELEASE or simply NEWS or RELEASE, but it can as easily be on a letterhead with NEWS typed at the top. The exact form is not very important, but it should follow certain journalistic practices to maximize its inherent media acceptability. It should have the following characteristics (see Figure 7-2):

1. Copy double spaced, with generous margins to permit editing without difficulty.
2. Type on only one side of sheet.
3. Issuing entity clearly identified.
4. Date of issue stated.
5. Contact provided.
6. End of copy or more to come clearly indicated at bottom of each page.

Style in writing a release is important. The following says it all about style in a news release, but is equally applicable to writing for newsletters and for most other applications:

Avoid hype, adjectives, adverbs, and other literary pretensions. State "just the facts," be as brief as possible, get to the point as quickly as possible, and when you have finished *stop*.

Newsworthiness

One point has not been covered adequately as yet: That is the important matter of "newsworthiness," an essential for success.

In its literal sense, in the world of journalism, information that is a candidate for publishing must be judged as to its newsworthiness—whether it does or does not truly qualify as news. However, newspapers publish a great deal of material that is not news at all. They publish a wide variety of features, from sidebar stories—supplements to major news stories, providing sidelights, ancillary facts, and/or background information—to crossword puzzles and advice-to-the-lovelorn columns. And so the term *newsworthiness*, refers to "publishability"—whether or not material is worthy of being published.

The standard must be applied to releases. Inasmuch as the word *news release* is more often than not a euphemism for *publicity release*—the information in most releases can be called "news" only by stretching that term considerably—using the word *newsworthiness* is also something of a euphemism. It refers to whatever quality will induce an editor to use the release, to publish the information in it. Since the release does not often deliver what the journalist calls "hard news," we must consider what else might persuade an editor or columnist (for releases ought to be sent to appropriate columnists, as well as to on-the-air commentators) to use the release in his newspaper, newsletter, magazine, column, or broadcast.

Editors do not just select material that they personally find interesting or useful; they select material that they believe their readers will find interesting and useful. That is the main focus of their work. Therefore, you must judge what will interest the editor's readers, including but not confined to news items. Before exploring such items, consider the one kind of item that will almost surely and unfailingly propel your release to the nearest "circular file" (wastebasket, that is!). It is this: An unabashed and unrelieved commercial for yourself.

That is probably the most common mistake many consultants make in writing releases. They write them as though they were paid commercials. See Figure 11-1 for an example of this type of release. This notice would have to be sent out in the form of a letter, a paid space advertisement, or a broadcast commercial. It is highly unlikely that an editor would run it as editorial matter, as written.

Yet, it is possible to rewrite this and give it a fighting chance to be found newsworthy. See Figure 11-2 for an example of this rewrite. The rewrite has a good chance of landing in the newspaper's business section. The release of Figure 11-1 was couched entirely in terms of what Barker and Windfall Associates offered and even sneered—or at least

WINDFALL ASSOCIATES, CONSULTANTS
3201 Serendipity Lane
Happenstance Falls, OH 45555

NEWS RELEASE

June 20, 1989

Contact: J. Silver, 555-0001

WINDFALL ASSOCIATES EXPANDS SERVICE OFFERING

Harken T. Barker announced today that his firm, Windfall Associates,

Inc., special marketing consultants, will now provide services on weekends and

in evenings, in emergencies, by special arrangement. This is the result of the

firm's experience, Barker said, with many clients who underestimate the

difficulties and volume of detail work required in putting together a complete

marketing campaign. So often have they been called on at the last minute and

been unprepared to respond that the firm decided to set up a plan to provide

services under such circumstances.

Barker advises clients that 24 hours' advance notice is required. Calls

during regular office hours should be made to 555-0001. After office hours

calls may be made to 555-0002.

###

Figure 11-1. Advertisement masquerading as news release

WINDFALL ASSOCIATES, CONSULTANTS
3201 Serendipity Lane
Happenstance Falls, OH 45555

NEWS RELEASE

June 20, 1989

                                    Contact: J. Silver, 555-0001

MODERN MARKETING DIFFICULTIES IDENTIFIED

Local business executives are finding that assembling a complete
marketing campaign in today's complex business environment is increasingly
difficult, according to Harken T. Barker, President of Windfall Associates,
marketing consultants. For one thing, lead times for many items, such as
printing, art work, and space advertising, has almost doubled in recent years.

Barker suggested that to avoid the problem executives should allow a
great deal more lead time in the future than they have been allowing
themselves, and probably would reduce the problem considerably by vending out
certain tasks, such as mailing. He said that his firm has been called on so
much for emergency help requiring evening and weekend work that he has been
forced to set up a special program to provide such services, although he urges
clients to consult with him early in the program and so probably avoid the
need for rescue operations. However, if worst comes to worst, the firm can be
reached after office hours at 555-0002.

                                                                    ###

Figure 11-2.   Rewrite to lend newsworthiness to release

sniffed a bit—at, the implied marketing ineptitude of most business
executives. The rewrite, however, identifies a problem and makes suggestions for avoiding the problem entirely. Focusing on a legitimate
problem that readers will recognize and then suggesting a solution or
way to avoid the problem is an excellent approach to achieving news-

worthiness or "publishability." But there are other characteristics that serve to qualify a release as newsworthy or otherwise publishable. The single standard is that the information must be useful and/or interesting to readers.

You must also address the specific interests of the publication. If your release offers information about securities investments, it does not belong in a periodical devoted to woodworking or political science, so expect the editor to spend little time considering a release so far out of the range of his or her publication's interests. Of course, the same considerations apply when you direct your releases and press kits to the news media, columnists, and commentators. The assignment editor of a tabloid directed to coin collectors is not likely to send someone to cover a convention or trade show staged by an association of professional trainers.

Press Kit Contents

In practice, press kits vary in what they include. Some are quite thick with photographs, brochures, and other paper, while others are quite modest. Some are packaged in costly presentation folders with pockets; others are enclosed in simple brown kraft envelopes. There are no absolute rules and no standards, other than common practice; you use your own best judgment as to what is most necessary and what you can afford. Examples of news releases have been shown, and the subject of releases has been covered adequately. However, several suggested forms for other press-kit elements are offered here for other elements of the press kit, and you may use these or adapt them to your own preferences. In the case of Figure 11-3, a suggested form for a tip sheet to announce an event, you would identify the event as a conference, symposium, convention, seminar, trade show, exhibit, or other. A space is provided near the top of the form to note any special event, such as a celebrity speaker, a special award, or other especially newsworthy feature. Space is also provided for notes to supplement, expand on, or otherwise amplify other information.

Biography

It is customary to provide a "bio"—biographical data about yourself—and here you depart from a limitation to data that concerns only your

NOTICE OF _____ (event title)

Summary description: _____
_____
_____

Sponsoring organization: _____
_____

Special events: _____
_____
_____

Date and time: _____
Place: _____
_____

Contact for more information: _____
Name and organization: _____
Address/telephone: _____
Name and organization: _____
Address/telephone: _____
Notes: _____
_____
_____
_____
_____

Figure 11-3.   Form for "tip sheet" notification to press

professional image, for the media often feels the need to introduce a
"human interest" element. Therefore, they often wish to know more
about you as an individual. Typical data appears in the suggested form
of Figure 11-4. You may prefer to put all this data into a narrative
format or even incorporate it into a release, in which case you may
find the form useful as a worksheet for collecting and organizing the
bio data, preparatory to constructing a narrative.

Use the provision for notes, as necessary. If you are engaged in
other PR or events with PR value, such as previous or current appearances on broadcasts of some kind, authorship of a book or column,
publication of a newsletter, frequent public speaking, or other note-

BIO OF _____ (your name)

Main professional affiliation, title, business address _____
_____

Other affiliations (civic, hobbies, associates, etc) _____
_____

Age _____ Marital status _____ Children _____
Current residence (city, not specific address), length of residence ____
_____

Native of (city/state) _____
Education (university[ies], dates, majors, related facts) _____
_____
_____

Awards and honors _____
_____

Publications _____
_____

Notes: _____
_____
_____
_____
_____

Figure 11-4. Form for bio data

worthy items, be sure to include the information prominently in the form or narrative.

Fact Sheet

In many cases there is a need for a fact sheet or "backgrounder" to set the scene and to provide journalists and other recipients of the press kit important and necessary background data. This is information a journalist would normally want and have to research independently if it were not provided. It differs from the information supplied in the other forms suggested earlier in that it furnishes facts and/or background on the overall occasion or media event, rather than on you as a speaker, presenter, or otherwise prominent participant. For example, if the event or the occasion is a convention of some association, the fact sheet would provide information about the association, its history, mission, membership, and other data that would enable journalists to understand the event, its purpose, background, and/or anything else necessary to observe, report, and/or comment intelligently on its happenings. Figure 11-5 is a suggested but quite general format, general because the events may be of a wide variety of types, and each might require a substantially different form. The form does suggest the nature of the information that would be provided. Note, that frequently the backgrounder is delivered verbally in a press conference, and the fact sheet, in this case, would help the presenter organize his or her presentation.

FACT SHEET FOR _____ (identity of event)

Type of event (convention, awards dinner, other) _____
_____

Sponsoring organization (name, address, etc) _____
_____
_____

Contact person, address, telephone _____
_____

Notes/explanation/comments on event _____
_____
_____

History/reason for event _____
_____

Typical attendance _____
Features/special events scheduled or anticipated _____
_____
_____

Notes _____
_____
_____
_____
_____

Figure 11-5. Generalized form for fact sheet

In any case, the design of this form, like that the others discussed and illustrated, is arbitrary, and is a rough model only, which you can (and should) use as a guide to designing your own fact sheet for each occasion—and it will necessarily be different for different occasions.

Again, a "notes" section is supplied, and it is especially important here because the form is so general that provision for special explanations is almost mandatory.

Position Paper

Some press kits include a position paper, when the occasion calls for it. A position paper is a narrative, a philosophical statement, establishing a position, as the name implies clearly enough, where there is involved an issue on which you must declare your views—i.e., your position. Because it is part of a press kit and intended to support your PR initiative, you must somehow keep it brief enough to gain and hold attention—to enable the press to digest it easily. (Jeffrey Lant suggests a maximum of 500 words, which sounds reasonable enough.)

There is no fixed format for this, especially since it is a narrative, but it should identify you clearly, may call for a release date, since it is a public statement and you may not wish it to become public prematurely, and should include any pertinent citations.

Prepared Statement

This, like the position paper, is in narrative format, and is prepared in advance when you anticipate being asked by the press to make a statement or when you judge that it is appropriate for you to make a statement. This assumes that there is a dispute, controversy, issue, debate, or some other situation that calls for public statements from you and possibly others. Like the position paper, it had no fixed format, but is narrative, and may or may not have a release date. (Premature release of any of these special papers tends to deprive you of the benefits of maximum impact, which would derive from release at the right psychological moment, as part of the coverage of your media event.

Text of Speech

If you are to deliver a formal speech, you should normally include a copy of your text in the press kit. Usually, this is in the form of a news release, and usually it is "embargoed"—has a release date to follow the day of your delivery of the speech so that it is not reported before you present it. (When a release does not carry a release date, it is presumed to be "for immediate release," whether the release does or does not so state specifically.)

WRITING NARRATIVE TEXTS

Many people who are otherwise self-assured and positive individuals have a dread of mounting the dais to speak publicly to a large group of fellow humans. That fear of public speaking is more than occasionally matched by an equally intense distaste for, and possibly even dread of, writing. The ability and willingness to write such texts is an essential and central part of PR, and success depends largely on writing.

I am not referring here to "literary" talent, whatever that may be. It is not necessary to be a writer per se or to study the art of writing generally. You are not required to hone your language, searching for that exactly right word, that melodious phrase, or that polished sentence. But it is necessary to write clearly—you must make yourself understood—and to follow a few simple rules and master a few simple principles. It is also necessary—absolutely necessary—that you surmount that fear of, or distaste for, writing. And bear in mind that we are not talking about writing "well," but writing *effectively*, which anyone with an average knowledge of our language can do.

First Principle

Writing is an art, not a science. That does not mean that it is without organized method and basic principles. And those most germane to our discussion here deal with the basic structure of all narrative. Releases, speeches, and all other narrative texts have this common basis: Each needs a *lead*, a *body*, and a *conclusion*, otherwise known as a *beginning*, a *middle*, and *end*.

The Lead

Learning to write a proper lead is probably the most difficult part of writing to master as well as the most important part. Speaking for myself and probably for a great many other professional writers, without the *right* lead I am unable to get very far, but with the right lead the rest begins to fall into place quite rapidly. Note here that I used the adjective *right*, not *good*, in referring to the needed lead. That was a deliberate choice. There may be many *good* leads possible, but they may or may not be the right leads for my purposes.

The lead is the introduction to whatever it is you wish to say with your narrative. For the typical news story written in classic journalistic style, it would be a summary of that narrative, introducing it while it presented the main facts—"John Spokesman, President of Giltedge Industries, today announced a merger of Giltedge Industries with Fantastic Corporation." The rest of the story would expand on that lead steadily, adding details with each succeeding sentence. An editor could chop the rest of the story at any point to make it fit available space. That is, in fact, the reason for that kind of writing, the traditional "inverted pyramid" of that school of writing. However, not every lead is designed to do that, to relate all the salient facts in the first breath of introducing the subject. There are other kinds of leads, designed for other purposes.

First, the example here was a straight narrative lead, in the style of a straight news story. It could have been written in numerous other ways, including the following few samples:

Quotation lead: "We are pleased to announce our merger with Fantastic Corporation," said John Spokesman, President of Giltedge Industries today.

Question lead: How does a small company take over a huge corporation? That question was answered today when John Spokesman, President of Giltedge Industries, announced a merger with Fantastic Corporation.

Humorous lead: A mouse can swallow an elephant, apparently. It was announced today that Giltedge Industries has acquired the much larger Fantastic Corporation.

Novelty lead: It isn't often that a small company swallows up a huge corporation and emerges as the surviving organization, as Giltedge Industries has just done, using a new and special technique that overpowered the other corporation before its executives realized that they were a takeover target.

The lead may be a single sentence but is not necessarily so constrained; it can be several sentences, a paragraph, or even longer, depending on the length of the total narrative. Moreover, the lead should do much more than simply introduce and summarize the narrative to follow; to be truly effective it must meet other criteria, accomplish other purposes as well:

1. It should set a *theme* or *mood* for the narrative. A humorous lead signals a lighthearted treatment to follow, for example. The reader of a humorous lead will expect that.

2. It should capture the reader's interest. A humorous lead may do that by virtue of being humorous, even if the reader does not know or care about Giltedge Industries or whatever/whomever is the subject of the story. On the other hand, the reader of the novelty lead exemplified here would read on to learn about this new takeover technique.

3. It should represent the *essence* of what is to follow. And it must be your own guiding star in writing the narrative. That is its most important objective—helping you, the writer, think out not only what you wish to say, but *how* you wish to present the narrative—the "slant" or "angle," and the theme or mood. At least, I find it so in my own writing. I am simply unable to proceed without a lead that *satisfies me that it is right*.

It is that last-named function and objective of the lead that I find most important. I know that I am not alone in that. Those wastebaskets full of crumpled sheets (from the days when we all used typewriters) often represented the frustrations of searching for the right lead. Word processing has changed that, insofar as it is—jocularly—the "bit bucket," rather than the wastebasket, into which we now cast all our discarded efforts to begin, to find the right lead. But it has not changed the quest. I cannot proceed until I have found the right lead, the one that tells *me*, as well as my reader, what the narrative is to be about. I still shudder at the memory of discarding approximately 50 full manuscript pages of a book I had started because I became increasingly aware, as I proceeded, that my lead was all wrong. Many days' work went into the trash because my lead—much longer than a sentence or two when it is the introduction to an entire book—was ill conceived.

I call that "thinking on paper," because it used to be literally paper that I consumed, often trying out and discarding as many as a dozen leads before "finding" one that satisfied me. I still do, although the blessing of word processing has made the quest far easier, for I can and often do salvage portions of earlier attempts in finally constructing the lead I find to be the right one. Even in the case of writing on a subject with which I am most familiar and have written about previously, I struggle for a lead. (I tried several in beginning this discussion of writing, for example.)

The Body

The body or middle of the narrative is one or more paragraphs that deliver what the lead promises. The lead promises information, theme, mood, and style, and the body should deliver that in an organized and progressive narrative. Each paragraph has its own lead, the first sentence, which should telegraph the content of the paragraph. Note the lead of this paragraph, for example. Note, too, that much more space and attention was devoted to the subject of writing leads than to that of writing the body of the narrative. Each paragraph should address a single topic, introduced by its own lead, and should deliver the discussion in simple, declarative sentences, with the single objective of making simple, clear statements.

The unpardonable sin is failing to deliver what the lead promised. The reader feels betrayed, tricked into reading something other than what you promised. Be sure that your text body delivers what it should deliver. If your lead says that a new takeover technique was revealed, be sure that your text explains exactly what you meant—what that technique is.

The Conclusion

The conclusion, for a brief narrative text, is usually a single paragraph. It should close out the subject by summarizing the story, presenting a moral or lesson learned, or conclusion drawn. The one thing it must not do is leave things hanging so that the reader is left with an unsatisfied feeling that there is more to be told or more to learn. Again, as an example, if you had promised and explained that alleged new takeover technique, summarized what it was, what it means for future takeovers, what someone else has commented on it, or something that concludes the narrative and *makes it clear that the narrative is concluded*.

Reprints

There are two kinds of reprints you may find useful to include in your press kit. One is the reprint of articles you have written that have some relevance to the event for which the press kit is prepared and distributed. The other is the reprint of articles about you/your work or which mentions you or your work—for example, a review/discussion of a book you have written or reference to your book in connection with a discussion of something else.

The reference is not necessarily about a book you have written. Depending on your field, it may be a computer program you have developed, a training system you designed, some original research you did, a paper you delivered, an award you received, or any of many other things.

Such items are valuable elements in the press kit. They lend you prestige and help you earn respect from the media, who are notoriously unimpressed even by celebrities, let alone by those of us who labor more or less anonymously. (The opportunity to create such reprints is itself sometimes ample justification for contributing articles on a complimentary basis—without payment—to trade or professional journals.) It is worthwhile making the efforts necessary to collect these. And that is not always an easy job. The enormous flood of printed paper that gushes forth from the presses each day precludes your being able to monitor more than a soupcon of the publications. That is where the clipping service enters the picture.

Clipping Services

Every metropolitan area boasts a few clipping bureaus, and every full-scale PR program subscribes to a clipping service. Luce Press Clippings of New York City, for example, proudly advertises that it has existed since 1881, over 100 years, and announces that it is one of the world's largest clipping bureaus, even offering prospective subscribers the convenience of a toll-free telephone number. Traditionally, such bureaus search the newspapers and certain classes of periodicals every day, clipping items that mention your name or whatever you have hired them to search for. You pay by the item clipped and sent to you.

It is in some ways not the most efficient service because you often find that you are paying many times over for what is essentially the same item, one that was released by a syndicate or press service to its subscriber publications and appeared in identical form in numerous publications. Despite this unavoidable drawback, such a service does get the job done, and is helpful, even indispensable, to serious PR work in the opinion of many public relations specialists.

RADIO AND TV APPEARANCES

Several decades ago the essence and main objective of PR was newspaper publicity. Today, radio and television publicity is at least the equal of newspaper publicity in effectiveness, and is or should be a major target of any PR program. It's quite easy to verify this. Listen to and observe radio and TV talk shows and be alert for the PR plugs; virtually every guest has something to sell, which is the main reason for the appearance. Newcomers and struggling beginners in the entertainment business are trying to gain personal recognition—to sell themselves—but almost all entertainers appearing as guests are sure to mention or have the host mention their new movie, their current or upcoming appearance somewhere, their new book, or something they wish to plug.

It's a swap, a barter exchange. The producers and hosts are providing valuable—often priceless—publicity free of charge, while the guest is providing some entertainment value—an interesting personality or some interesting information to present. The guest—except for professional entertainers—is paid in publicity, a few seconds of advertising that would cost hundreds or even thousands of dollars if it were commercial advertising time at commercial rates, while the producer is getting program material—guests—at no cost. Understand and appreciate that—that it is a fair exchange, not a gift. You are giving, as well as getting, so in pursuing publicity you are making an *offer*—proposing an exchange—and not begging favors. You need to be highly conscious of this to have the right mental set in selling yourself.

Winning Radio and TV PR

That press kit that you prepare for media events is readily adaptable to the purpose of selling yourself for radio and TV interviews, which are simply another media event for you. Just as the journalists in the print media wish to know *why* they should interview you, producers of the talk shows want to know why they should book you—who you are, what you have done, what you will present, etc. Your press kit must answer such questions—as the second or third step in the process. The first step is, usually, a telephone call to the producer or to the main contact to whom you should send your information. There are many possible functionaries, depending on several factors—producers, assistant or associate producers, talent coordinators, news directors, news producers, editors, and others. It is helpful if you can first chat briefly with the individual who happens to be the right one for you to speak with. Even if you cannot, leave word that you called, and why you called, and promise to send your kit of materials to support your proposal. (It is helpful to think of this as a proposal, rather than as a request or application.) Follow up then with your information kit, even if your original call was not returned (it is likely that it will not be) and then with telephone calls again to follow up your mailing.

Even when you have done everything properly, you will almost surely have to be persistent in your efforts. The radio and TV program staffs are busy, harried people, facing many requests similar to yours, while they are trying to organize and assemble their programs. Their failure to respond promptly does not necessarily reflect rejection or indecision; it may signify a simple shortage of time and freedom to follow up immediately, and may even reflect a belief that *you* will follow up and persist. You must keep the initiative in any case.

Of course, there are many exceptions to the "rule" that you must persist and persevere, for often fortune and chance step in to take a hand. I persuaded the Washington *Star* (now one of the many demised big-city newspapers) to interview me by writing a letter to a business-news reporter, who then got permission from his editor to conduct and print the interview. However, a free lance writer who happened to guest regularly on the air with a prominent local news broadcaster read that newspaper account and interviewed me for a magazine article he had been assigned. Subsequently, he arranged to have me appear on the program with him on several occasions, and did so on his own initiative. So, one PR success often leads to the next one even without special effort on your part. However, you can and should try to pyramid such successes by making other producers aware of your appearances on the air and in print.

PR INFORMATION RESOURCES

Success in PR campaigns—in gaining adequate publicity, that is—depends heavily on access to comprehensive information resources. Certain publications have been created especially for use in PR activity, while others, created and marketed for other uses, have also proved to be extremely useful in pursuing publicity campaigns. The information resources most useful in PR projects fall into three major categories:

1. Lists of media and related outlets of PR information—principally newspapers, news services, newsletters, magazines, associations, radio stations, TV stations, columnists, commentators, programs and producers, with names, addresses, telephone numbers, and as much other, related data as possible.
2. Directories of such lists as those described in item 1 here.
3. Publications guiding readers in the methodologies, new ideas, news items, and other information concerning the PR industry and its activities.

Cautionary Notes

Some of the relevant information, principally that which is useful but only indirectly related to PR as such, is listed in the bibliography. Here, there are listed a number of sources of information directly related to and useful for PR functions. In some cases, where it appears they will be useful, comments appear with the listing. In other cases the title listed itself furnishes the significant information.

It is not necessary to own all of these directories, but it may be useful to know of the existence of all of them. However, this is by no means a complete list. Decisions as to whether a given item belongs in this chapter or in the bibliography are arbitrary and are mine, alone. In fact, the decisions as to which list is the proper one for any given item are necessarily arbitrary as well. Many are not clearly one kind or another—and arbitrary judgment is unavoidable. Finally, there is no significance to the order in which items appear: that, too, is arbitrary and random.

Directories and Other PR Publications

Modern times, with radio and TV bringing news into our homes, often even as it is happening, have not been kind to the print media—newspapers, especially. Even in the large metropolitan areas, of which there are about 125 in the United States, major newspapers have increasingly been forced to fold their tents. Cities such as New York, Philadelphia and Washington, which once supported as many as a half-dozen or more metropolitan dailies, are reduced to a very few. Still, there are several hundred suburban daily newspapers and many weeklies surviving that are, collectively, still a strong media force, reaching millions of readers.

Anything lost as a result of the demise of many newspapers has been more than compensated for by the rise of radio and TV broadcast stations. There are many thousands of newsletters also, so there is no shortage of potential outlets for releases and other PR material to reach millions of readers, viewers, and listeners daily. That means that many directories are needed. A relative handful are listed here. Some of them are highly specialized, while others are more general in nature, but all pertain to PR/publicity in some way.

The National Directory of Addresses and Telephone Numbers
Concord Reference Books, Inc.
850 Third Avenue
New York, NY 10022
(212) 223-5100

This publication is listed also in the bibliography, without comment, but is valuable enough and important enough to merit being listed in both places. It is an annual publication that grows thicker and more useful each year. (The 1986 edition on my desk has well over 1,000 pages.) It is a paperback, large format (8-½×11 inches), on newsprint, and is generalized, rather than specialized, as a multi-faceted directory. The section on "Media & Information Sources" alone lists newspapers, business newsletters, radio and TV stations, cable TV systems, magazines, business reference books, database information services, and research services. But there are also thick sections listing advertising agencies, associations and organizations, government agencies, corporations by SIC (Standard Industrial Classification) code number and alphabetically, and a number of other useful listings.

It is probably fair to consider this an entire set of directories in one volume, rather than a single directory. Certainly, it is the most useful single directory that I know of, and if I could own only one directory it would be this one.

The Unabashed Self-Promoter's Guide
Jeffrey Lant Associates
50 Follen Street, Suite 507
Cambridge, MA 02138
(617) 547-6372

This is one of Dr. Jeffrey Lant's earlier books for consultants (1983), but is no less unrelenting and remorseless (two of his own adjectives) in pressing home his vigorous and aggressive messages. In this book he provided the wealth of detailed how-to information that has become his hallmark. The entire book—nearly 400 *large* pages—deals with marketing promotion, much of it closely related to the content of this chapter.

Bacon's Publicity Checker
332 S. Michigan Avenue
Chicago, IL 60604
(312) 922-2400

An old-timer in the field of publicity, newspaper listings, and related information.

Ayer Directory of Publications
Ayer Press
One Bala Avenue
Bala Cynwyd, PA 19004
(215) 664-6203

An old, established, and often-recommended source of information about periodicals.

Literary Market Place
Ulrich's International Periodicals Directory
R.R. Bowker Co.
1180 Avenue of the Americas
New York, NY 10036
(212) 764-5100

The first publication listed here, familiarly referred to as the "LMP," is an annual and the leading journal of the book publishing industry and related activities. It is loaded with directory information, and is something of a "bible" in the industry. Ulrich's is something of a bible in listing periodicals worldwide, including newsletters.

Editor & Publisher International Year Book
Editor & Publisher Market Guide
Editor & Publisher Co.
575 Lexington Avenue
New York, NY 10022
(212) 752-7050

Information on newspapers, clipping services, other publications and related activity.

Hudson's Washington News Media Contacts Directory
7315 Wisconsin Avenue
Bethesda, MD 20814
(301) 986-0666

This publication of Howard Penn Hudson, the well-known authority on newsletters and publisher of the *Newsletter on Newsletters*, is an annual, listing newspapers, news bureaus and news services, newsletters, columnists, magazines, and other PR assets in Washington, DC, where dozens and dozens of major periodicals maintain offices.

Syndicated Columnists Directory
News Bureaus in the U.S.
Public Relations Publishing Co.
888 Seventh Avenue
New York, NY 10106
(212) 582-7373

Highly useful directories of what the titles suggest.

Media Personnel Directory
Encyclopedia of Business Information Sources
Encyclopedia of Associations
National Directory of Newsletter and Reporting Services
Gale Research Co.
Book Tower
Detroit, MI 48226
(313) 961-2242

Typically large and comprehensive directories.

TV Publicity Outlets Nationwide
Public Relations Plus, Inc.
New York Publicity Outlets
POB 327
Washington Depot, CT 06794
(203) 868-0200

Directories and guides.

North American Radio, TV Station Guide
Howard W. Sams & Co., Inc.
4300 W. 62nd Street
Indianapolis, IN 46206
(317) 298-5400

Television Contacts
Radio Contacts
Larimi Communications Associates, Ltd.
151 East 50th Street
New York, NY 10022
(212) 935-9262

Directories of commercial and non-commercial stations.

How to Get Publicity
Times Books, Div. of Random House, Inc.
201 East 50th Street
New York, NY 10022
(212) 872-8110

Excellent how-to book on the subject.

PART IV

GOVERNMENT CONTRACTING OPPORTUNITIES

In modern times federal legislators have recognized that modern purchasing power of the federal government is such a great economic force that government procurement alone can greatly influence the economy of the country. This has led to a succession of socioeconomic programs linked to federal buying power, in which goals generally are to encourage and nourish free enterprise and small business growth, and to afford greater equality of economic opportunity for all.

In the next few chapters you will be presented with information about, and directories to, an enormous number of prospects in thousands of governments—"government entities," in Census Bureau terms. The federal government has many programs of assistance to small businesses and minority-owned businesses, administered through the Small Business Administration, the Department of Commerce, and many small-business-assistance officers in the Department of Defense and other agencies. These include loans, loan guarantees, preference for government contracts, and many kinds of free business services. State governments and, in many cases, local governments too, have similar programs.

CHAPTER 12

FEDERAL GOVERNMENT PROSPECTS

Federal government agencies use all kinds of consulting services frequently and in quantity. They represent thousands of excellent prospects for technical and professional services.

GOVERNMENT OFFICES AND FACILITIES

The lists that appear in this chapter are by no means a complete directory of all U.S. Government offices and facilities, nor is there much purpose in listing all, for many are of no interest to consultants, are small and insignificant installations, or do virtually no purchasing. Moreover, the government's structure grows and changes as much as the private sector does. (Overall, it continues to grow in size and complexity.)

The U.S. military services are a special problem insofar as providing coherent and complete listings is concerned because of the special problems of DOD being a department, within which there are the three military organizations also called "departments," and because of the complex structure of military organizations. Bear in mind that every military base does at least some independent purchasing and therefore has its own procurement office and sometimes more than one such office, especially where the base serves as a headquarters for some major function within the military department.

On the other hand, with only the relative handful of exceptions noted here, federal government agencies do a great deal of purchasing and contracting independently, using their own internal budgets. The agencies listed here are therefore all good prospects for services. But before turning to the lists, there is some other information here that should be an aid in pursuing government prospects.

PROCUREMENT CLASSIFICATIONS

The columns of the *Commerce Business Daily* that should be of interest to you cover both goods and services. The services categories under which you are likely to find relevant requirements include all of the following:

A   Experimental, Developmental, Test and Research Work
H   Expert and Consultant Services
L   Technical Representative Services
M   Operation and/or Maintenance of Government Owned Facility
T   Photographic, Mapping, Printing and Publication Services
U   Training Services
X   Miscellaneous
69 Training Aids and Devices
70 General Purpose Automated Data Processing (ADP) Equipment, Software, Supplies, and Support Equipment
76 Books, Maps, and Other Publications

Aside from that, the General Services Administration buys certain services, under identifying codes, including the following:

0478 Miscellaneous Services Incidental to Transportation
0489 Communications Services
0635 Surety Insurance
0641 Insurance Agents and Service
0731 Advertising
0737 Computer and Data Processing Services
0739 Miscellaneous Business Services
0781 Motion Picture Production and Allied Services

GLOSSARY OF SPECIAL TERMS

As in every special field, government marketing and contracting has its own special jargon and acronyms. Sometimes the acronym or colloquial term becomes known better and is recognized more easily than the formal term or name for which it stands. Moreover, there is no true consistency in the methods employed. The Agriculture Department, for example, is USDA, but the Labor Department is DOL, and the Treasury Department is simply Treasury. The following is a brief glossary of terms you will encounter most commonly in doing business with the federal government.

Advertised bid, advertised procurement, sealed bids: also formally advertised procurement: Procurement requiring sealed bids and public opening on an announced date and time at an announced place, with award normally to the low bidder; usually requires price quotes only and is solicited by IFB (Information for Bid).

ADP: Automated data processing.

ADTS: Automated Data and Telecommunications Service.

AEC: Atomic Energy Commission.

AFB: Air Force Base.

AID: Agency for International Development.

ASPR: Armed Services Procurement Regulations; former procurement regulations, replaced by DAR—Defense Acquisition Regulations and, more recently, by FAR—Federal Acquisition Regulations.

Below the line: Providing goods or service to customer at cost; sometimes required for certain kinds of items, especially in some cost-plus contracts.

Best and final offer: Invitation often extended to finalists in negotiated procurement to review and adjust their prices before final decision.

BIA: Bureau of Indian Affairs.

Bid set: Package of information and forms required to make bid; same as solicitation package.

Bidder's conference, prebid conference: Conference held in advance of some awards to answer questions and provide more detailed information to bidders and/or proposers.

BLM: Bureau of Land Management.

BLS: Bureau of Labor Statistics.

BOA: Basic Ordering Agreement; contract to supply goods/services at set (contracted) rates, as called for by customer; an indefinite-quantity term contract.

CBD: Commerce Business Daily.

C/E: Corps of Engineers.

COB: Close of business; by that time at which the office in question ends its work day, which varies from one office to another; often cited as time bid or proposal is due on given date.

CONUS: Continental United States.

COR: Contracting Officer's Representative; also COTR and GTR; government technical manager or project manager.

COTR: Contracting Officer's Technical Representative; see COR.

CPAF: Cost plus award fee, a cost-reimbursement type of contract often used when government wants to furnish incentives to contractor.

CPFF: Cost plus fixed fee; another type of cost-reimbursement contract often used when it is difficult to estimate costs in advance.

DARPA: Defense Advanced Research Projects Agency.

DCA: Defense Communications Agency.

DCAA: Defense Contract Audit Agency; DOD contractor auditors, who often audit contractors for other government agencies.

DCASR: Defense Contract Administration Service Region; field office of DOD that carries out many duties for DOD, including security inspections and inspections to approve shipment of contracted-for goods.

D/E: Department of Education.

DEA: Drug Enforcement Administration.

DIA: Defense Intelligence Administration.

DLA: Defense Logistics Agency.

DOC: Department of Commerce.

DOD: Department of Defense.

DOL: Department of Labor.

DOT: Department of Transportation.

End-product: Item to be delivered; also "deliverable" item.

Evaluation criteria: Factors used to evaluate proposals objectively.

FAA: Federal Aviation Administration.

FDA: Food and Drug Administration.

FmHA: Farmers Home Administration.

Form 33: Form usually used as first sheet of solicitation package for both IFB and RFP solicitations.

Form 60: Cost form used by most nonmilitary agencies.

Form DD-633: Cost form used by military agencies.

Form 129: Bidders application form.

FP: Fixed price, as in fixed-price contract.

FPDC: Federal Procurement Data Center.

FPR: Federal Procurement Regulations; now replaced by FAR—Federal Acquisition Regulations.

FRA: Federal Railroad Administration.

FTS: Federal Telecommunications System.

GAO: General Accounting Office.

GSA: General Services Administration.

GPO: Government Printing Office.

GSA Schedule: Term contract for common-use commodities.

GTR: Government Technical Representative; same as COR and COTR (which see).

HHS: Department of Health and Human Services.

HRA: Health Resources Administration.

HSA: Health Services Administration.

HUD: Department of Housing and Urban Development.

Indefinite quantity: Term contract for goods/services to be supplied as called for and at prices agreed on.

IFB: Information for Bid; see Advertised bid.

Labor-hour contract: Type of BOA listing labor rates.

MBDA: Minority Business Development Agency.

NASA: National Aviation and Aeronautics Administration.

Negotiated procurement: Usually solicited via RFP and requiring a proposal competition; contract to be negotiated and not bound by lowest bid.

NHTSA: National Highway Traffic Safety Administration.

NIDA: National Institute of Drug Abuse.

NIH: National Institutes of Health.

NIMH: National Institutes of Mental Health.

NIOSH: National Institute of Safety and Health.

NLM: National Library of Medicine.

NOAA: National Oceanic and Atmospheric Administration.

NOL: Naval Ordnance Laboratory.

Non-responsive: Characteristic of a bid or proposal which fails to respond as requested; also applied to performance of a contractor who fails to respond to the government's direction or requests.

NRL: Naval Research Laboratory.

OFPP: Office of Federal Procurement Policy.

OMB: Office of Management and Budget.

OPM: Office of Personnel Management; new name for Civil Service Commission.

OSHA: Occupational Safety and Health Administration.

PHS: Public Health Service.

Pre-award survey: Visit to bidder's facility, prior to contract award, to inspect and verify that all is as represented by bidder.

Proposal: Response to RFP describing what bidder proposes and pledges to do and at what cost.

Purchase order: Informal type of contract which may be used for smaller purchases (to $10,000 in most agencies, to $25,000 in DOD, under present law).

RFP: Request for Proposals.

RFQ: Request for Quotation; often followed by issuing a purchase order to firm submitting lowest quotation.

SBA: Small Business Administration.

SOW: Statement of Work, which is specification issued with RFP.

Task order: One of the orders issued under a BOA for services; also used as contracting term, as in Task Order Contract.

T&M: Time and Material, another type of BOA.

TVA: Tennessee Valley Authority.

USAF: U.S. Air Force.

USA: U.S. Army

USCG: U.S. Coast Guard.

USDA: U.S. Depaetment of Agriculture.

USN: U.S. Navy.

USMC: U.S. Marine Corps.

USPS: U.S. Postal Service.

SMALL BUSINESS UTILIZATION OFFICES

All federal agencies are required to maintain small business utilization functions, with individuals appointed to act as advocates for small business in satisfying federal needs, directly and indirectly. That means making direct contract awards to small businesses, where possible, and assisting small business in winning subcontracts from the large prime contractors to the government. When making calls on any agency it is always a good idea to talk to the contracting officer and any small-business representatives who are available. In agencies doing a large amount of procurement there is likely to be an individual or even an office of several individuals charged with the responsibility. In agencies doing only occasional or relatively small amounts of procurement the small-business representative may well be the agency's contracting officer wearing another hat. However, the function is required to exist, by law, and it is often well worth the time and effort to spend a few minutes with the small-business representative and/or contracting officer.

The Department of Defense (DOD) is especially active in utilizing small businesses as suppliers because DOD accounts for such a significantly large portion of the overall federal procurement budget that it is in DOD's own interest to maximize competition and support a maximum number of suppliers. (One major consideration of military procurement is the maintenance of the maximum industrial base to be ready with near-instant support in event of an emergency.) Of course, the law also requires small-business utilization, and DOD is unquestionably by far the largest customer in the federal establishment, so it follows that DOD would have the most highly developed system of small-business-utilization specialists.

SMALL BUSINESS ADMINISTRATION

Among the earliest efforts to use the federal purchasing power for socioeconomic benefits was the formation of the Small Business Administration (SBA) in 1953, under the Small Business Act. The SBA operates a variety of programs in carrying out its missions, which are to aid small business generally and minority- and women-owned business especially in a variety of ways. These are the general types of programs and activities SBA carries out:

1. Financing of enterprises through a variety of loans, loan guarantees, and other programs.
2. Special preference, where possible and practicable, and special

help in winning government contracts and in carrying them out successfully.

3. Special services, such as consulting and training in general business functions.

4. Publications, many free, others at nominal cost.

Among its functions SBA sets the standards that determine what qualifies a venture as a small business. The general language of the law is that to qualify as a small business the company must not be in a dominant position within its industry, so SBA must determine what size determines dominance or nondominance within each industry and how that may be measured. The standards therefore vary from one industry to another so that there are many standards of small-business size. Some are based on annual sales in dollars, some on number of employees, and some on other factors.

To help small businesses win government contracts, some contracts are set aside for small businesses only; larger businesses cannot bid for them. In addition, small businesses are entitled automatically to progress payments on government contracts, and are also entitled to enlist SBA aid when they are having difficulties of any kind, such as finding the financing necessary to handle a contract or to demonstrate qualifying "financial responsibility" and financial capability to a contracting officer. Similarly, if in bidding for a contract it becomes necessary to demonstrate qualifying technical capability to a contracting officer, a small business may seek assistance from SBA in an SBA certification of technical capability.

The Small Business Administration also operates a special program for minorities, the so-called "8(a)" program, to help minority entrepreneurs succeed in winning government contracts by certifying minority firms as qualifying under that clause — 8(a) — of the law and exempting them from normal competition for many awards set aside as 8(a) contracts. (The competition, when and if there is any for such contracts, is technical only, not cost, and is confined to certified minority firms only.)

The Small Business Administration operates approximately 100 offices throughout the United States, with the central or headquarters office in Washington, DC. (Other offices are Regional or District offices.) Following is a list of those offices.

Alabama
Birmingham 35205
908 S. 20th Street, Room 202

Alaska
Anchorage 99501
1016 W. 6th Avenue, Suite 200

Fairbanks 99701
Federal Building & Courthouse

Arizona
Phoenix 85004
112 N. Central Avenue

Arkansas
Little Rock 72202
611 Gaines Street, Suite 900

California
Fresno 93712
1229 N. Street

Los Angeles 90071
350 S. Figueroa Street

Sacramento 95825
2800 Cottage Way, Room 2535

San Diego 92188
880 Front Street, Room 4-S-38

San Francisco 94102
*450 Golden Gate Avenue
211 Main Street, 4th Floor

Colorado
Denver 80202
*1405 Curtis Street, 22nd Floor
721 19th Street

Connecticut
Hartford 06103
1 Financial Plaza

Delaware
Wilmington 19801
844 King Street, Room 5207

District of Columbia
Washington 20416
**1441 L Street, NW

Washington 20417
1030 15th Street, NW

Florida
Coral Gables 33134
2222 Ponce de Leon Boulevard

Jacksonville 32202
400 West Bay Street, Room 261

Tampa 33607
700 Twiggs Street

West Palm Beach 33402
701 Clematis Street

Georgia
Atlanta 30309
*1375 Peachtree Street, NE
1720 Peachtree Street, NW

Guam
Agana 96910
Pacific Daily News Building

Hawaii
Honolulu 96850
300 Ala Moana, Box 50207

Idaho
Boise 83702
1005 Main Street

Illinois
Chicago 60604
*219 South Dearborn Street

Springfield 62701
1 North Old State Capital Plaza

Indiana
Indianapolis 46204
575 North Pennsylvania Street

Iowa
Des Moines 50309
210 Walnut Street, Room 749

Kansas
Wichita 67202
110 East Waterman Street

Kentucky
Louisville 40202
600 Federal Plaza, Room 188

Louisiana
New Orleans 70113
1001 Howard Avenue, 17th Floor

Shreveport 71101
500 Fannin Street

Maine
Augusta 04330
40 Western Avenue, Room 512

---

* Regional Office
** Central (Headquarters) Office

Maryland
Baltimore/Towson 21204
8600 LaSalle Road

Massachusetts
Boston 02114
*60 Batterymarch, 10th Floor

Boston 02203
150 Causeway Street

Holyoke 01050
302 High Street, 4th Floor

Michigan
Detroit 48226
477 Michigan Avenue

Marquette 49855
540 West Kave Avenue

Minnesota
Minneapolis 55402
12 South 6th Street

Mississippi
Biloxi 39530
111 Fred Haise Boulevard, 2nd Floor

Jackson 39201
200 East Pascagoula Street

Missouri
Kansas City 64106
*911 Walnut Street, 23rd Floor
1150 Grande Avenue

St. Louis 63101
1 Mercantile Center

Montana
Helena 59601
301 South Park, Drawer 10054

Nebraska
Omaha 68102
Empire State Building, 2nd Floor

Nevada
Las Vegas 89101
301 East Stewart Street

Reno 89505
50 South Virginia Street, Room 213

New Hampshire
Concord 03301
55 Pleasant Street, Room 213

New Jersey
Camden 08104
1800 East Davis Street

Newark 07102
970 Broad Street, Room 1635

New Mexico
Albuquerque 87110
5000 Marble Avenue, NE

New York
Albany 12210
99 Washington Avenue, Room 301

Buffalo 14202
111 West Huron Street, Room 1311

Elmira 14904
1051 South Maine Street

Melville 11746
425 Broad Hollow Road

New York 1007
*27 Federal Plaza, Room 29-118
26 Federal Plaza, Room 3100

Rochester 14614
100 State Street, Room 601

Syracuse 13260
100 South Clinton Street

North Carolina
Charlotte 28202
230 South Tryon Street

Greenville 27834
215 South Evans Street, Room 206

North Dakota
Fargo 58102
65 72nd Avenue North, Room 218

Ohio
Cincinnati 45202
550 Main Street, Room 5028

Cleveland 44199
1240 East 9th Street, Room 317

Columbus 43215
85 Marconi Boulevard

Oklahoma
Oklahoma City 73102
200 NW 5th Street, Room 670

---

* Regional Office

Oregon
Portland 97205
1220 SW 3rd Avenue, Federal Building

Pennsylvania
Harrisburg 17101
100 Chestnut Street

Philadelphia/Bala-Cynwyd 19004
*1 Bala-Cynwyd Plaza

Pittsburgh 15222
1000 Liberty Avenue Room 1401

Wilkes-Barre 18702
20 North Pennsylvania Avenue

Puerto Rico
Hato Rey 00919
Chardon and Bolivia Streets

Rhode Island
Providence 02903
40 Fountain Street

South Carolina
Columbia 29201
1801 Assembly Street, Room 131

South Dakota
Rapid City 57701
515 9th Street, Room 246

Sioux Falls 57102
101 S. Maine Avenue

Tennessee
Knoxville 37902
502 South Gay Street, Room 307

Memphis 38103
167 North Main Street, Room 211

Nashville 37219
404 James Robertson Parkway

Texas
Corpus Christi 78408
3105 Leopard Street

Dallas 75202
1100 Commerce Street, Room 3C36

Dallas 752335
*1720 Regal Row, Room 230

El Paso 79901
4100 Rio Bravo, Suite 300

Harlingen 78550
222 E. Van Buren Street

Houston 77002
500 Dallas Street
1 Allen Center

Lubbock 79401
1205 Texas Avenue, Room 712

Marshall 75670
100 South Washington Street

San Antonio 78206
727 East Durango, Room A-513

Utah
Salt Lake City 84138
125 South State Street

Vermont
Montpelier 06502

Virginia
Richmond 23240

Virgin Islands
St. Thomas 00801
Veterans Drive, U.S. Federal Building

Washington
Seattle 98104
*710 2nd Avenue, 5th Floor
915 2nd Avenue, Room 1744

Spokane 99210
Court House Building, Room 651

West Virginia
Charleston 25301
Charleston National Plaza

Clarksburg 26301
109 North 3rd Street

Wisconsin
Eau Claire 54701
500 South Barstow Street

Madison 53703
212 East Washington Avenue

Milwaukee 53202
517 East Wisconsin Avenue

Wyoming
Casper 82602
100 East B Street

---

* Regional Office

AGENCY NAMES AND ADDRESSES

U.S. DEPARTMENT OF AGRICULTURE
Central Offices:
Independence Avenue & 12th-14th Streets, SW
Washington, DC 20250
(202) 655-4000

U.S. DEPARTMENT OF COMMERCE
Central Office:
14th Street & Constitution Avenue, NW
Washington, DC 20230
(202) 377-2000

MINORITY BUSINESS DEVELOPMENT AGENCY

The Minority Business Development Agency (MBDA) is an office in the U.S. Department of Commerce. Its mission is to support the development of minority-owned businesses. This organization has changed direction in recent years (marked by the change from the former name, the Office of Minority Business Development (OMBD) to the present name). Where the original organization tended to support any kind of enterprise, the current organization tends to encourage the growth of minority-owned high-technology enterprises. In any case, the program consists primarily of supporting a number of nonprofit centers (roughly 100 in number, at this time) around the country. A request must be made of the organization in Washington, DC for an up-to-date list of their contractors and centers. The central office address is as follows:

Minority Business Development Agency
U.S. Department of Commerce
14th Street & Constitution Avenue
Washington, DC 20230

Field and Regional offices of MBDA are as follows:

MBDA, Department of Commerce
2940 Valley Bank Center, Suite 2490
Phoenix, AZ 85073

MBDA, Department of Commerce
14 NE 1st Avenue, Room 1100
Miami, FL 33132

MBDA, Department of Commerce
450 Golden Gate Avenue, Room 15045
San Francisco, CA 94102

MBDA, Department of Commerce
1730 K Street, NW
Washington, DC 20006

MBDA, Department of Commerce
600 South Street, Room 901
New Orleans, LA 70130

MBDA, Department of Commerce
441 Stuart Street, 10th Floor
Boston, MA 02116

MBDA, Department of Commerce
505 Marquette Street
Albuquerque, NM 87101

MBDA, Department of Commerce
26 Federal Plaza
New York, NY 10007

MBDA, Department of Commerce
1371 Peachtree Street, NW, Suite 505
Atlanta, GA 30309

MBDA, Department of Commerce
55 East Monroe Street, Suite 1440
Chicago, IL 60603

MBDA, Department of Commerce
600 Arch Street
Philadelphia, PA 19106

MBDA, Department of Commerce
United American Bank Building, #714
Memphis, TN 38103

MBDA, Department of Commerce
1412 Main Street, Room 1702
Dallas, TX 75202

MBDA, Department of Commerce
727 East Durango Street, Room B-412
San Antonio, TX 78206

DEPARTMENT OF DEFENSE
Defense Logistics Agency, Cameron Station, Alexandria, VA 22314
Defense Supply Service, The Pentagon, Washington, DC 20310
Headquarters, Defense Personnel Support Center, Defense Logistics Agency, 2800 S. 20th
    Street, Philadelphia, PA 19101
Defense Electronics Supply Center, 1507 Wilmington Pike, Dayton, OH 45444
Defense Atomic Support Agency, Sandia Base, Albuquerque, NM 87115

U.S. AIR FORCE
Headquarters, Audiovisual Service, Norton AFB, CA 92409
Electronic Systems Division, L.G. Hanscom Field, Bedford, MA 01731
Air Force Communications Service, Scott AFB, Belleville, IL 62225
Army and Air Force Exchange Service:
Fort Sam Houston, TX 78234 (Alamo Exchange Region)
Bldg 6, Cameron Station, VA 22314 (Capitol Exchange Region)
POB 3553, San Francisco, CA 94119 (Golden Gate Region)
Bldg 2501, Indiana Army Ammunition Plant, Charleston, IN 47111 (Ohio Valley Exchange
    Region)
1280 Kershaw Street, Bldg T-5, Montgomery, AL 36108 (Southeast Exchange Region)

U.S. ARMY
Computer Systems Selection and Acquisitions Agency, The Pentagon, Washington, DC 20310
Development and Readiness Command, 5001 Eisenhower Avenue, Alexandria, VA 22333
Corps of Engineers, Department of the Army, Washington, DC 20314
Office of the Surgeon General, The Pentagon, Washington, DC 20310
Medical Material Agency, Frederick, MD 21701
Medical Research and Development Command, Fort Detrick, MD 21701
Walter Reed Army Institute of Research, Washington, DC 20012
Health Services Command, Fort Sam Houston, TX 78234
Communications Command, Fort Huachuca, AZ 85613
Ballistic Missile Defense Systems Command, POB 1500, Huntsville, AL 35807
Military Traffic Management Command, 5611 Columbia Pike, Falls Church, VA 22041
Publications Directorate, Forrestal Bldg, Washington, DC 20314
Defense Mapping Agency, 6500 Brooks Lane, NW, Washington, DC 20315
Fort Lesley J. McNair, Washington, DC 20319

U.S. NAVY
Navy ADP Selection Office, Crystal Mall #4, Washington, DC 20376

Navy Regional Contracting Office, Washington Navy Yard, Washington, DC 20374
Naval Regional Contracting Office, Terminal Island, Long Beach CA 90822
Navy Resale System Office, 29th Street & 3rd Avenue, Brooklyn, NY 11232
Naval Air Systems Command, Washington, DC 20361
Naval Facilities Engineering Command, 200 Stovall Street, Alexandria, VA 22332
Naval Sea Systems Command, Washington, DC 20376
Naval Material Command, Crystal Place #5, Washington, DC 20360
Naval Electronic Systems Command, National Center, Washington, DC 20361
Naval Research Laboratory, Washington, DC 20375

U.S. DEPARTMENT OF EDUCATION
Central Office:
400 Maryland Avenue, SW
Washington, DC 20202
Office of Contracts, 7th & D Streets, SW, GSA Administration Bldg, 5th Floor, Washington,
   DC 20407
National Institute of Education, 1200 19th Street, NW, Washington, DC 20208

U.S. DEPARTMENT OF ENERGY
Central Office:
Forrestal Building
1000 Independence Avenue, SW
Washington, DC 20585
Regional Offices and Special Facilities
111 Pine Street, San Francisco, CA 94111
POB 26247, Belmar Branch, Lakewood, CO 80226
1655 Peachtree Street, NE, Atlanta, GA 30309
Argonne National Laboratory, 9800 S. Cass Avenue, Argonne, IL 60439
175 West Jackson Blvd, Chicago, IL 60604
150 Causeway Street, Rm 700, Analex Bldg, Boston, MA 02114
112 E. 12th Street, Kansas City, MO 64142
26 Federal Plaza, New York, NY 10007
1421 Cherry Street, Philadelphia, PA 19102
POB E. Oak Ridge National Laboratory, Oak Ridge, TN 37830
2626 W. Mockingbird Lane, Dallas, TX 75235
915 2nd Avenue, Federal Bldg, Seattle, WA 98174

U.S. DEPARTMENT OF HEALTH AND HUMAN SERVICES
Central Office:
200 Independence Avenue, SW
Washington, DC 20201
Public Health Service, 200 Independence Avenue, SW, Washington, DC 20201
Alcohol, Drug Abuse, and Mental Health Administration, 5600 Fishers Lane, Rockville, MD
   20857
Center for Disease Control, 1600 Clifton Road, NE, Atlanta, GA 30333
Food and Drug Administration, 5600 Fishers Lane, Rockville, MD 20857
Health Resources Administration, 3700 East-West Hwy, Hyattsville, MD 20782
Health Services Administration, 5600 Fishers Lane, Rockville, MD 20857
National Institutes of Health, 9000 Rockville Pike, Bethesda, MD 20205
Social Security Administration, 6401 Security Blvd, Baltimore, MD 21235
Regional Offices
John F. Kennedy Federal Building, Boston, MA 02203
26 Federal Plaza, New York, NY 10007

3535 Market Street, Philadelphia, PA 19101
101 Marietta Towers, NE Atlanta, GA 30323
300 S. Wacker Drive, Chicago, IL 60606
1200 Main Tower Bldg, Dallas, TX 75202
601 E. 12th Street, Kansas City, MO 64106
1961 Stout Street, Denver, CO 80202
50 United Nations Plaza, San Francisco, CA 94102
1321 2nd Avenue, Seattle, WA 98101

U.S. DEPARTMENT OF HOUSING AND URBAN DEVELOPMENT
Central Office:
451 Seventh Street, SW
Washington, DC 20410
Regional Offices
John F. Kennedy Federal Building, Boston, MA 02203
26 Federal Plaza, New York, NY 10007
Curtis Building 6th & Walnut Streets, Philadelphia, PA 19106
1800 Pennsylvania Avenue, Delaware Trust Plaza, Atlanta, GA 30303
300 S. Wacker Drive, Chicago, IL 60606
221 West Lancaster Avenue, Fort Worth, TX 76113
1103 Grant Avenue, Kansas City, MO 64106
450 Golden Gate Avenue, San Francisco, CA 94102
3003 Arcade Plaza Bldg, Seattle, WA 98101

U.S. DEPARTMENT OF THE INTERIOR
Central Office:
18th & C Streets, NW
Washington, DC 20240
(202) 343-1100

U.S. DEPARTMENT OF JUSTICE
Central Office:
10th Street & Constitution Avenue, NW
Washington, DC 20530
Community Relations Service, 550 11th Street, NW, Washington, DC 20530
Federal Bureau of Investigation, 9th Street & Pennsylvania Avenue, NW, Washington, DC
    20535
Bureau of Prisons, 320 First Street, NW, Washington, DC 20534
Immigration and Naturalization Service, 425 I Street, NW, Washington, DC 20536
Drug Enforcement Administration, 1405 I Street, NW, Washington, DC 20537
Office of Assistance, Research and Statistics, 633 Indiana Avenue, NW, Washington, DC
    20531

U.S. DEPARTMENT OF LABOR
Central Office:
200 Constitution Avenue, NW
Washington, DC 20210
Occupational Safety and Health Administration and Employment Standards Administration,
    200 Constitution Avenue, NW, Washington, DC 20210
Employment and Training Administration and Office of Job Corps, 601 D Street, NW,
    Washington, DC 20213
Bureau of Labor Statistics, 441 G Street, NW, Washington, DC 20212

U.S. DEPARTMENT OF TRANSPORTATION
Central Office:
400 7th Street, SW
Washington, DC 20590
Federal Highway Administration, Federal Railroad Administration, National Highway Traffic
   Safety Administration, Urban Mass Transportation Administration, Saint Lawrence Seaway
   Development Corporation, Coast Guard, and Research and Special Programs
   Administration, 400 7th Avenue, SW, Washington, DC 20590
Transportation Systems Center, Kendall Square, Cambridge, MA 02142
Federal Aviation Administration
800 Independence Avenue, SW, Washington, DC 20591
National Aviation Facilities Experimental Center, Atlantic City, NJ 08405
Aeronautical Center, 6400 S. MacArthur Blvd, Oklahoma City, OK
U.S. Coast Guard
400 7th Street, SW, Washington, DC 20590
Coast Guard Academy, New London, CT 06320
Training Center, Petaluma, CA 94952
Supply Center, 830 3rd Avenue, Brooklyn, NY 11232
Aircraft Repair and Supply Center, Elizabeth City, NC 27909

U.S. DEPARTMENT OF THE TREASURY
Central Office:
Main Treasury Building
15th Street and Pennsylvania Avenue, NW
Washington, DC 20220
Bureau of Alcohol, Tobacco and Firearms, 1200 Pennsylvania Avenue, NW, Washington, DC
   20226
U.S. Customs Service, 1301 Constitution Avenue, NW, Washington, DC 20229
Federal Law Enforcement Training Center, Glynco, GA 31520
United States Secret Service, 1800 G Street, NW, Washington, DC 20223
Internal Revenue Service, 1111 Constitution Avenue, NW, Washington, DC 20224

ENVIRONMENTAL PROTECTION AGENCY
Central Office:
401 M Street, SW
Washington, DC 20460
Laboratories and Special Facilities
POB 3009, Montgomery, AL 36109
West Ridge University of Alaska, College, AK 99701
Sabine Island, Gulf Breeze, FL 32561
College Station Road, Athens, GA 30605
9311 Groh Road, Ann Arbor, MI 48105
6201 Congdon Blvd, Duluth, MN 55804
11640 Administration Drive, St. Louis, MO 63141
POB 15027, Las Vegas, NV 89114
Research Triangle Park, NC 27711
26 W. St. Clair Street, Cincinnati, OH 45268
POB 1198, Ada, OK 74820
200 SW 35th Street, Corvallis, OR 97330
South Ferry Road, Narragansett, RI 02882

GENERAL SERVICES ADMINISTRATION
Central Office:
18th and F Streets, NW
Washington, DC 20405
Public Buildings Service and Automated Data and Telecommunications Service, 18th and F
    Streets, NW, Washington, DC 20405
National Archives and Records Service, 8th Street and Pennsylvania Avenue, NW,
    Washington, DC 20408
Federal Property Resources Service, 1755 Jefferson Davis Hwy, Arlington, VA 22209
Transportation and Public Utilities Service, 425 Eye Street, NW, Washington, DC 20406
Federal Supply Service
1941 Jefferson Davis Hwy, Arlington, VA 22209
7th and D Streets, SW, Washington, DC 20407
26 Federal Plaza, New York, NY 10007

The General Services Administration (GSA) operates a network of Business Service Centers throughout the United States. The purpose of each of these Centers is to assist vendors who wish to pursue government contracts. Each Center has a supply of helpful literature and counselors who will meet with you to answer questions and provide guidance. The locations of these Centers are as follows:

300 North Los Angeles Street
Los Angeles, CA 90012

525 Market Street
San Francisco, CA 94102

Denver Federal Center, Building 41
Denver, CO 80225

7th & D Streets, SW
Washington, DC 20407

1776 Peachtree Street, NW
Atlanta, GA 30309

230 South Dearborn Street
Chicago, IL 60604

John W. McCormack P.O. & Courthouse
Boston, MA 02109

1500 East Bannister Road
Kansas City, Mo. 64131

26 Federal Plaza
New York, NY 10007

600 Arch Street
Philadelphia, PA 19106

819 Taylor Street
Fort Worth, TX 76102

515 Rusk Street, FOB Courthouse
Houston, TX 77002

915 2nd Avenue
Seattle, WA 98174

NATIONAL AERONAUTICS AND SPACE ADMINISTRATION
Central Office:
400 Maryland Avenue, SW
Washington, DC 20546
Centers and Facilities
George C. Marshall Space Flight Center, Huntsville, AL 35812
Hugh L. Dryden Research Center, POB 273, Edwards, CA 93523
Ames Research Center, Moffet, CA 94035
Jet Propulsion Laboratory, 4800 Oak Grove Drive, Pasadena, CA 91103
John F. Kennedy Space Center, Cape Canaveral, FL 32899

Goddard Space Flight Center, Greenbelt, MD 20771
National Space Technology Laboratories, Bay St. Louis, MS 39520
Lewis Research Center, 21000 Brookpark Road, Cleveland, OH 44135
Lyndon B. Johnson Space Flight Center, Houston, TX 77058
Langley Research Center, Langley Station, Hampton, VA 23665
Wallops Flight Center, Wallops Island, VA 23337

NATIONAL SCIENCE FOUNDATION
1800 G Street, NW
Washington, DC 20550

OFFICE OF PERSONNEL MANAGEMENT
1900 E Street, NW
Washington, DC 20415

PENSION BENEFIT GUARANTY CORPORATION
2020 K Street, NW
Washington, DC 20006

U.S. POSTAL SERVICE
475 L'Enfant Plaza West, SW
Washington, DC 20260

VETERANS ADMINISTRATION
Central Office:
810 Vermont Avenue, NW
Washington, DC 20420
Office of Data Management and Telecommunications, 810 Vermont Avenue, NW, Washington,
 DC 20420
Data Processing Centers:
941 N. Capitol Street, NW, Washington, DC 20421
11000 Wilshire Blvd, Los Angeles, CA 90013
Lock Box 66303, AMF O'Hare, Chicago, IL 60666
Federal Bldg, Fort Snelling, St. Paul, MN 55111
5000 Wissahickon Avenue, Philadelphia, PA 19101
1615 E. Woodward Street, Austin, TX 78772
Records Processing Center, POB 172, St. Louis, MO 63166

DIRECTORY OF STATE AND LOCAL GOVERNMENT PROSPECTS

Agencies of state and local governments are even more numerous than those of the federal government and are, in the aggregate, an even larger market.

79,912 OTHER GOVERNMENT SOURCES OF PROSPECTS

There are 38,776 state and local governments, with all their own subordinate agencies, and 79,912 school districts and special districts that the U. S. Bureau of the Census reports and lists as "government entities." Together, they constitute hundreds of thousands of prospects for consulting services.

Like the many federal government procurement officials, most state and local government purchasing agents have shown an active interest in eliciting as many vendor applications as possible. That is, they tend to encourage and maximize competition among vendors for at least two reasons:

1. Competition has classically been the way to produce the best prices and best quality of goods and services. For purely selfish reasons of making the best buys, procurement officials value maximum competition.

2. Most states and local governments, like the federal government (and often in emulation of the lead provided by the federal government), have statutes requiring that the agencies encourage both opportunity and competition in their procurement functions.

The federal government spends a great deal of money and makes a considerable effort to help entrepreneurs learn how to become aware of and take advantage of opportunities to do business with federal agencies. Unfortunately and mysteriously, most of that money is wasted because the federal government is remarkably ineffectual at publicizing the help offered. Unfortunately, the state and local governments are perhaps even less successful in making people generally aware of the opportunities to do business with their agencies. Many have information services and offer other help rivaling that of the federal government, but those services are helpful only when the individual succeeds in learning enough to seek out the help, learning where and how to begin uncovering the opportunities.

Some states and even local governments offer quite elaborate information packages, virtual starter kits for the vendor, while others have extremely little to offer. However, the lists tend to resemble the federal listings, and in some cases, that of California, for instance, to be almost a carbon copy of the federal supply lists and classifications, even to the extent of using the same supply-group numbers and designations.

AN IMPORTANT DIFFERENCE

One major difference between the federal procurement system and that of most states is that the federal system tends strongly to decentralize purchasing, while the state systems tend to the opposite direction. The mandatory use of centralized supply sources is the exception in the federal system; in many if not most states the authority of state agencies to buy independently is the exception, or is regarded as an exception to the general rule. In many cases when purchase authority is delegated to other agencies of the state the authority is limited to certain, specific classes of procurement, such as professional services and items which are peculiar to the needs of that agency.

These are important exceptions, for the vendor, however, for most states and even many local governments have a large number of agencies, representing a proportionately large potential market in the state or local government. It is not unusual for a state to have as many as 300 or more agencies of various kinds, agencies which tend to parallel the federal agencies, including various departments, bureaus, commissions, and institutions. These are too numerous to list here, but they include at least the following classes:

Prisons and other correctional institutions	State department of education
Highway/transportation departments	Hospitals and sanitariums
Insurance commissioners	Colleges and universities
Fish and wildlife departments	Public school systems
Assessments & taxation departments	Agriculture departments
Bank commissioners	Conservation departments
Income/general tax bureaus	Aviation administrations
	Budget and fiscal planning offices
	Data processing divisions
	Port authorities

WHAT, WHERE, HOW STATE AND LOCAL GOVERNMENTS BUY

For the most part, and with the exception of purely military goods, state and local governments buy the same services and goods federal agencies buy. But whereas federal government purchasing is largely decentralized (at least 15,000 federal procurement offices exist throughout the United States, with relatively few in Washington, DC), most state and local governments tend to concentrate their purchasing in capitals—the state capitals, the county seats, and the city and town halls. The first list offered here is one of the state governments' purchasing offices, Almost without exception each purchasing office requires vendors to register as bidders and to fill out suitable forms to get on the bidders list. (In a few cases a registration fee is exacted.) And all strongly recommend, even urge, personal visits to the purchasing office, if possible, to meet personally with the various buyers. (Most of these purchasing offices employ staffs of buyers, each buyer assigned a group of items.)

In many cases the state purchasing office does centralized purchasing for all agencies in the state on term contracts and permits local governments to utilize those contracts to place their own orders. This benefits both the governments because both get the advantages of group buying. But it also benefits the vendors because they can thus utilize their contracts with the state to sell to the local governments. Therefore, in many cases it is the state government's purchasing office that opens doors to the local government markets. (Also, all state and local governments can utilize the federal supply contracts negotiated and listed as "Federal Supply Schedules.")

STATE PROGRAMS

Like the federal government, many state governments and even local governments have instituted programs to support minority entrepreneurs, small businesses, and local businesses in a variety of ways. The programs fall into several categories:

Loans and loan-guarantees
Counseling and consultative assistance
Preferences in government procurement
Handling complaints
Legislative activity for future programs

Table 13-1 reports on the latest general status of such programs for those states which have adopted or are in the process of adopting programs at the time this is being written.

Following are additional details of each state's programs, on the basis of whatever information is available at this time. Once again, it is advisable to verify this information, which may very well be completely outdated by the time you read this.

Table 13-1.   State socioeconomic programs

State	Loan	Procurement Preference	Assistance Office	Complaint Handling	Other
Alabama		X			
Alaska	X		X		
Arizona		X	X	X	
Arkansas			X	X	X
California	X	X	X		X
Colorado			X		X
Connecticut	X	X	X	X	X
Florida			X	X	X
Georgia		X			X
Hawaii	X				
Illinois	X	X	X	X	X
Indiana		X		X	X
Iowa				X	X
Kansas		X			X
Kentucky	X	X	X	X	X
Louisiana		X	X	X	
Maine	X				X
Maryland	X	X	X		
Massachusetts	X	X	X	X	X
Michigan	X	X	X	X	X
Minnesota	X	X	X	X	X

Alabama

Alabama gives preference for small business, which is defined as one with fewer than 50 employees or less than $1 million in gross annual receipts. The Department of Industrial Relations is authorized to render a variety of services to help small businesses win state contracts. Contact Office of State Planning, 3734 Atlanta Highway, Montgomery 36130.

Alaska

Alaska has several loan programs, all of them rather comprehensive and well defined, and including both direct loans from the state and bank-participation loans, wherein the state and the bank are co-lenders. Alaska also operates a small business assistance office. Contact the Division of Economic Enterprise, Department of Commerce and Economic Development, 675 7th Avenue, Station A, Fairbanks 99701.

Arizona

Little information on Arizona's socioeconomic programs is available at this moment. Contact Arizona's Office of Economic Planning and Development, 1700 West Washington, Room 400, Phoenix 85007.

Arkansas
Arkansas has established a small business office. Contact Arkansas's Small Business Assistance division, Arkansas Department of Economic Development, One State Capital Mall, Little Rock 72201.

California
California offers a comprehensive set of socioeconomic programs, including loan programs and a Small Business Procurement Office to give procurement preference to small business in the State. Requirements are that the business be located in California and not dominant in the relevant industry, to qualify for such preference. (Of course, you may always bid for state contracts without qualifying for preference.) Contact the Small Business Procurement Office, Department of General Services, 1823 14th Street, Sacramento 95807.

Colorado
Colorado has a Small Business Council and also provides a number of other services to small business. Contact The Small Business Assistance Center, University of Colorado, Campus Box 434, Boulder 80309; and the Colorado Department of Local Affairs, Division of Commerce and Development, 1313 Sherman Street, Room 500, Denver 80203.

Connecticut
Connecticut has a definite small-businesses set-aside requirement, and defines small buisnesses as those which have been domiciled, and are doing business, in the state for at least one year and whose annual revenues are not in excess of $1 million for the previous fiscal year. Contact the Office of Small Business Affairs, Department of Economic Development, State Office Building, Hartford 06115.

Florida
Contact the Office of Business Assistance, Executive Office of the Governor, Tallahassee 32301.

Georgia
Georgia defines small business as having fewer than 100 employees or less than $1 million in gross annual receipts. An advisory council of small business representatives offers counsel on procurement matters to Georgia's Department of Administrative Services.

Hawaii
Hawaii uses the federal (SBA) definition of small business as their own and operates a loan program also. Contact the Department of Planning and Economic Development, 250 South King Street, Honolulu 96813.

Illinois
Illinois has a Department of Commerce and Community Affairs within which is included the Illinois Office of Business Services. This office incorporates the duties and services formerly provided by the old Small Business Information Office. Contact the Illinois Office of Business Services, 180 North LaSalle Street, Chicago 60701; and/or the Small Business Coordinator, Department of Administrative Services, Stratton Office Building, Room 802, Springfield 62707.

Indiana
Indiana now has a Small Business Ombudsman office to help small business in a variety of ways, including help in bidding for state contracts. Contact Ombudsman Office, 503 State Office Building, Indianapolis 46204.

Iowa
Iowa operates an Office of Ombudsman and a legislative program for small business. Address inquiries to Iowa Citizens' Aide Office, State Captial, Des Moines 50319.

Kansas
Kansas establishes as a goal the setting aside for small business of at least 10 percent of state purchases, and has a legislative program as well. Among several other criteria, businesses must

meet standards of numbers of employees and/or annual dollar volume set for different industries to qualify as small business in the state.

Kentucky

Kentucky has a small business office to oversee and manage its small business programs, which
includes small business set-asides in state procurement. Contact the Small Business Development Section, Small and Minority Business Development Division, Kentucky Department of
Commerce, Capital Plaza, Frankfort 40601.

Louisiana

Louisiana has a small business set-aside program and defines small business according to standards of numbers of employees and annual volume, which vary for different types of enterprises. Contact the Louisiana Department of Commerce, Office of Commerce and Industry,
POB 44185, Baton Rouge 70804.

Maine

Contact the Maine Development Foundation, One Memorial Circle, Augusta 04333.

Maryland

In-state small businesses in Maryland get a 5 percent preference over out-of-state bidders for
state contracts. Contact the Office of Business Liaison and the Office of Business and Industrial
Development, Department of Economic and Community Development, 1748 Forest Drive, Annapolis 21401. An Office of Minority Business Enterprise is located at the same address.

Massachusetts

Massachusetts operates a broad spread of small-business programs and other programs for
business generally, including general assistance to small business in winning both state and
federal contracts and offering extensive consultative assistance. Contact the Division of Small
Business Assistance, Department of Commerce and Development, 100 Cambridge Street, Boston 02202. Also contact the Business Information Center/Network (BIC/NET) and Business
Service Center within the same Department and at the same address. Also Massachusetts Technology Development Corporation, 131 State Street, Boston 02109 and Massachusetts Business
Development Corporation, One Boston Place, Boston 02108.

Michigan

Michigan offers a variety of business-assistance programs, including help in winning state
contracts. For small- and minority-business assistance programs contact the Business Enterprise Specialist, Purchasing Division, Department of Management and Budget, Mason Building, 2nd Floor, Lansing 48909 and the Small Business Development Division, Office of Economic Development, Michigan Department of Commerce, POB 30225, Lansing 48909.

Minnesota

Minnesota has a goal of awarding 20 percent of the state's procurement dollars to small business, which it defines as one with not more than 20 employees nor more than $1 million in
annual revenues. The program is administered by the Department of Economic Development,
480 Cedar Street, St. Paul 55101.

Mississippi

Mississippi operates a broad spread of programs for small business, including publications,
consultation, training, and procurement preference, and has a number of offices with related
functions in different areas of the state. Contact the Small Business Assistance Division, Agri-
cultural and Industrial Board, Agriculture and Commerce Department, 301 Walter Sillers
Building, Jackson 39205.

Missouri

Little information is available currently about Missouri's small business programs (relevant
legislation was pending at the time of this writing), but the state advises that small businesses

should seek assistance from the program of Existing Business Assistance, Division of Community and Economic Development, Jefferson City 65102.

Montana

Montana includes within its small business programs one that pledges that "all agencies will insure that a fair proportion of the state government's total purchases and contracts for property and services are placed with small business concerns." Contact the Office of Commerce and Small Business Development, Governor's Office, Room 212, Capitol Station, Helena 59601.

New Jersey

New Jersey has a small business assistance office with rather a general and broadly defined mission to aid small business. Contact the New Jersey Department of Labor and Industry, John Fitch Plaza, Trenton 08625.

New Mexico

New Mexico has no specific programs for small business, but vendors are invited to contact Existing Industry Liaison, Economic Development Division, Santa Fe 85703.

New York

New York's several small business programs include one offering help in winning state contracts. Contact the Division of Ombudsmen and Small Business Services, 230 Park Avenue, New York 10017.

North Carolina

North Carolina has a small business program, but without any specific dollar or percentage goals. Contact the Business Assistance Division, North Carolina Department of Commerce, 430 North Salisbury Street, Raleigh 27611.

Ohio

Contact the Office of Small Business Assistance, Ohio Department of Economic and Community Development, Columbus 43215.

Oregon

Contact Small Business Office, Director for Business/Government Relations, Department of Economic Development, Salem 97310.

Pennsylvania

Pennsylvania does not have a special small business program but takes the position that all businesses should have all possible assistance and services from the state. There is, however, a Small Business Service Center, South Office Building, Room G-13, Harrisburg 17120.

Tennessee

Contact Small Business Information Center, Department of Economic & Community Development, 107 Andrew Jackson State Office Building, Nashville 37219.

Texas

Texas has a small business procurement program, among others, which has the goal of awarding at least 10 percent of the state's procurement dollars to small business, defined as those with fewer than 100 employees or less than $1 million in annual revenues. Contact the Purchasing and General Services Commission, 1711 San Jacinto Street, Austin 78701.

Utah

Utah has a small business office. Contact the Business Development Coordinator, No. 2 Arrow Press Square, Suite 260, 165 South West Temple, Salt Lake City 84101.

Vermont

Contact Vermont Economic Opportunity Office, Montpelier 05602.

West Virginia

West Virginia sets general goals for awards to small business, which is defined by using federal SBA standards. Contact Small Business Service Unit, Governor's Office of Economic and Community Development, Building 6, Suite B-564, Capitol Complex, Charleston 25305.

Wisconsin
Wisconsin includes a small business procurement program. Contact Small Business Ombudsman, Department of Business Development, Madison 53702.

DIRECTORY OF STATE PURCHASING OFFICES

Select the purchasing offices of immediate interest—for example, those of your own state and perhaps surrounding states, if their capitals are not too far—and try to visit the purchasing offices personally, if at all possible, and get acquainted with the appropriate buyers. In any case, register with the offices, by mail if necessary, and apply for inclusion on the bidders' lists.

Alabama
Finance Department, Purchase & Stores Division, Room 125, Capitol Building, Montgomery, AL 36130, (205) 832-3580

Centralized purchasing, term contracts. Small purchases (under $500) may be made by informal bids. The office awards term contracts, permits other jurisdictions to place orders under those contracts.

Alaska
Department of Administration, Division of General Services & Supply, Pouch C, Juneau, AK 99811 (907) 465-2253, and 330 East 4th Avenue, Suite A, Anchorage, AK 99501, (907) 272-1491

This office spends some $40+ million annually and welcomes new suppliers enthusiastically. The commodity index has about 35 supply classes, including furniture, machines, supplies, and services required for data processing applications. The state issues purchase orders, term contracts, and definite-quantity contracts. Small purchases are those under $300. Professional services are exempt from bidding, are negotiated, using proposals, with requests issued by using agencies, who are authorized to do at least some purchasing independently.

Arizona
Department of Administration, Finance Division, Purchasing Office, 1688 West Adams Street, Room 220, Phoenix, AZ 85007, (602) 255-5511

All purchases over $5,000 must be by formal sealed bids; those over $500 but not more than $2,500, may be by oral bids. And those less than $5,000 but more than $2,500 must be by written bids, although informal. The state purchasing office may enter into consortia to buy jointly with other political jurisdictions of the state, and these 12 Arizona agencies are authorized to buy independently:

Department of Corrections	State Compensation Fund
Department of Education	Department of Economic Security
Department of Public Safety	Arizona State University
Northern Arizona University	University of Arizona
Correctional Industries	Department of Health Services
Division of Military Affairs	Game and Fish Department

Arkansas
Office of State Purchasing, Department of Finance and Administration, POB 2940, Little Rock, AR 72203, (501) 371-1771

Although this office buys for the state, many agencies may buy independently, to at least some extent. The following state agencies may be approached directly:

Arkansas Highway Department	University of Arkansas
Arkansas State University	University of Arkansas Medical Science
Arkansas Tech University	University of Arkansas at Monticello
East Arkansas Community College	Henderson State University
West Arkansas Community College	Garland County Community College
North Arkansas Community College	Mississippi County Community College
University of Arkansas at Pine Bluff	University of Central Arkansas
Phillips County Community College	Southern Arkansas University

California

Office of Procurement, Department of General Services, 1823 14th Street, POB 1612, Sacramento, CA 95807, (916) 445-2500, and 107 S. Broadway, Los Angeles, CA 90012 (213) 620-5660

California furnishes an abundant package of procurement information on request, and the state's list of commodities, classification numbers, and system in general resemble the federal system rather closely. Like many other states, California delegates much buying authority to various state agencies: Although the state's purchasing office does buy a wide array of goods, it does not buy professional services, land, or buildings, nor does it negotiate leases, leaving these purchases to its delegates, the individual user agencies. Sealed bids are the usual method, and the small-purchase limit is normally $1,000.

Procurement regulations designate EDP equipment purchases as meriting special policies, and normally makes all such purchases via the proposal-and-negotiation method. Such supplies are listed as supply Group 70: EDP Equipment, Software, Supplies, and Support Equipment.

Colorado

Department of Administration, Division of Purchasing, 1525 Sherman Street, R, 712, Denver, CO 80203, (303) 839-3261

This organization reports annual purchases of well over $200 million, but delegates separate purchasing authority to the state's Department of Highways, colleges and universities, and other state institutions. Formal, sealed bids are required for procurements over $1,500.

Connecticut

Bureau of Purchases, 460 Silver Street, Middletown, CT 06457, (203) 344-2080

The State of Connecticut reports that it is a "multi-million dollar participant in the market place as a buyer of supplies, equipment, and services – including construction – to meet the needs of more than 300 budgeted agencies of the executive branch of State government." State law permits open-market purchases where the total value is less than $6,000. Larger purchases must be advertised and bid competitively. The Bureau of Purchases is part of Connecticut's Department of Administrative Services and is assigned major procurement responsibility, but purchasing authority is assigned to other bureaus of the Department: Bureau of Public Works, and Bureau of Information Services and Data Processing.

Delaware

Administrative Services Department, Division of Purchasing, Governor Bacon Health Center, Delaware City, DE 19706, (302) 834-4512

The State of Delaware maintains centralized purchasing for common-use commodities, but delegates purchase authority to many other agencies of the state and also permits other agencies to buy independently by processing purchase requests through the Division of Purchasing, after direct contact with vendors.

Florida

Department of General Services, Division of Purchasing, 613 Larson Building, Tallahassee, FL 32304, (904) 488-1194

Florida advises all corporations who wish to do business with the state to register with Florida's Secretary of State, and suggests calling (904) 488-9000 to get relevant information and request vendor applications.

The Division of Purchasing is made up of a Bureau of Procurement and a Bureau of Standards, the latter charged with developing specifications, as necessary. Both have relatively large staffs of specialists. However, the many agencies within the state each have some purchasing power of their own, and each such agency has an individual named as a purchasing agent or has assigned the purchasing responsibility to an administrative official.

Georgia

Department of Administrative Services, Purchasing & Supplies Division, 116 Mitchell Street, Room 504, Atlanta, GA 30335 (404) 656-3240

Purchasing for all agencies, with certain exceptions provided by law or Departmental regulation, is done centrally by the Division. Purchases between $100 and $5,000 may be made by informal bids, which may be oral and made via telephone. Larger procurements must be made by formal, sealed bids, with public bid openings. And local governments within the state may utilize the state's contracts for their own purchasing. The law also provides that any contractor with the state has the option to offer to do business with local governments under the same contract and/or terms as those the state government enjoys. As in the case of many other state governments, various state agencies may contract independently for professional services.

Hawaii

Department of Accounting and General Services, Purchasing and Supply Division, 1151 Punchbowl Street, POB 119, Honolulu, HI 96810, (808) 548-7428

The State of Hawaii does not envision its purchasing organization as making purchases for the entire state but rather as a service agency, assisting the various other state agencies in making procurements by soliciting bids, publishing price lists, and providing other services.

The state may issue purchase orders for procurements up to $8,000 but must negotiate formal contracts for larger purchases, which must also be advertised in two local newspapers for at least three days. (Purchases between $4,000 and $8,000 must be advertised for at least one day.)

Idaho

Department of Administration, Division of Purchasing, 650 West State Street, Room 100, Boise, ID 83720, (208) 384-2465

Idaho has a comprehensive Registration Packet available for vendors who wish to register with the state. The Division of Purchasing has sole authority to contract for goods and services for the state, with certain specific exemptions of those other agencies authorized to buy independently.

In general the law requires that all purchases of more than $500 but less than $5,000 be made only after soliciting competitive bids from at least three registered vendors. Purchases of more than $5,000 require at least 20 registered vendors be invited to bid. The law provides that where appropriate (as in the case of federal procurement procedures) proposals may be solicited, proposals evaluated, and contracts negotiated.

Idaho furnishes a lengthy commodities list, covering data processing equipment and services, the latter as consulting services in "data processing, computer, information systems, and programming," under supply group 94.

Illinois

Department of Administrative Services, Office of Procurement, 810 Stratton Office Building, Springfield, IL 62706 (217) 782-2301

Illinois procurements of $2,500 or more require competitive sealed bids and advertising in an English-language newspaper designated as the "official newspaper," for such purposes, as required by Illinois law. The exceptions include the existence of emergency conditions of some sort which make normal competitive procurement impractical or when the item is available from only a single source, such as would be the case for a proprietary for which there is no suitable equivalent.

Indiana

Department of Administration, Procurement Division, 100 N. Senate Avenue, 507 State Office Building, Indianapolis, IN 46204, (317) 232-3032

At the time the above information was furnished, Indiana had no formal brochures or other literature to furnish aspirants to their supplier lists, but explained a policy of sending inquirers a form letter and a registration form to fill out. Out-of-state firms must also register with Indiana's Secretary of State and a form is furnished for that purpose also. Purchases under $500 do not require competitive bids, as do those above that figure.

Indiana also uses negotiated procurement, after soliciting proposals and selecting contenders with whom to negotiate. Typically, those are two-step processes, where an unpriced proposal is submitted first, and then prices are solicited from those whose technical proposals are acceptable.

The Procurement Division may delegate purchasing authority to other state agencies and may also buy for local governments, open its contracts to local governments, and/or buy from the federal supply schedules, utilizing federal supply contracts for its own procurement.

Iowa

Department of General Services, Purchasing Division, Hoover State Office Building, Des Moines, IA 50319, (515) 281-5856

The State of Iowa furnishes a *Vendor Information Booklet* to assist suppliers in understanding Iowa's procurement policies and regulations. Under Iowa law the Department of General Services is charged with central procurement of all supplies and services for all state agencies, except as otherwise exempted specifically by law. Procurements are of both one-time purchases and term contracts, and of both definite- and indefinite-quantity types. In some cases local governments are offered the opportunity to order under the state's contracts to satisfy their own needs.

Formal (sealed and advertised) bids are required for all procurements of $15,000 or more, to include both newspaper advertising and Information for Bid (IFB) solicitations—mailed to registered vendors. Procurements between $2,500 and $14,999 need not be advertised but will be solicited from those on the Vendor's List. In both cases the bids will be opened publicly and awards made to the lowest responsive and responsible bidders.

For procurements less than $2,500 Requests for Quotations (RFQs) will be sent out to registered vendors and informal written bids can be accepted. And for those procurements under $500 oral bids are acceptable.

RFPs—Requests for Proposals—are used also when the sealed-bid procedure is inappropriate to the procurement, and the familiar processes of proposal evaluation, selection, and negotiation follow.

Kansas

Department of Administration, Division of Purchasing, State Office Building, Topeka, KS 66612, (913) 296-2376

Kansas furnished little information regarding any aspect of their state purchasing and procurement functions, other than to identify their purchasing office. However, they may have some literature available by the time you read this, if they follow the general trend extant.

Kentucky

Finance and Administration Cabinet, Department for Administration, Division of Purchases, 348 Capitol Annex, Frankfort, KY 40601, (502) 564-4510

Procurements of over $1,000 are required to be made via sealed bids and public openings under Kentucky law. Procurements less than $1,000 may be made under small-purchase procedures, and procurements over $10,000 must be advertised in at least two widely circulated Kentucky newspapers.

Kentucky makes a comprehensive *Bidders Application Packet* available to applicants who wish to register as vendors, and advises that it has a comprehensive manual of instructions for evaluating proposals, which the Division of Purchases often solicits for procurements requiring negotiation, rather than bids.

Louisiana

Division of Administration, State Purchasing, One American Place (Waterside Mall Entrance), Plaza West, POB 44095, Baton Rouge, LA 70804, (504) 342-4441

A request to the above office will bring you a copy of Louisiana's *Vendor's Guide, How to do Business With the State of Louisiana*, which furnishes detailed information about state government procurement. As do most other purchasing offices, this one urges personal visits by prospective suppliers, and adds that it is helpful to bring along price lists, photographs, samples, specification, and anything else that will help state purchasing officials review and evaluate the goods and services you offer.

Louisiana has a lengthy and highly detailed commodities list, describing some 200 supply classes and as many as 60 items within a class. Computers and computer-related goods and services are therefore covered under several classes of supply, such as consulting, leasing, maintenance, office equipment and supplies, and others.

Procurements expected to run over $5,000 must be made via bids solicited from at least eight vendors.

Maine

Department of Finance and Administration, Bureau of Purchases, State Office Building, State House Station 9, Augusta, ME 04333, (207) 289-3521

Maine's Bureau of Purchases is empowerd by law to do all purchasing for Maine's agencies, but may also delegate purchase authority to the agencies, if and as necessary and justified. Small purchase policy is limited to purchases not more than $250, and with written authorization to make the purchase, such purchases may be made on the open market.

The commodities purchased regularly by the Bureau of Purchases are purchased on fixed schedules, described in the state's vendor brochure, *How to do Business With Maine*, issued by the Bureau. The brochure describes some 125 supply classes, and anticipates that agencies will contract out independently for services.

Maryland

Department of General Services, Purchasing Bureau, 301 West Preston Street, Baltimore, MD 21201, (301) 383-3573

Maryland has four principal procurement authorities. The other three (other than that listed above, that is) are these:

Department of General Services
Department of Transportation
Department of Budget and Fiscal Planning

Advertising bids by the state purchasing bureaus in Maryland is done by publishing the announcements in the *Maryland Register*, an official state publication, analogous to the federal government's *Federal Register*. Subscriptions to the *Maryland Register* at the time of this writing are $50 per year and are ordered by addressing a request and check as follows:

Circulation Manager
MARYLAND REGISTER
Division of State Documents
POB 802, Annapolis, MD 21404.

Procurements are made via competitive sealed bids, competitive negotiation, small-purchase procedures, and sole-source (non-competitive) procurement when justified. Contracts over $25,000 must be advertised in the *Maryland Register* for at least 30 days before the bid-opening date, but many contracts less than $25,000 must also be advertised. Contract awards must be listed in the *Maryland Register* also, to furnish leads for subcontracting opportunities.

A list of the state's purchasing agents for the school systems of each of Maryland's 24 counties and another listing of some 300 other state agencies, boards, and commissions are available on request.

Massachusetts
Purchasing Division, McCormack State Office Building, One Ashburton Place, Room 1011, Boston, MA 02108, (617) 727-2882

The Commonwealth of Massachusetts has an active and well-organized procurement system, with a large number of vendors and customers in the commonwealth. The excellent vendor's manual offered suppliers, *How to do Business With the State*, is unusually well done and highly informative.

Massachusetts buys as most states do, with both single-purchase and term contracts. State agencies may issue purchase orders for purchases under $500; purchases above that amount must follow bid procedures. One basic, relevant policy is this: For soliciting professional services with a maximum obligation of $40,000 or more formal proposals are required, solicited from at least three qualified vendors.

Massachusetts maintains an active Business Service Center to assist suppliers. It is part of the Massachusetts Department of Commerce and is located at 100 Cambridge Street, Boston, Massachusetts 02202. A free hot line is available, too: 1-800-632-8181.

A lengthy list of state agencies (approximately 200) which are to at least some degree independent in their purchasing authority (and some are entirely independent) is available also.

Michigan
Department of Management and Budget, Purchasing Division, Stevens T. Mason Building, 2nd Floor, POB 30026, Lansing, MI 48909, (517) 373-0330

A vendor's guide brochure is available from the above office, and it is quite complete in the information it offers, despite its modest size. A commodity list of some 1,000 items in over 50 supply groups is also available to vendors.

Purchases of $4,000 or more must be made by formal, sealed bids; those of lesser amount may be on an "open bid" or informal basis. That is, the latter kind of bid may be opened immediately on receipt, and does not require the formality of public opening at a preannounced time and place. Both types of bid are solicited by a Request for Quotation (RFQ).

Term contracts are used for most commodities, and a list of contracts is published for the use of all state agencies, who are instructed to order from those for appropriate procurements. For procurement of items not covered by the existing contracts the agencies must order through the Purchasing Division (unless the agency is specifically exempted), except for purchases not more than $400. Among the several buying units is one (Unit 9) designated specifically for data processing. However, certain relevant items, such as books, tab cards, office furniture, magazines, office machines, office supplies, and paper, are listed for other units.

Minnesota
Department of Administration, Division of Procurement, 50 Sherburn Avenue, St. Paul, MN 55155, (612) 296-6152

Small purchases in Minnesota are those up to $500. Above that amount newspaper advertising and sealed bids and/or negotiations are required to make procurements. Although the Division of procurement does buy for the state's agencies many of the state's agencies do buy independently and/or make purchase requests to the Division of Purchasing, identifying specific sources of supply for the requested purchases. (This makes it advisable to market directly to these agencies, of course.)

Mississippi

Commission of Budget and Accounting, Division of Purchase Supervision, 902 Walter Sillers Building, Jackson, MS 39202, (601) 354-7107

Mississippi does not operate a central purchasing office as such, but advises that the above-named office supervises purchasing by the agencies and institutions within the state. The Division includes among its functions such tasks as coordinating and consolidating purchasing or arranging for cooperative purchasing to take advantage of the benefits that can be derived therefrom, and ensuring that pertinent Mississippi statutes are observed when making purchases. These include the requirement that purchases over $1,500 must be advertised and made by formal competitive methods. Purchases of less than $500 may be made by small-purchase producers, and those between $500 and $1,500 may be made without advertising if at least two competitive written bids are obtained.

A procurement manual was being written at the time this information was provided and should be available by the time you read this.

Montana

Department of Administration, Purchasing Division, Mitchell Building, Room 165, Helena, MT 59620, (406) 449-2575

Montana reports annual spending by the Purchasing Division for supplies and services in excess of $52 million. (Whether this does or does not include the various procurement budgets of all the state agencies served by the Purchasing Division is not made clear.) In-state suppliers are given a 3-point preference over out-of-state suppliers, a practice followed in several states, although not always announced in brochures.

Procurements of $2,000 or more must be advertised in three in-state newspapers, at least one of them a daily publication. Bids under that amount do not require advertising, but both must be by sealed bids and public openings.

State agencies may make competitive purchases of less than $200 for items not available under existing state term contracts. Term contracts are normally entered into for computer magnetic tape, continuous paper, tab cards, and other related items.

Nebraska

Department of Administrative Services, State Purchasing Bureau, 301 Centennial Mall, South, POB 94847, Lincoln, NE 68509

Nebraska offers a publication, *Nebraska Procurement Manual for Vendors*, and invites all interested vendors to compete for its business. Vendors must register for inclusion on bid lists to receive solicitations, although they may make bids without being formally registered, the manual advises; that is, notices of all goods and services required are posted at offices of the State Purchasing Bureau and vendors may visit and examine these listings and postings.

The procedures are typical, favoring formal, sealed bids and/or negotiation for all except small purchases.

Nevada

Department of General Services, Purchasing Division, 205 Blasdel Building, Carson City, NV 89701, (702) 885-4070

Nevada reports annual expenditures of over $35 million for central purchasing. Procurements are advertised in local newspapers and solicitations sent out to those on appropriate bidders' lists. The figure cited does not include the procurement budgets of the various state agencies, who must place their procurement orders through the Purchasing Division.

New Hampshire

Department of Administration and Control, Division of Purchase and Property, State House Annex, Concord, NH 03301, (603) 271-2700

New Hampshire offers a comprehensive *Manual of Procedure* to prescribe purchasing procedures to purchasing division personnel and to vendors who wish to do business with the state.

The manual covers New Hampshire procurement law and regulations, purchasing procedures and requirements, commodities normally purchased, and other useful data, such as names and telephone numbers of buyers in the division.

Purchases of $500 or more are generally made by sealed bids, with formal public openings and awards to the lowest responsible bidders. Procurements under $500 may be made by soliciting quotations and selecting an awardee.

Many commodities are bought on term contracts, and these are scheduled for various times throughout the year.

New Jersey

Department of the Treasury, Purchase Bureau, CN 230, State House, Trenton, NJ 08625, (609) 292-4700

The Purchase Bureau reports an annual procurement budget of over $425 million to buy supplies and services for all the state's agencies. As in the case of other states, local governments may utilize state term contracts for their own purchasing. In fact, the state reports that some 1,427 user agencies had made such cooperative purchases at the time this information was supplied, representing additional expenditures of some $460 million through state contracts.

As in many other states, vendors are required to register by filling out a bidders application form, available from the Purchase Bureau on request.

Purchases over $2,500 must be made via the advertised and sealed-bid processes, using local newspapers to make the announcements of solicitation. Purchases under this amount may be made by telephone requests to registered vendors. Out-of-state corporations wishing to do business with the Bureau must register as foreign corporations with the New Jersey Secretary of State.

Other agencies may buy independently, issuing their own purchase orders against the existing term contracts, and under some circumstances may get authority from the Purchase Bureau to make completely independent procurements, using competitive bidding procedures.

New Mexico

Department of Finance and Administration, Purchasing Division, Lamy Building, Santa Fe, NM 87503, (505) 827-2626

New Mexico has a brochure for you, *How to do Business With the State of New Mexico*, several forms for registering as a vendor and applying for inclusion on bidders lists, and information that the state charges a $58 registration fee to cover the costs of issuing solicitations.

In-state suppliers are given a 5-point preference over out-of-state suppliers. Single purchases up to $1,000 may be made by small-purchase procedures, purchases to $1,500 using only three oral bids, and purchases over $1,500 up to $2,500 only under sealed bids. Large purchases require advertising in three newspapers in the state.

A lengthy commodity list is supplied on request, which includes as a supply class: 58 Data Processing Equipment and Supplies and lists under this class the following specific items:

02 Cards, tabulating	04 Data processing accessory equipment
06 Data processing machine supplies	08 Data processing machines and
10 Data processing machines and	systems
systems—RENTAL only	12 Data processing services
14 Maintenance and repairs	

New York

Standards and Purchase Group, Office of General Services, 41st Floor, Tower Building, Empire State Plaza, Albany, NY 12242, (518) 474-6262

New York State's brochure, *How to Sell to New York State*, says, "The State is a good customer. It knows what it wants and it maintains strict standards of quality to protect the taxpayer. It pays promptly, and otherwise maintains a good relationship with its vendors." The brochure reports annual purchases ". . . of over $650 million worth of commodities for State agencies, political subdivisions, private non-profit educational institutions," and others authorized by law. (The figure may be a bit low for today, since it is not a recent one and does not include all state purchasing.)

The state buys in much the same manner that most states do, with term contracts for common-use commodities, special one-time purchases, and open-market purchasing in cases where such purchasing is authorized by law. For purchases up to $500 small-purchase procedures may be used. Purchases ranging from $500 to $1,000 require three bids, and those from $1,000 to $1,500 require five bids. Above that figure special authorization is required.

Typically, the central purchasing authority does all buying of commodities for state agencies and institutions, but for small purchases buying authority may be released to the agency, where justified. However, the agencies all negotiate on their own for services, and you must approach the many agencies and institutions directly to sell services. (A list of well over 500 such agencies and institutions is available.)

North Carolina

Department of Administration, Division of Purchase and Contract, 116 West Jones Street, Raleigh, NC 27611, (919) 733-3581

The North Carolina purchasing program employs seven purchasing teams, a purchasing consulting group, a data processing group, and a staff group. Team number 6 buys consulting services and team number 7 buys data processing equipment. Included on that team is one individual whose responsibility is described as "Purchases by local municipalities & other non-state agencies." The Division also has its own internal data processing group.

All purchases in excess of $2,500 must be advertised and made competitive, and RFPs are issued to contract for technical and professional services, such as consulting.

North Dakota

Office of Management and Budget, Purchasing Division, State Capitol, Bismarck, ND 58505, (701) 224-2680

Although buying for one of the less-populous states and with a relatively small procurement budget, the Purchasing Division of North Dakota's state government is well organized and operates with well-defined procedures. As in most states, in-state vendors are given preference over out-of-state vendors. Advertising methods are not specified, however, and the principal method of soliciting bids is by mailing invitations out to registered vendors.

Sealed bids may be formal or informal, the distinction being cost: Informal bids without bonds are acceptable for purchases of $1,000 to $5,000. Bids in excess of this must be made via formal procedures, and they require bid bonds of 5 percent and performance bonds of 25 percent. Bids of less than $1,000 may be made orally, by telephone, with written confirmation to follow. Other state agencies are empowered to do their own separate purchasing.

Ohio

Department of Administrative Services, State Purchasing, 364 S. Fourth Street, Columbus, OH 43216, (614) 466-8218

A request to Ohio's purchasing office brings an abundance of information about the purchasing system. Among the basic policies and regulations are these: Purchases of $5,000 or more must be by formal, sealed bids, solicited by mailing bid sets to registered vendors and posting notices on a bulletin board in a public area of the purchasing offices. Purchase authority may be delegated to other agencies, and some agencies are exempt by statute and are thus authorized to buy independently.

The state has been divided into 12 bid districts, and a map of the districts is furnished, with the various state agencies and institutions of each district identified. Eleven of the bid districts are actual geographic areas, but the 12th is a hypothetical subdivision and actually represents the state as a whole, and is identified as the "district" to be served when the purchase is for the state as a whole, rather than for some geographic subdivision.

Oklahoma

State Board of Public Affairs, Central Purchasing, State Capitol Building, Room 306, Oklahoma City, OK 73105, (405) 521-2115

Oklahoma's purchasing office furnishes a 236-page manual to vendor applicants, most of which is devoted to listing over 7,000 commodities and services in 191 supply classes, listed both by supply classes and in an alphabetical index. The manual's title is *How to Sell to the State of Oklahoma*, with the subtitle *Partners in Procurement*. Except for those agencies exempted specifically by statute, the purchasing office buys all commodities for the state. However, that the purchasing office considers itself to be the agent of other state agencies, performing a service for them, is clearly indicated by the graphic device on the cover of the manual, three meshing gears, labeled "Agency," "Vendor," and "Central Purchasing."

Four procurement methods are used: open market bids, annual and semi-annual term contracts, formal competitive bids (for one-time purchases), and small purchases under emergency conditions, of not more than $750. (Emergency purchases may run to $2,000, if the governor certifies the need in writing.)

Among those who may buy independently are the State Transportation Commission, all state educational institutions, the Department of Corrections, and the University Hospital. However, the purchase of professional services is exempt from the general requirements for competitive bids and awards to low bidders, but the published regulations are less than crystal clear on exactly what procedures must be followed, and the logical inference is that negotiated procurement methods may be used here.

Rhode Island

Department of Administration, Division of Purchases, 289 Promenade Street, Providence, RI 02908, (401) 277-2321

A brochure titled *A Guide on How to Sell to the State of Rhode Island* is provided to inquirers. The brochure explains the following procurement procedures and policies:

Formal Bids: Sealed bids with stated opening date and time for public opening in the Division's bid room.

Informal Bids: As above but for small purchases, not necessarily formal public bid openings.

Telephone Bids: Emergency procurements where situation precludes usual procedures.

South Carolina

Budget and Control Board, Division of General Services, Materials Management Office, 800 Dutch Square Boulevard, Suite 150, Columbia, SC 29210, (803) 758-6060

The Materials Management Office spends some $200+ million annually for goods and services for the state agencies. Specifically exempt from procurement via this office and authorized to make purchases independently are the following agencies of the state:

South Carolina Department of Corrections, Division of Prison Industries
South Carolina State Ports Authority
South Carolina Public Railways Commission
South Carolina Public Service Authority

Procurement policies and statutes provide for both formal, sealed bids, with awards to the lowest bidders, and for negotiated procurement. In-state vendors are given preference, where they are competitive with out-of-state bidders, and contract forms used are fixed-price, cost-reimbursement, one-time purchase, annual supply term contracts, and even multiyear term contracts.

Tennessee

Department of General Services, Purchasing Division, C2-211 Central Service Building, Nashville, TN 37219, (615) 741-1035

The State of Tennessee lists thousands of items purchased annually, and furnishes its commodity lists on microfiche. However, it also offers a vendor's guide, *Rule of the Department of General Services Purchasing Division*. The Purchasing Division has supply responsibility, as well as purchasing authority, for the entire state. However, other agencies and institutions may negotiate their own contracts for the purchase of professional services, and the following state agencies and institutions are authorized generally to use the services of the Purchasing Division or to buy autonomously, as they wish:

The General Assembly of the State

The University of Tennessee

The State University and Community College System

The State Technical Institutes

The local governments within the state may purchase through the Purchasing Division also, for both one-time purchases and for term contracts, and/or may utilize the state's contracts to place their own orders.

Purchases not over $2,000 must be by competitive bid, but may be made informally by written or verbal (telephone) means. Purchases above that amount must be made through formal, sealed bids, with public openings and awards to lowest responsible and responsive bidders. Purchases up to $300 are classed as small purchases.

Texas

State Purchasing and General Services Commission, Lyndon Baines Johnson State Office Building, POB 13047, Capitol Station, Austin, TX 78711, (512) 475-2211

Except for certain professional and consulting services and a few other exclusions, the Commission is the purchasing agent for the entire state. In general, formal competitive bidding is required, under one of the following options:

Open Market Purchases: Bids invited for fixed-quantity, fixed-price purchase, with award to lowest responsive and responsible bidder.

Term Contract Purchase: Supply contract, usually for one year, for common-use commodities at fixed prices, but indefinite quantity. (State agencies issue purchase orders under the basic contract, in much the same manner as the federal supply contracts known as GSA "schedules.")

Multiple Award Contract Purchases: Variant of Term Contract Purchase, wherein there is to be more than one level of performance or more than one supply service, and separate contracts are awarded for each level or service.

Utah

Department of Administrative Services, Division of Purchasing, 147 State Capitol Building, Salt Lake City, UT 84114, (801) 533-4620

Utah advises that its procurement budget is more than $150 million, exclusive of highway funds, and offers vendors a guidance publication, *Procurement regulations*. Purchases expected to be in excess of $8,000 are advertised each Monday in the legal-notices columns of the *Salt Lake Tribune* and the *Deseret News*. The favored method of procurement is via formal sealed bids, with public openings and awards to the lowest bidders. However, Utah also uses a multistep sealed-bid method, consisting of unpriced technical proposals followed by sealed bids from those whose proposals were found acceptable, so Utah issues RFPs as well as invitations to bid.

Small purchases are those under $8,000, and are made according to these guidelines:

To $500: Made through expedited procedures, not clearly defined because the regulation simply directs that the contracting official may "adopt operational procedures."

$500 to $2,000: Minimum of two bids, which may be made by telephone.

$2,000 to $8,000: Minimum of two bids, written.

On any of these purchases, up to $5,000, purchase authority may be delegated to the requesting agency.

Vermont

Agency of Administration, Purchasing Division, 7 School Street, Montpelier, VT 05602, (802) 828-2211

Vermont furnished no information, other than to identify its purchasing office.

Virginia

Department of General Services, Division of Purchases and Supply, 805 East Broad Street, POB 1199, Richmond, VA 23209, (804) 786-3845

Virginia's central purchasing office provides a guidance publication, *Vendor's Manual* and reports an annual procurement budget of over $400 million, spent to buy some 5,000 individual items of supply in approximately 100 supply classes, and extends a welcome to all prospective new suppliers. The office also recommends that sales efforts be directed to the Director of Purchasing, Virginia's Department of Highways and Transportation (1221 E. Broad Street, Richmond, VA 23219, (804) 786-2801) because that agency does its own purchasing.

The purchasing office reports that it does not buy services for the other state agencies and institutions, although the commodities list does include such items as printing and bookbinding, and in general small purchases (those under $500) do not require their authorization. More-over, computers and related equipment are purchased for the state through Virginia's Department of Management Analysis and Systems Development. Too, Virginia's publicly operated colleges and universities are exempt and may buy independently with their own purchase orders. General guidelines include these:

Purchases less than $200: Small purchases, may be noncompetitive where justified.

$200 to $500: Informal quotations/bids, verbally or in writing.

$500 to $5,000: May be by unsealed bids on special Virginia form.

$5,000 up: Must be formal, sealed bids.

Other Virginia agencies which make at least some of their purchases independently include these:

Agriculture and Commerce Department	Conservation Department
Economic Development Department	Public Utilities Division
Insurance Division	Consumer Affairs Office
Labor & Industry Department	Arts and Humanities Commission
Taxation Department	

Washington

Department of General Administration, Purchasing Division, 216 General Administration Building AX-22, Olympia, WA 98504, (206) 753-0900

The Purchasing Division has an annual procurement budget of well over $100 million, but many of the state's agencies and institutions buy independently. The Purchasing Division buys from approximately 10,000 vendors registered with it. (Registration is required, to be placed on the bidders list.)

The Division is divided into four purchasing groups, with Contract Group A and Contract Group B buying items and services relevant to computers and data processing. However, a special file of prequalified individuals and organizations is maintained for the procurement of a variety of technical and professional services, and the following are the relevant contacts to make, relevant to computers and data processing:

For management services: Management Services, Office of Financial Management, 101 House Office Building AL-01, Olympia, WA 98504, (206) 753-5448.

For data processing services and equipment: Data Processing Authority, 2604 12th Court, SW FV-11, Olympia, WA 98504.

For software and maintenance: Room 25, Office Building 2, Olympia, WA 98504, (206) 753-7277

West Virginia

Department of Finance and Administration, Purchasing Division, Capitol Station, POB 5280, Charleston, WV 25311

West Virginia's purchasing office furnishes a small but informative booklet, *Selling to the State of West Virginia*, upon request. The staff of the Division includes a roster of buyers, each of whom is assigned a "File Number." Bids for commodities are solicited via Request for Quotations (RFQs), and Request for Proposals (RFPs) are used to solicit problem-solving and other special services. Purchases over $2,000 must be advertised in the newspaper of the county where the procuring agency is located. Most procurements are made by State Purchase Order, but such purchases as those of consulting and other technical/professional services are made via contracts, which the state refers to as "Agreements."

Wisconsin

Department of Administration, State Bureau of Procurement, 101 South Webster Street, 6th Floor, POB 7867, Madison, WI 53707

The procurement bureau of Wisconsin uses an automated bidders list and procurement management system, spending over $300 million annually to purchase goods and services for the state. As in the case of other states, many of the state's agencies are authorized to make their purchases independently, and the bureau furnished a list of about 100 such agencies and institutions, along with an extensive commodity list.

Wyoming

Department of Administration and Fiscal Control, Purchasing and Property Control Division, Emerson Building, Room 301, Cheyenne, WY 82002, (307) 777-7523

Wyoming's *Vendor's Guide*, available from the office listed here, advises the reader that Wyoming has five separate purchasing authorities. In addition to the centralized purchasing by the bureau listed here, purchasing authority is extended to the following agencies of the state:

The Judicial Districts throughout the state

The Legislative Branch, in Cheyenne

The Highway Department, in Cheyenne

The University of Wyoming, in Laramie

The Bureau employs seven buyers, one of whom is assigned the purchase of data processing equipment and related supplies. Most purchases are made by state purchase orders, and solicitations are issued in both general forms, invitations to bid, and requests for proposals, and some preference is given to in-state vendors, except when the purchase is made with federal funds.

MISCELLANEOUS JURISDICTIONS

The following are procurement offices for other United States jurisdictions, local governments which are not states, counties, cities, towns, or townships.

District of Columbia

Bureau of Material Management, Department of General Services, 613 G Street, NW, Washington, DC 20001, (202) 629-5014.

American Samoa

Department of Purchases, Government House, Pago Pago, Samoa 96799, 633-4116.

Guam

Procurement and Supply, Department of Administration, Agana, Guam 96910.

Puerto Rico
Purchases and Supply Services, Department of Treasury. Box 2112, San Juan, PR 00903, (809) 723-2789.

Virgin Islands
Department of Property and Procurement, Government House, St. Thomas, Virgin Islands 00801, (809) 774-0828.

A FEW RELEVANT NAMES AND ADDRESSES

The following organizations may be of considerable help to you. In any case, you certainly should be aware of their existence.

American Chamber of Commerce Executives, 1133 15th Street, NW, Suite 620, Washington, DC 20005.

Council of State Chambers of Commerce, 499 South Capitol Street, Washington, DC 20003.

American Society for Public Administration, 1225 Connecticut Avenue, NW, Washington, DC 20036.

United States Conference of Mayors, 1620 Eye Street, NW, Washington, DC 20006.

International City Management Association, 1140 Connecticut Avenue, NW, Washington, DC 20036.

National Association of Counties, 1753 New York Avenue, Washington, DC 20006.

National Institute on Governmental Purchasing, Crystal Square Building #3, Suite 101, 1735 Jefferson Davis Highway, Arlington, VA 22202.

National Association of State Purchasing Officials, POB 11910, Lexington, KY 40578.

National Association of Towns and Townships, 1522 K Street, NW, Suite 730, Washington, DC 20005.

Coalition for Common Sense in Government Procurement, 1990 M Street, NW, Suite 570, Washington, DC 20036.

National Association of County Administrators, 1735 New York Avenue, NW, Washington, DC 20006.

National Association of City Planning Directors, 1735 New York Avenue, NW, Washington, DC 20006.

American Society for Hospital Purchasing and Materials Management, 840 North Lake Shore Drive, Chicago, IL 60611.

Society for Marketing Professional Services, 1437 Powhaten Street, Alexandria, VA 22314.

National Purchasing Institute, POB 20549, Houston, TX 77025.

National Association of Purchasing Management, 11 Park Place, New York, NY 10007.

National Contract Management Association, 2001 Jefferson Davis Highway, Arlington, VA 22202.

CHAPTER 14

DIRECTORY OF CITY AND COUNTY GOVERNMENT PROSPECTS

The needs of the cities and counties parellel those of the states generally, as do the procurement systems. In many cases the city and county procurement budgets rival those of the states in size and diversity as well.

A FEW RELEVANT STATISTICS

There are approximately 125 major urban or metropolitan areas, large cities surrounded by heavily populated suburbs in the United States. There are some 2,500 municipalities of over 10,000 population and approximately 7,000 municipalities of over 2,500 population. And there are also more than 3,000 counties in the United States. Without counting the towns and townships of less than 2,500 population we can count in excess of 12,500 governments within our national borders, all of whom purchase goods and services every day. With the enormous procurement budget of the federal government, we are talking about an annual government procurement of goods and services that can be counted in the hundreds of billions of dollars. In numerals, which are somewhat more expressive in helping us to grasp the enormous size of this overall procurement budget, it would look something like this: $550,000,000,000. A large part of that total, probably about one-half or something in excess of $250,000,000,000 represents the annual procurement of goods and services by the local governments or over 99 percent of those jurisdictions the Census Bureau refers to as "governmental units."

While it is possible to list the major customers of the federal and state governments of our country and provide some fairly detailed guidance information about each, it would be impractical to attempt to present information at the level of detail for all those cities, towns, townships, and counties and still have a book of manageable size. But it is not necessary to do so. Instead, in this chapter there are listed a number of those city/county jurisdictions, with details of their procurement systems and potential as markets, serving as examples of what you may expect typically in such jurisdictions. This chapter begins with presentations of city/county markets on the level of detail followed generally for the states in the preceding chapter and then goes on to list the key addresses for the remaining cities and counties.

PHILOSOPHICALLY, AT LEAST, THE SYSTEMS ARE SIMILAR

In general, cities and counties follow the same pattern to be found among the various state governments: Procurement is primarily by sealed bids as the procurement method of choice. (Purchasing officials usually favor this method whenever it is appropriate and practical to use it because it is the most competitive method and therefore the most effective way to persuade bidders to offer their best prices.) Negotiated procurement is resorted to when circumstances make sealed bids impractical, as when technical competence is at least as much a consideration as cost in influencing the final selection. Most cities and counties, like most cities and states, employ a philosophy of centralized procurement, but recognize the inevitability of authorizing many agencies to do at least some of their purchasing autonomously. The City of Oakland, California, for example, has a centralized purchasing office and a rather comprehensive and complete central purchasing organization, but delegates purchasing authority to 11 agencies in the city, nevertheless.

Those agencies most likely to have some independent spending authority for other than routine procurements, such as office supplies and furniture, include highway or public roads agencies (also called transportation departments in many jurisdictions), school districts, utilities, (when publicly owned), and airports, although there are many others often found to be authorized at least some independent purchasing authority. This includes public libraries, police departments, fire departments, port authorities, and others whose needs are likely to be so highly specialized as to be virtually unique within that government. Obviously, this will vary considerably, from one local government to another, as it does from one state government to another, as local conditions and local concerns vary.

In counties the purchasing bureau, by whatever name it may be called, is generally found at the county seat, the county's capital, and in cities the purchasing office is generally found in the city hall. Names and ideas about organizational assignments vary widely and a purchasing function may be assigned to someone and/or some office with a title that does not directly suggest the purchasing function. In some cases, for example, purchasing is the responsibility of someone called "Chief of Administration" or "Manager of Services." Generally speaking, if you do not know the formal name of the purchasing office or purchasing official, a letter or inquiry addressed to "Purchasing Office" or "Purchasing Officer" will generally be routed to the proper office and individual.

SOME TYPICAL CITY/COUNTY PURCHASING SYSTEMS

Following are somewhat detailed descriptions of several city and county purchasing organizations and their systems, intended to serve as examples of what you are likely to find in most of the approximately 21,000 cities, towns, townships, and counties of the United States (not to mention the remaining 59,000 "governmental units" the U.S. Census Bureau identifies). But while the examples here are typical, bear in mind that there is also a wide range of differences among all these 21,000 government entities. As in the case of the state governments some of these jurisdictions are quite generous in accommodating your needs, and will offer you extensive literature to help you market your goods and services to their governments, while others will have extremely little to offer as organized information or even reasonably detailed definition of their procurement and purchasing policies. And, as in the case of the states, the amount and scope of the information made available has no apparent relationship to the size of the government or the volume of their annual purchasing. For example, New York and Texas (especially Texas, which not only furnished little information, but was not very cooperative in furnishing even that little) furnished less help than did some relatively small states, such as Massachusetts, which was quite generous and gracious with its help.

In some cases a simple request will bring you all the information you could possibly want, while in other cases you will have to dig extensively to get the information you need. However, each jurisdiction does buy, of course, and they are spending public money, which means that you have a legal right to get information about their purchasing and to participate in bidding for their business.

The lists furnished here are therefore offered as starting points to begin your marketing to these governments and to serve you as examples of what you can expect and/or may pursue in other cities and counties. Bear in mind, in the meanwhile, that most of the literature furnished to me in researching this field—guidance brochures, procurement manuals, commodity lists, procurement regulations, and other such literature—was developed before the advent of the desktop/personal microcomputers, and did not anticipate the changes in computer procurement that would result from this revolutionary development. Be alert, therefore, for relevant deviations from some of the prescribed practices.

Oakland, California
Purchasing Department, 7101 Edgewater Drive, Oakland, CA 94621, (415) 273-3521
  The City of Oakland Purchasing Department buys for the following agencies:

Office of Public Works	Office of General Services
Office of Parks and Recreation	Office of Community Development
Social Services Department	Housing Department
Library Department	Oakland Museum
Police Department	Fire Department
Data Processing Department	Finance Department

  On the other hand, all the following agencies buy independently, and each of these has its own purchasing department, which you should contact directly:

Oakland Unified School District	Oakland/Alameda County Coliseum
Oakland Housing Authority	Port of Oakland and Airport
Bay Area Rapid Transit System (BART)	East Bay Municipal Utility District (Water)
Pacific Gas & Electric Co.	Alameda-Contra Costa Transit
(gas and electricity)	(bus transportation)
County of Alameda (general government,	East Bay Regional Park District
incl. hospitals)	Oakland Scavenger Co.

The Oakland purchasing organization has as its objective maximizing competition and making awards to the lowest responsible bidders. For purchases less than $1,000, Requests for Quotations (RFQs) are sent out to vendors and oral bids (usually via telephone) are accepted. Above that amount, up to $15,000, written bids are required. And for purchases in excess of $15,000 the procurement is advertised in local newspapers, formal specifications are mailed to vendors, and bids are opened publicly every Monday at 2:00 P.M. by the City Clerk in Room 306, Oakland City Hall, 14th and Washington Streets.

Jacksonville, Florida

Department of Central Services, Purchasing Division, 220 East Bay Street, Jacksonville, FL 32202, (904) 633-2704

Under Jacksonville's form of government the Purchasing Division buys for the city, the county, the Duval County School Board, and for several other agencies of the jurisdiction. There are three groups of buyers constituting the purchasing staff, and purchases in excess of $8,000 must be made by formal sealed bids. Procedures are not specifically defined by statute for smaller purchases, although a series of Purchasing Bulletins have been issued, describing decisions and prescribing procedures to be followed.

Milwaukee, Wisconsin

Central Board of Purchases, Room 607, City Hall, 200 East Wells Street, Milwaukee, WI 53202, (414) 278-3501

Milwaukee classifies bids over $20,000 as "Formal Bids," and those under that figure as "Informal Bids." Formal Bids are also referred to as "Class A Purchases," and must be awarded by the Central Board of Purchases after using formal sealed bids to find the lowest responsible bidder. The Informal Bids, which are those under $20,000 and referred to also as "Class B Purchases," must also be subjected to the formal sealed bid process, but awards may be made by the City Purchasing Agent.

Preference, in case of tie bids, is given to those who manufacture their goods in the city, those who manufacture in the County of Milwaukee, or are otherwise "local," rather than "foreign" bidders, in an order of priority prescribed by the City.

Other Class B purchases are informal bids referred to as "Buyer Bids," for purchases expected to cost less than $1,000. In these purchases the buyer may make awards and telephone bids may be accepted, under these guidelines:

$100 to $1,000:   Three or more quotes from vendors
$35 to $100:   Quote from one or more vendors
$35 or less: Petty-cash expenditure (no quote required)

Emergency purchases may run between $1,000 and $20,000, and require that quotes be solicited from at least three vendors.

Tulsa, Oklahoma

Department of Purchasing, 200 Civic Center, Room 1023, Tulsa, OK 74103, (918) 581-5511

Tulsa spends on the order of $20 million or more annually for centralized purchasing, using formal sealed bids after advertising in the *Tulsa Legal News*, when the purchase is expected to be over $4,000. Informal bids are solicited from at least three sources for procurements less than this.

Dallas, Texas

Department of Purchasing, City Hall, 1500 Marilla Street, Dallas, TX 75201, (214) 670-3326

The Dallas centralized purchasing office spends some $40 million annually for goods and services, exclusive of construction contracts. Purchases in excess of $2,000 must be advertised in one of the city's daily newspapers. The Director of Purchasing may approve purchases up to $2,000. The City Manager may approve purchases up to $10,000. And the City Council must approve larger purchases. Moreover, the City Council must also approve the advertising notices when the purchase is to be in excess of $100,000.

The Dallas commodity list covers more than 1,000 items of goods and services, many of the latter in technical/professional categories of many kinds.

San Diego, California
Purchasing Department, City Operations Buildings, 1222 1st Avenue, San Diego, CA 92101, (714) 236-6210

San Diego's annual budget for centralized purchasing is approximately $45 million. The Purchasing Department operates with a staff of eight buyers and an assistant purchasing agent, who buy from a commodity list of several hundred commodity supply groups. All purchases of $5,000 or more are advertised in the San Diego *Daily Transcript*, the City's official newspaper, and bid competitively.

New York City
Department of General Services, Office of Vendor Relations, Room 1919, Municipal Building, 1 Centre Street, New York, NY 10007, (212) 566-3062

New York City, not surprisingly, is a market for a wide array of goods and services, spending more than $350 million annually in such procurements. The City furnishes vendor-applicants a brochure, *How to do Business With New York City, A Vendor's Guide*, and urges vendors to apply to the address listed here for a form issued to register and qualify you as a vendor and place your name on the bidder's list. The publication assures the reader that New York City is constantly seeking new and additional sources of supply and is most receptive to offers from vendors.

Two kinds of contracts are offered: Formal Contracts are used for purchases of $10,000 or more, and Open Market Contracts are used for smaller purchases. In some cases, prebid conferences are held.

In addition to being placed on the bidder's list to receive bid solicitations by mail you may subscribe to New York City's official publication, *The City Record*, which lists bid proposals from all the city agencies and/or you may visit the Bid Room (Room 1911, Municipal Building), where copies of all bid proposals are posted for your inspection.

Local (New York City) vendors are given a preference of up to 5 percent in determining the lowest bid. (To qualify for this the vendor must have a New York City business address and be a New York taxpayer.)

At least nine other city agencies do their own purchasing, independently, and it is advisable to market to these agencies directly and separately:

Board of Education
44th Road & Vernon Blvd
Long Island City, NY 11101

Board of Higher Education
535 East 80th Street
New York, NY 10021

Transit Authority
25 Chapel Street
Brooklyn, NY 11201

Port of New York Authority
1 World Trade Center, Suite 73N
New York, NY 10048

Housing Authority
250 Broadway, Room 707
New York, NY 10007

Health and Hospitals Corporation
125 Worth Street
New York, NY 10013

Triboro Bridge & Tunnel Authority
Randall's Island
New York, NY 10035

Off-Track Betting Corp.
1501 Broadway
New York, NY 10036

Bureau of Water Resources Development
1250 Broadway
New York, NY 10001

Cleveland, Ohio

Department of Finance, Division of Purchasing, Room 128, City Hall, 601 Lakeside Avenue, Cleveland, OH 44114 (216) 664-2620

The City of Cleveland spends approximately $200 million annually for centrally purchased goods and services. All purchases expected to exceed $3,500 must be advertised in the *City Record*.

Washington, DC

Department of General Services, Bureau of Materiel Management, 613 G Street, NW, Room 1001, Washington, DC 20001, (202) 727-1000

Washington's commodity list identifies about 250 supply classes and about 6,000 individual items of goods and services purchased by the City, for an estimated annual total of approximately $300 million (exclusive of about $300 million more for construction contracts).

Many of the City's agencies buy independently, and each of the following has its own designated purchasing agent:

Office of Consumer Protection
Office of Administrative Services, Personnel Office
Office of Inspector General
Council of the District of Columbia
Department of Licenses, Investigations, and Inspections
DC Court of Appeals, DC Courthouse
Office of Business and Economic Development
Board of Education, DC Public Schools
Department of Housing and Community Development
Materiel Support and Contracts Division
DC National Guard, USPFODC
Public Defender Services
Public Library
Office of the People's Counsel
Department of Recreation
University of the District of Columbia
DC Commission on Judicial Disabilities and Tenure
DC Bail Agency
Executive Office of the Mayor
Office of Human Rights

Office of Emergency Preparedness
Office of the City Administrator
Board of Appeals and Review
Office of Documents
Office of the Corporation Counsel
Department of Corrections
Board of Elections
Department of Environmental Services
Department of Finance and Revenue
DC Court System
Fire Department
Department of General Services
Department of Employment Services
Board of Public Employee Relations
Metropolitan Police Department
Department of Insurance
Board of Parole
DC Commission for Women
Rental Accommodation Office
Office of the Surveyor
Department of Transportation
Office of the District of Columbia Auditor
Armory Board
Public Service Commission
Metropolitan Police Department

Memphis, Tennessee

Division of Finance & Administration, Purchasing Agent, Room 304, City Hall, 125 North Main Street, Memphis, TN 38103, (901) 528-2683

Purchases over $2,000 for the City of Memphis must be made by formal contracts, after advertising notices are run for three days in the *Memphis Daily News*, with solicitations also mailed to appropriate vendors. Purchases under $500 may be made informally, after verbal (telephone) solicitations and quotes, or informally by written quotations for purchases between these two figures. Several agencies are authorized to buy independently, including the City School System; City of Memphis hospitals; the Memphis Light, including the Sheriff's Department, the City/County Health Department, and the Library System.

MUNICIPALITIES

Following is a list of about 800 municipalities, most of them over 25,000 population. The list is alphabetical, by states and municipalities, with population figures noted for each municipality, following the zip code. Where street addresses are given they are generally those of city or town halls. Address inquiries to the city or town and purchasing offices or purchasing agents at the addresses or box numbers given, with requests for information. However, as in the case of the state purchasing offices, most purchasing agents recommend making visits to meet the buyers personally, and you should follow up inquiries with visits when possible.

Alabama

Anniston 36201 (32,000)
POB 670

Bessemer 35020 (33,000)
1800 3rd Avenue North

Birmingham 3203 (301,000)
City Hall

Decatur 35602 (38,000)
POB 488

Dothan 36301 (37,000)
POB 2128

Florence 35630 (34,000)
POB 98

Gadsden 35902 (54,000)
POB 267

Huntsville 35804 (138,000)
308 Fountain Row

Mobile 36601 (190,000)
POB 1827

Montgomery 36102 (133,000)
POB 1111

Prichard 36610 (42,000)
POB 10427

Tuscaloosa 35401 (66,000)
2201 University Blvd

Alaska

Anchorage 99701 (15,000)
Pouch 6-650

Fairbanks 99701 (15,000)
410 Cushman Street

Juneau 99801 (14,000)
155 S. Seward Street

Arizona

Flagstaff 86001 (26,000)
POB 1208

Glendale 85311 (36,000)
POB 1556

Mesa 85201 (63,000)
POB 1466

Phoenix 85003 (582,000)
251 West Washington Street

Scottsdale 85251 (68,000)
3939 Civic Center Plaza

Tempe 85281 (63,000)
POB 5002

Tucson 85703 (263,000)
POB 5547

Yuma 85364 (29,000)
180 First Street

Arkansas

El Dorado 71730 (25,000)
City Hall

Fayetteville 72701 (31,000)
Drawer F

Fort Smith 72901 (63,000)
POB 1908

Little Rock 72201 (132,000)
500 West Markham Street

North Little Rock 72114 (60,000)
3rd and Main Streets

Pine Bluff 71601 (57,000)
200 East 8th Street

California

Alameda 94501 (71,000)
Oak and Santa Clara Streets

Alhambra 91801 (62,000)
111 South First Street

Anaheim 92803 (43,000)
POB 3222

Arcadia 91006 (43,000)
240 West Huntington Drive

Bakersfield 93301 (70,000)
City Hall

Baldwin Park 91706 (47,000)
1 Civic Center

Bellflower 90706 (51,000)
9838 East Belmont

Berkeley 94704 (117,000)
2180 Milvia Street

Beverly Hills 90210 (33,000)
450 North Crescent Drive

Buena Park 90620 (64,000)
6650 Beach Boulevard

Burbank 91502 (89,000)
275 East Olive Avenue

Carson 90745 (71,000)
21919 South Avalon Boulevard

Chula Vista 92012 (68,000)
POB 1087

Compton 90224 (79,000)
600 North Alameda Avenue

Concord 94519 (85,000)
1950 Parkside Drive

Costa Mesa 92626 (73,000)
POB 1200

Covina 91723 (30,000)
125 East College Street

Culver City 90230 (35,000)
POB 507

Cypress 90630 (31,000)
5275 Orange Avenue

Downey 90241 (88,000)
8425 Second Street

El Cajon 9202 (52,000)
200 East Main Street

El Monte 91734 (70,000)
11333 Valley Boulevard

Escondido 92025 (54,000)
100 Valley Boulevard

Fairfield 94533 (44,000)
1000 Webster Street

Fountain Valley 92708 (32,000)
10200 Slater Avenue

Fremont 94538 (101,000)
39700 Civic Center Drive

Fresno 93721 (166,000)
2326 Fresno Street

Fullerton 92632
303 West Commonwealth Avenue

Gardena 90247 (41,000)
1700 West 162nd Street

Garden Grove 92640 (123,000)
11391 Acacia Parkway

Glendale 91205 (133,000)
613 East Broadway

Glendora 91740 (31,000)
249 East Foothill Boulevard

Hawthorne 90250 (53,000)
4460 West 126th Street

Hayward 94541 (93,000)
22300 Foothill Boulevard

Huntington Beach 92648 (116,000)
POB 190

Huntington Park 90255 (34,000)
6550 Miles Avenue

Inglewood 90301 (90,000)
1 Manchester Boulevard

La Habra 90631 (41,000)
Civic Center

La Mesa 92041 (39,000)
8130 Allison Avenue

La Mirada 90638 (31,000)
13700 La Mirada Boulevard

La Puente 91744 (31,000)
15900 East Main Street

Lakewood 90714 (83,000)
5050 Clark Avenue

Livermore 94550 (38,000)
2250 First Street

Lodi 95240 (32,000)
221 West Pine Street

Long Beach 90802 (359,000)
333 West Ocean

California (Cont'd)

Los Angeles 90012 (2,816,000)
200 North Spring Street

Lynwood 90262 (43,000)
11330 Bullis Road

Manhattan Beach 90262 (35,000)
1400 Highland Avenue

Merced 95340 (30,000)
POB 2068

Modesto 96353 (30,000)
POB 642

Monrovia 91016 (30,000)
415 South Ivy Avenue

Montebello 90640 (43,000)
1600 Beverly Boulevard

Monterey Park 91745 (49,000)
320 West Newmark Avenue

Mountain View 94042 (51,000)
POB 10

Napa 94558 (36,000)
POB 660

National City 92050 (43,000)
1243 National Avenue

Newport Beach 92663 (49,000)
3300 Newport Boulevard

Norwalk 90650 (92,000)
12700 Norwalk Boulevard

Novata 94947 (31,000)
POB 578

Oakland 94621 (362,000)
7101 Edgewater Drive

Oceanside 92054 (40,000)
706 3rd Street

Ontario 91761 (64,000)
222 South Euclid Avenue

Orange 92666 (77,000)
300 East Chapman Avenue

Oxnard 93030 (71,000)
225-305 West Third Street

Pacifica 94044 (36,000)
170 Santa Maria Avenue

Palm Springs 92262 (50,000)
POB 1786

Palo Alto 94301 (56,000)
250 Hamilton Avenue

Paramount 90723 (35,000)
16420 Colorado Avenue

Pasadena 91009 (113,000)
100 North Garfield Avenue

Petaluma 94951 (25,000)
Post and English Streets

Pico Rivera 90660 (54,000)
6615 Passons Boulevard

Pleasantown 94566 (32,000)
200 Bernal Avenue

Pomona 91766 (87,000)
POB 660

Rancho Palos Verdes 90274 (40,000)
30940 Hawthorne Boulevard

Redlands 92373 (36,000)
POB 280

Redondo Beach 90277 (56,000)
425 Diamond Street

Redwood City 94064 (56,000)
POB 468

Richmond 94804 (79,000)
27th Street and Barrett Avenue

Riverside 92522 (155,000)
3900 Main Street

Rosemead 91770 (41,000)
8838 East Valley Boulevard

Sacramento 95814 (254,000)
915 I Street

Salinas 93901 (59,000)
200 Lincoln Avenue

San Bernardino 92418 (104,000)
300 North D. Street

San Bruno 94066 (39,000)
567 El Camino Real

San Buenaventura 93001 (56,000)
POB 99

San Diego 92101 (697,000)
1222 First Avenue

San Francisco 94102 (716,000)
400 Van Ness Avenue

San Gabriel 91778 (30,000)
POB 130

San Jose 95110 (446,000)
801 North First Street

San Leandro 94577 (69,000)
835 East 14th Street

San Mateo 94403 (79,000)
330 West 20th Avenue

San Rafael 94901 (39,000)
1400 Fifth Avenue

Santa Ana 92701 (157,000)
20 Civic Center Plaza

Santa Barbara 93102 (88,000)
POB P-P

Santa Clara 95050 (88,000)
1500 Warburton Avenue

Santa Cruz 95060 (32,000)
809 Center Street

Santa Maria 93454 (33,000)
110 East Cook Street

Santa Monica 90401 (88,000)
1685 Main Street

Santa Rosa 95403 (50,000)
POB 1678

Seaside 93955 (36,000)
440 Harcourt Avenue

Simi Valley 93065 (56,000)
3200 Cochran Street

South Gate 90280 (57,000)
8650 California Avenue

South San Francisco 94080 (47,000)
POB 711

Stockton 95202 (108,000)
425 North El Dorado Street

Sunnyvale 94086 (95,000)
456 West Olive Avenue

Thousand Oaks 91360 (36,000)
401 West Hillcrest Drive

Torrance 90503 (135,000)
3031 Torrance Boulevard

Upland 91786 (33,000)
POB 460

Vallejo 94590 (67,000)
555 Santa Clara Street

Visalia 93277 (35,000)
707 West Acequia Street

Walnut Creek 94596 (40,000)
1445 Civic Drive

West Covina 91790 (68,000)
POB 1440

Westminster 92683 (60,000)
8200 Westminster Avenue

Whittier 90602 (73,000)
13230 Penn Street

Colorado

Arvada 80002 (47,000)
8101 Ralson Road

Aurora 80012 (75,000)
1470 Emporia Street

Boulder 80302 (67,000)
POB 791

Colorado Springs 80901 (135,000)
POB 1575

Denver 80202 (515,000)
1437 Bannock Street

Englewood 80110 (34,000)
3400 South Eluti

Fort Collins 80522 (43,000)
POB 580

Grand Junction 81501 (20,000)
POB 968

Greeley 80632 (39,000)
Civic Center Complex

Lakewood 80228 (93,000)
44 Union Boulevard

Northglenn 80233 (32,000)
10701 Melody Drive

Pueblo 81001 (97,000)
One City Hall Plaza

Wheat Ridge 80033 (30,000)
POB 610

Connecticut

Bridgeport 06604 (157,000)
45 Lyon Terrace B

Bristol 06010 (55,000)
111 North Main Street

Danbury 06810 (51,000)
155 Deer Hill Avenue

East Hartford 06108 (58,000)
740 Main Street

Enfield 06082 (46,000)
820 Enfield Street

Fairfield 06430 (56,000)
610 Old Post Road

Greenwich 06830 (60,000)
Greenwich Avenue

Groton 06340 (39,000)
295 Meridian Street

Connecticut (Cont'd)
Hamden 06518 (49,000)
2372 Whitney Avenue

Hartford 06103 (158,000)
550 Main Street

Manchester 06040 (48,000)
41 Center Street

Meridien 06450 (56,000)
142 East Main Street

Middletown 06457 (37,000)
POB 141

Milford 06460 (51,000)
River Street

New Britain 06051 (83,000)
27 West Main Street

New Haven 06508 (130,000)
City Hall

New London 06320 (32,000)
181 Captain's Walk

Norwalk 06856 (79,000)
41 North Main Street

Norwich 06360 (41,000)
City Hall

Southington 06489 (31,000)
Main Street

Stamford 06904 (109,000)
429 Atlantic Street

Stratford 06497 (50,000)
2725 Main Street

Torrington 06790 (32,000)
140 Main Street

Trumbull 06611 (31,000)
5866 Main Street

Wallingford 06492 (36,000)
350 Center Street

Waterbury 06702 (108,000)
236 Grand Street

West Hartford 06107 (68,000)
28 South Main Street

West Haven 06516 (53,000)
355 Main Street

Delaware
Dover 19901 (17,000)
POB 475

Wilmington 19801 (80,000)
800 French Street

District of Columbia
Washington 20004 (757,000)
14th and E Streets, NW

Florida
Clearwater 33618 (52,000)
POB 4748

Coral Gables 33134 (42,000)
405 Biltmore Way

Daytona Beach 32015 (45,000)
POB 551

Fort Lauderdale 33302 (140,000)
POB 14250

Gainesville 33602 (65,000)
POB 490

Hialeah 33011 (102,000)
POB 40

Hollywood 33022 (107,000)
POB 2207

Jacksonville 32202 (529,000)
220 East Bay Street

Key West 33040 (28,000)
POB 1550

Lakeland 33802 (42,000)
City Hall

Melbourne 32901 (40,000)
900 East Strawbridge Avenue

Miami 333133 (335,000)
3500 Pan American Drive

Miami Beach 33139 (87,000)
505 17th Street

North Miami 33161 (35,000)
776 NE 125th Street

North Miami Beach 33162 (31,000)
17011 NE 19th Avenue

Orlando 32801 (99,000)
400 South Orange Avenue

Panama City 32401 (32,000)
9 Harrison Avenue

Pensacola 32521 (60,000)
POB 12910

Pompano Beach 33061 (38,000)
POB 1300

St. Petersburg 33731 (216,000)
POB 2842

Sarasota 33577 (40,000)
1565 First Street

Tallahassee 32304 (72,000)
City Hall

Tampa 33602 (278,000)
315 East Kennedy Boulevard

Titusville 32780 (31,000)
555 South Washington Avenue

West Palm Beach 33402 (57,000)
POB 3366

Georgia

Albany 31702 (73,000)
POB 447

Athens 30601 (44,000)
City Hall

Atlanta 30303 (497,000)
68 Mitchell Street, SW

Augusta 30902 (60,000)
Municipal Building

Columbus 31902 (154,000)
POB 1340

East Point 30344 (39,000)
2777 East Point Street

Macon 31202 (122,000)
City Hall

Rome 30161 (31,000)
POB 1433

Savannah 31402 (118,000)
POB 1027

Valdosta 31601 (32,000)
POB 1125

Warner Robbins 31093 (33,000)
POB 1488

Hawaii

Honolulu 96813 (325,000)
530 South King Street

Idaho

Boise 83702 (75,000)
POB 500

Idaho Falls 83401 (36,000)
POB 220

Lewiston 83501 (26,000)
1134 F Street

Pocatello 83201 (40,000)
POB 4169

Illinois

Alton 62002 (40,000)
101 East Third Street

Arlington Heights 60005 (65,000)
333 South Arlington Heights Road

Aurora 60504 (74,000)
44 East Downer Place

Belleville 62220 (42,000)
101 South Illinois Street

Berwyn 60402 (53,000)
6700 West 26th Street

Bloomington 61701 (40,000)
109 East Olive Street

Calumet City 60409 (33,000)
204 Pulaski Road

Champaign 61820 (57,000)
102 North Neill Street

Chicago 60602 (3,367,000)
121 North LaSalle Street

Chicago Heights 60411 (41,000)
1601 Chicago Road

Cicero 60650 (67,000)
4937 West 25th Street

Danville 61832 (43,000)
402 North Hazel Street

Decatur 62523 (90,000)
707 East Wood Street

De Kalb 60115 (33,000)
200 South Fourth Street

Des Plaines 60018 (57,000)
1412 Miner Street

Downers Grove 60515 (33,000)
801 Burlington Avenue

East St. Louis 62201 (70,000)
7 Collinsville Avenue

Elgin 60120 (56,000)
150 Dexter Court

Elmhurst 60126 (51,000)
119 Schiller Street

Evanston 60204 (80,000)
2100 Ridge Avenue

Galesburg 61401 (36,000)
City Hall

Granite City 62040 (40,000)
2000 Edison Avenue

Harvey 60426 (35,000)
15320 Broadway

Highland Park 60035 (32,000)
1707 St. Johns Avenue

Illinois (Cont'd)

Hoffman Estates 60172 (32,000)
1200 North Gannon Drive

Joliet 60435 (80,000)
150 West Jefferson Street

Kankakee 60901 (31,000)
385 East Oak Street

Lombard 60148 (36,000)
48 North Park Avenue

Maywood 60153 (30,000)
115 South Fifth Avenue

Moline 61265 (46,000)
619 16th Street

Mount Prospect 60056 (46,000)
100 South Emerson Street

Niles 60648 (31,000)
7601 Milwaukee Avenue

Normal 61761 (31,000)
124 North Street

North Chicago 60064 (47,000)
1850 Lewis Avenue

Oak Lawn 60453 (60,000)
5252 West James Street

Oak Park 60301 (63,000)
Village Hall Plaza

Park Forest 60466 (31,000)
200 Forest Boulevard

Park Ridge 60068 (42,000)
505 Park Place

Pekin 61554 (31,000)
City Hall

Peoria 61602 (127,000)
419 Fulton Street

Quincy 62301 (45,000)
507 Vermont Street

Rockford 61104 (147,000)
425 East State Street

Rock Island 61201 (50,000)
1528 Third Avenue

Schaumberg 60193 (37,000)
101 Schaumberg Court

Skokie 60067 (69,000)
5127 Oakton Street

Springfield 62701 (92,000)
Municipal Building

Urbana 61801 (33,000)
400 South Vine Street

Waukegan 60085 (65,000)
106 North Utica Street

Wheaton 60187 (31,000)
303 West Wesley Street

Wilmette 60091 (32,000)
1200 Wilmette Avenue

Indiana

Anderson 46011 (71,000)
POB 2100

Bloomington 47401 (43,000)
Municipal Building

East Chicago 46514 (43,000)
4527 Indianapolis Boulevard

Elkhart 46514 (43,000)
Municipal Building

Evansville 47708 (139,000)
302 Civic Center Complex

Fort Wayne 46802 (178,000)
City-County Building

Gary 46902 (175,000)
City Hall

Hammond 46320
5925 Calumet Avenue

Indianapolis 46204 (745,000)
200 East Washington Street

Kokomo 46901 (44,000)
City Building

Lafayette 47901 (45,000)
20 North Sixth Street

Marion 46952 (40,000)
City Hall

Michigan City 46360 (39,000)
Warren Building

Mishawaka 46544 (36,000)
First and Church Streets

Muncie 47305 (69,000)
City Hall

New Albany 47150 (38,000)
City-County Building

Richmond 47374 (44,000)
50 North Fifth Street

South Bend 46601 (126,000)
227 West Jefferson Boulevard

Terre Haute 47807 (70,000)
17 Harding Avenue

Iowa

Ames 50010 (40,000)
Fifth and Kellog Streets

Burlington 52601 (32,000)
4th and Washington Streets

Cedar Falls 50613 (34,000)
220 Clay Street

Cedar Rapids 52401 (111,000)
City Hall

Clinton 52732 (35,000)
POB 337

Council Bluffs 51501 (60,000)
209 Pearl Street

Davenport 52801 (98,000)
226 West Fourth Street

Des Moines 50307 (201,000)
First and Locust Streets

Dubuque 52001 (62,000)
13th and Central Avenue

Fort Dodge 50501 (31,000)
813 First Avenue South

Iowa City 52240 (47,000)
410 East Washington Street

Mason City 50401 (30,000)
19 South Delaware Avenue

Ottuma 52501 (30,000)
105 East Third Street

Sioux City 51102 (86,000)
POB 447

Waterloo 50705 (76,000)
City Hall

Kansas

Hutchinson 67501 (37,000)
125 East Avenue B

Kansas City 66101 (168,000)
Civic Center Plaza

Lawrence 66044 (46,000)
POB 708

Leavenworth 66048 (25,000)
Fifth and Shawnee

Overland Park 66212 (77,000)
8500 Santa Fe Drive

Salina 67401 (38,000)
300 West Ash Street

Wichita 67202 (277,000)
455 North Main Street

Kentucky

Bowling Green 42101 (36,000)
POB 130

Covington 41011 (53,000)
City-County Building

Lexington 40507 (108,000)
Municipal Building

Louisville 40202 (361,000)
601 West Jefferson Street

Owensboro 42301 (50,000)
4th and St. Ann Streets

Paducah 42001 (32,000)
POB 891

Louisiana

Alexandria 71301 (42,000)
POB 71

Baton Rouge 70821 (166,000)
POB 1471

Bossier City 71010 (42,000)
635 Barksdale Boulevard

Houma 70360 (31,000)
City Hall

Lafayette 70501 (69,000)
733 Jefferson Street

Lake Charles 71201 (56,000)
POB 1178

Monroe 71201 (56,000)
POB 123

New Iberia 70560 (30,000)
POB 11

New Orleans 70112 (593,000)
1300 Perdido Street

Shreveport 71163 (182,000)
POB 1109

Bangor 044012 (33,000)
73 Harlow Street

Maine

Augusta 04330 (22,000)
One Cony Street

Biddeford 04005 (20,000)
POB 586

Maine (Cont'd)

Lewiston 04240 (42,000)
Pine Street

Portland 04111 (65,000)
389 Congress Street

Sanford 04073 (16,000)
267 Main Street

Waterville 04901 (18,000)
City Hall

Maryland

Annapolis 21202 (30,000)
166 Duke of Gloucester Street

Baltimore 21202 (906,000)
100 Holliday Street

Bowie 20715 (35,000)
Tulip Grove Drive

College Park 20740 (26,000)
4500 Knox Road

Cumberland 21502 (30,000)
City Hall

Hagerstown 21740 (36,000)
City Hall

Rockville 20850 (42,000)
111 Maryland Avenue

Massachusetts

Arlington 02174 (54,000)
730 Massachusetts Avenue

Attleboro 02703 (33,000)
29 Park Street

Beverly 01915 (38,000)
191 Cabot Street

Billerica 01821 (32,000)
Concord Road

Boston 02201 (641,000)
City Hall, Government Center

Braintree 02185 (35,000)
One J. F. Kennedy Memorial Drive

Brockton 02401 (89,000)
45 School Street

Brookline 02146 (59,000)
City Hall

Cambridge 022139 (100,000)
795 Massachusetts Avenue

Chelmsford 01824
One North Road

Chelsea 02150 (31,000)
City Hall

Chicopee 01013 (67,000)
City Hall

Everett 02149 (42,000)
484 Broadway

Fall River 02720 (97,000)
123 Main Street

Fitchburg 01420 (43,000)
718 Main Street

Framingham 01701 (64,000)
Memorial Building

Haverhill 01830 (46,000)
4 Summer Street

Holyoke 01040 (50,000)
536 Dwight Street

Lawrence 01840 (67,000)
200 Common Street

Leominster 01453 (33,000)
City Hall

Lexington 02173 (32,000)
1625 Massachusetts Avenue

Lowell 01853 (94,000)
City Hall

Lynn 01901 (90,000)
City Hall Square

Malden 02148 (56,000)
200 Pleasant Street

Medford 02155 (64,000)
85 George P. Hassett Drive

Melrose 02176 (33,000)
562 Main Street

Methuen 01844 (35,000)
90 Hampshire Street

Natick 01760 (31,000)
City Hall

New Bedford 02740 (102,000)
133 William Street

Newton 02159 (91,000)
1000 Commonwealth Avenue

Northampton 01060 (30,000)
210 Main Street

Norwood 02062 (31,000)
Municipal Building

Peabody 01960 (48,000)
24 Lowell Street

Pittsfield 01201 (57,000)
City Hall

Quincy 02169 (88,000)
1305 Hancock Street

Revere 01970 (41,000)
City Hall

Salem 01970 (41,000)
93 Washington Street

Somerville 02144 (89,000)
Highland Avenue

Springfield 01103 (164,000)
36 Court Street

Taunton 02780 (44,000)
15 Summer Street

Waltham 02154 (62,000)
City Hall

Watertown 02072 (39,000)
149 Main Street

Westfield 01085 (31,000)
59 Court Street

Weymouth 02189 (55,000)
75 Middle Street, East Weymouth

Woburn 01801 (37,000)
10 Common Street

Worcester 01608 (177,000)
Main Street

Michigan
Allen Park 48101 (41,000)
16850 Southfield Road

Ann Arbor 48107 (100,000)
100 Fifth Avenue

Battle Creek 49014 (39,000)
POB 1717

Bay City 48706 (49,000)
301 Washington Avenue

Burton 48519 (33,000)
4303 South Center Road

Dearborn 48126 (104,000)
13615 Michigan Avenue

Dearborn Heights 48127 (80,000)
6045 Fenton Street

Detroit 48226 (1,511,000)
912 City-County Building

East Detroit 48021 (46,000)
23200 Gratiot Avenue

East Lansing 48823 (48,000)
410 Abbott Road

Farmington Hills 48024 (51,000)
31555 Eleven Mile Road

Ferndale 48220 (31,000)
300 East Nine Mile Road

Flint 48502 (193,000)
1101 South Saginaw

Garden 48135 (42,000)
6000 Middlebelt Road

Grand Rapids 49503 (198,000)
300 Monroe, NW

Highland Park 48203 (35,000)
30 Gerald Avenue

Inkster 48141 (39,000)
2121 Inkster Road

Jackson 49201 (45,000)
132 West Washington Avenue

Kalamazoo 49006 (86,000)
241 West South Street

Lansing 48933 (132,000)
125 West Michigan Avenue

Lincoln Park 48146 (53,000)
1355 Southfield Road

Livonia 48154 (110,000)
33001 Five Mile Road

Madison Heights 48071 (39,000)
300 West Thirteen Mile Road

Menominee 49858 (11,000)
City Hall

Midland 48640 (35,000)
202 Ashman

Muskegon 49443 (45,000)
933 Terrace Street

Oak Park 48273 (37,000)
13600 Oak Park Boulevard

Pontiac 48058 (85,000)
450 East Widetrack Drive

Portage 49081 (34,000)
7800 Shaver Road

Port Huron 48060 (36,000)
201 McMorran Boulevard

Roseville 48066 (61,000)
29777 Gratiot Avenue

Royal Oak 48068 (85,000)
POB 64

Michigan (Cont'd)
Saginaw 48601 (92,000)
1315 South Washington Avenue

St. Clair Shores 48081 (88,000)
277600 Jefferson Street

Southfield 48076 (69,000)
26000 Evergreen Road

Southgate 48195 (34,000)
13763 Northline Road

Sterling Heights 48078 (61,000)
40555 Utica Road

Taylor 48180 (70,000)
23555 Goddard Road

Troy 48084 (39,000)
500 West Big Beaver Road

Warren 48093 (179,000)
29500 Van Dyke Avenue

Westland 48185 (87,000)
36601 Ford Road

Wyandotte 48192 (41,000)
3131 Briddle Avenue

Wyoming 49509 (57,000)
1151 28th Street, SW

Minnesota
Austin 55912 (25,000)
500 Fourth Avenue NE

Bloomington 55431 (82,000)
2215 West Old Shakopee Road

Brooklyn Center 55430 (35,000)
6301 Shingle Creek Parkway

Coon Rapids 55433 (31,000)
1313 Coon Rapids Boulevard

Crystal 55422 (31,000)
4141 Douglas Drive North

Duluth 55802 (101,000)
403 City Hall

Rhode Island
Cranston 02910 (73,000)
869 Park Avenue

East Providence 02914 (48,000)
60 Commercial Way

Newport 02840 (35,000)
City Hall

Pawtucket 02860 (77,000)
City Hall

Providence 02903 (179,000)
25 Dorrance Street

Warwick 02864 (84,000)
3275 Post Road

Woonsocket 02895 (47,000)
169 Main Street
817 Franklin Street

South Carolina
Charleston 29401 (67,000)
City Hall

Columbia 29217 (114,000)
POB 147

Greenville 29602 (61,000)
POB 2207

North Charleston 29406 (54,000)
POB 5817

Rockhill 29730 (34,000)
POB 11706

Spartanburg 29303 (45,000)
480 North Church Street

South Dakota
Aberdeen 57401 (26,000)
POB 1299

Rapid City 57701 (44,000)
22 Main Street

Sioux Falls 57102 (72,000)
24 West Ninth Street
201 Delafield Street

Tennessee
Chattanooga 37402 (119,000)
City Hall, Municipal Building

Clarksville 37040 (32,000)
City Hall

Jackson 38301 (40,000)
312 East Main Street

Johnson City 337601 (34,000)
Municipal-Safety Building

Kingsport 37660 (32,000)
225 West Center Street

Knoxville 37902 (175,000)
City Hall

Memphis 38103 (624,000)
125 North Main Street

Nashville 37201 (448,000)
107 Court House

Texas

Abilene 79604 (90,000)
POB 60

Amarillo 79186 (127,000)
POB 19171

Arlington 76010 (91,000)
POB 2880

Austin 78701 (252,000)
124 West Eight Street

Baytown 77520 (44,000)
POB 424

Beaumont 77704 (116,000)
POB 3287

Brownsville 78520 (53,000)
POB 911

Bryan 77801 (34,000)
POB 1000

Corpus Christi 78408 (205,000)
POB 9277

Dallas 75201 (844,000)
1501 Marilla Street

Denton 76201 (40,000)
215 East McKinney

El Paso 79901 (322,000)
500 East San Antonio Street

Fort Worth 76102 (393,000)
1000 Throckmorton

Galveston 77550 (62,000)
POB 779

Garland 75040 (81,000)
POB 40189

Grand Prairie 75050 (51,000)
POB 11

Harlingen 78550 (34,000)
POB 2207

Houston 77002 (1,233,000)
900 Brazos Street

Irving 75061 (97,000)
POB 3008

Killeen 76541 (36,000)
400 North Second Street

Laredo 78040 (69,000)
City Hall

Longview 75601 (46,000)
POB 1952

Lubbock 79457 (149,000)
POB 2000

McAllen 78501 (38,000)
POB 220

Mesquite 75149 (55,000)
POB 137

Midland 79701 (59,000)
POB 1152

Odessa 79760 (78,000)
POB 4398

Pasadena 77506 (89,000)
1211 East Southmore

Plano 75074 (44,000)
POB 358

Port Arthur 77640 (57,000)
POB 1089

Richardson 75080 (49,000)
POB 309

San Angelo 76901 (64,000)
POB 1751

San Antonio 78205 (654,000)
Military Plaza, POB 9066

Temple 76501 (33,000)
Municipal Building

Texarkana 75501 (30,000)
POB 1967

Texas City 77590 (39,000)
POB 2608

Tyler 75701 (58,000)
POB 2039

Victoria 77901 (41,000)
104 West Juan Linn Street

Waco 76703 (95,000)
POB 1370

Wichita Falls 76307 (98,000)
POB 1431

Utah

Bountiful 84010 (28,000)
745 South Main Street

Ogden City 84401 (69,000)
Municipal Building

Provo 84601 (53,000)
POB 799

Salt Lake City 84111 (176,000)
300 City and County Building

Vermont
Burlington 05401 (38,000)
City Hall
Montpelier 05602 (9,000)
Main Street

Virigina
Alexandria 22314 (111,000)
125 North Royal Street
Charlottesville 22902 (39,000)
POB 911
Chesapeake 23320 (90,000)
POB 15225
Danville 14541 (46,000)
Municipal Building
Hampton 23669 (121,000)
22 Lincoln Street
Lynchburg 24505 (54,000)
POB 60
Newport News 23607 (138,000)
2400 Washington Avenue
Norfolk 23501 (308,000)
City Hall Building
Petersburg 23803 (45,000)
City Hall
Portsmouth 23705 (11,000)
POB 820
Richmond 23219 (250,000)
900 East Broad Street
Roanoke 24011 (92,000)
Municipal Building
Suffolk 23434 (45,000)
POB 1858
Virginia Beach 23456 (172,000)
Municipal Center

Washington
Bellevue 98009 (61,000)
POB 1768
Bellingham 98225 (39,000)
210 Lottie Street
Bremerton 98310 (35,000)
239 Fourth Street
Everett 98201 (54,000)
City Hall
Richland 99352 (28,000)
POB 190

Seattle 98104 (531,000)
600 Fourth Avenue
Spokane 99201 (171,000)
North 221 Wall Street
Tacoma 98402 (155,000)
County-City Building
Vancouver 98660 (42,000)
210 East 13th Street
Yakima 98901 (46,000)
129 North Second Street

West Virginia
Charleston 25717 (74,000)
POB 1659
Morgantown 26505 (29,000)
389 Spruce Street
Parkersburg 26101 (44,000)
POB 1348
Wheeling 26003 (48,000)
City-County Building

Wisconsin
Appleton 54911 (57,000)
POB 1857
Beloit 53511 (36,000)
Municipal Center
Brookfield 53005 (32,000)
2000 North Calhoun Road
Eau Claire 54701 (45,000)
203 South Farwell Street
Fond du Lac 54935 (36,000)
POB 150
Green Bay 54301 (88,000)
Jefferson Street
Janesville 53545 (46,000)
18 North Jackson Street
Kenosha 53140 (79,000)
625 52nd Street
La Crosse 54601 (51,000)
City Hall
Madison 53709 (173,000)
210 Monona Avenue
Manitowoc 54220 (33,000)
817 Franklin Street
Menomonee Falls 53051 (32,000)
POB 100
Milwaukee 53202 (717,000)
200 East Wells Street

Oshkosh 54901 (53,000)
POB 1130

Racine 53403 (95,000)
730 Washington Avenue

Sheboygan 53081 (48,000)
828 Center Avenue

Superior 54880 (32,000)
1407 Hammond Avenue

Waukesha 53186 (40,000)
201 Delafield Street

Wausau 54401 (33,000)
407 Grant Street

Wauwatosa 53213 (59,000)
7725 West North Avenue

West Allis 53214 (72,000)
7525 West Greenfield Avenue

Wyoming
Casper 82601 (39,000)
City-County Building

Cheyenne 82001 (41,000)
City-County Building

COUNTIES AND THEIR GOVERNMENTS

States are too large to be governed from a single headquarters or capital and so are divided into counties, with only 3 counties in the tiny State of Delaware, but 254 counties in Texas. In California there is one county that is larger in area than Belgium and several other European countries. And just as each state has a capital city, so each county has a county seat in one of its cities or towns, which serves as the capital of the county and in which the county government is housed.

In many cases counties do as significant an amount of purchasing as do many busy cities. This is certainly true in the Washington, DC suburban county where this is being written (Montgomery County, Maryland), for example. This is a prosperous county, with a great deal of industrial and business activity, and a large population living in a large number of bedroom communities. A majority of this population, business, and industry lies in large, unincorporated areas of the county, such as the well-known and sprawling area called Silver Spring, Maryland. Virtually everything unincorporated in this part of the county is referred to as Silver Spring, and there is even a "downtown" Silver Spring, where there is a very city-like section of stores, restaurants, broad sidewalks, and other urban features. However, since there is actually no city or town of Silver Spring, the entire area depends on the Montgomery County government to patrol its streets, fight its fires, and provide all the other services a built-up community needs. That, plus the fact that Montgomery County is a rather large and prosperous county (with one of the largest per capita income levels in the country), makes it inevitable that purchasing is a major activity of the county government from its seat in Rockville, Maryland.

The nearby County of Fairfax, Virginia is another excellent example. It has its own Purchasing and Supply Management Agency, which is reasonably typical of government purchasing organizations. A few illustrative details of purchasing organization and practices of Fairfax County, whose county seat is in Fairfax, Virginia, are presented here as an example of county purchasing. It is easy to see the resemblance philosophically and functionally to the purchasing organizations and practices of the State and other local governments.

Fairfax County Procurement System

The County of Fairfax, Commonwealth of Virginia, operates its Purchasing and Supply Management Agency at 4100 Chain Bridge Road, Fairfax, Virginia 22030. The Agency offers vendors a *Vendor's Guide*, which lists as personnel and organizational units connected with purchasing a Director of the Agency, a Deputy Director, a Commodity Buying Section, and a Projects and Contracts Section, among other offices, staff, and functions. Vendors must register to get on bidders lists, and will then be invited to bid and/or submit proposals (for the County issues both invitations to bid and requests for proposals) in competition for contracts and purchase orders. Formal bids are classified as those larger than $5,000, and solicitations for both formal bids and proposals will be advertised in a local newspaper. Informal bids may be invited via RFQs, and oral (telephone) quotes may be accepted for those kinds of bids.

COUNTY LISTINGS AND THEIR USE

County governments tend to centralize their functions in a County Courthouse, and in most counties the Chief Executive tends to bear some title such as County Executive or County Supervisor. In the following listings three items are furnished: the name of the county; the city, town, or township which is the county seat; and the zip code for the County Courthouse, or other building in which county government offices are located. The listings are alphabetical by state and city or town, as in earlier listings. For example, this is the first listing:

Alabama
Calhoun, Anniston 36201

This tells you that the county seat of Calhoun County, Alabama is at Anniston, Alabama 36201, and you may address the county government along the following lines if you do not have a local telephone directory available to get a specific street address, with reasonable certainty that your request for information will usually find its way to the right office or official:

County Purchasing Agent		County Purchasing Office
County Courthouse	or:	Calhoun County Government
Calhoun County		Anniston, AL 36201
Anniston, AL 36201		

Of course, you should also watch for announcements in newspaper classified columns under the heading Bids and Proposals, if you have access to the newspapers published in the county.

The listings which follow are by no means a complete listing of all counties in the United States but are of approximately 500 counties. It would not serve any good purpose to list all 3,021 counties, for not all are suitable prospects. Those listed here are those which justify being called "major" counties, either because they do a great deal of buying directly or were otherwise deemed suitable for inclusion here. (Note that many counties bear the same name as the city or town that serves as the county seat.)

Surprisingly often, too, the city or town which serves as the county seat is also the state capital and/or the site of important federal facilities which are good market targets, which is, itself, a good reason for inclusion here.

Alabama
Calhoun, Anniston 36201
Dallas, Selma 36701
Houston, Dothan 36301
Jefferson, Birmingham 36701
Macon, Tuskeegee 36083
Madison, Huntsville 35801
Mobile, Mobile 36602
Montgomery, Montgomery 36102
Morgan, Decatur 35601
Russell, Phenix City 36837
Tuscaloosa, Tuscaloosa 35401

Alaska
Fairbanks North Star, Fairbanks 99701
Anchorage, Anchorage 99510
Greater Juneau, Juneau 99801
North Slope, Barrow 99723

Arizona
Coconino, Flagstaff 86001
Maricopa, Phoenix 85007
Pima, Tucson 85701
Yuma, Yuma 85364

Arkansas
Benton, Bentonville 72712
Craighead, Jonesboro 72401
Garland, Hot Springs 71901
Jefferson, Pine Bluff 71601
Mississippi, Blytheville 72315
Pulaski, Little Rock 72201
St. Francis, Forrest City 72335

Arkansas (Cont'd)
Sebastian, Fort Smith 72901
Washington, Fayetteville 72701

California
Alameda, Oakland 94612
Butte, Oroville 95965
Contra Costa, Martinez 94553
Fresno, Fresno 93721
Humboldt, Eureka 95501
Imperial, El Centro 92243
Kern, Bakersfield 93301
Los Angeles, Los Angeles 90012
Marin, San Rafael 94902
Merced, Merced 95340
Monterey, Salinas 93901
Orange, Santa Ana 92701
Riverside, Riverside 92501
Sacramento, Sacramento 95814
San Bernardino, San Bernardino 95801
San Diego, San Diego 92101
San Francisco, San Francisco 94102
San Joaquin, Stockton 95202
San Luis Obispo, San Luis Obispo 93401
San Mateo, Redwood City 94063
Santa Barbara, Santa Barbara 93101
Santa Clara, San Jose 95110
Santa Cruz, Santa Cruz 95060
Shasta, Redding 96001
Solano, Fairfield 94533
Sonoma, Santa Rosa 95402
Stanislaus, Modesto 95352
Tulare, Visalia 93227
Ventura, Ventura 93001
Yolo, Woodland 96596

Colorado
Adams, Brighton 80601
Arapahoe, Littleton 80120
Boulder, Boulder 80302
Denver, Denver 80203
El Paso, Colorado Springs 80902
Jefferson, Golden 80401
Larimer, Fort Collins 80521
Mesa, Grand Junction 81501
Pueblo, Pueblo 81003
Weld, Greeley 80631

Connecticut
Fairfield, Bridgeport 06430
Hartford, Hartford 06115
Litchfield, Litchfield 06759
Middlesex, Middletown 06457

New Haven, New Haven 06510
New London, New London 06320
Tolland, Rockville 06066
Windham, Putnam 06280

Delaware
Kent, Dover 19901
New Castle, Wilmington 19801
Sussex, Georgetown 19947

Florida
Alachua, Gainesville 32601
Bay, Panama City 32401
Brevard, Titusville 32780
Broward, Fort Lauderdale 33301
Dade, Miami 33132
Duval, Jacksonville 32202
Escambia, Pensacola 32502
Hillsborough, Tampa 33602
Lee, Fort Myers 33902
Leon, Tallahassee 32304
Manatee, Bradenton 33505
Monroe, Key West 33040
Okaloosa, Crestview 32536
Orange, Orlando 32801
Palm Beach, West Palm Beach 33401
Pinellas, Clearwater 33516
Polk, Bartow, 33830
St. Lucie, Fort Pierce 33450
Sarasota, Sarasota 33577
Volusia, De Land 32720

Georgia
Bibb, Macon 31201
Chatham, Savannah 31401
Cobb, Marietta 30060
De Kalb, Decatur 30030
Dougherty, Albany 31702
Fulton, Atlanta 30303
Houston, Warner-Robins 31093
Muscogee, Columbus 31902
Richmond, Augusta 30902
Whitfield, Dalton 30720

Hawaii
Hawaii, Hilo 96720
Honolulu, Honolulu 96813
Kauia, Lihue 96766
Maui, Wailuku 96793

Idaho
Ada, Boise 83702
Bannock, Pocatello 83201
Bonneville, Idaho Falls 83401
Canyon, Caldwell 83605

Kootenai, Coeur d'Alene 83814
Nez Perce, Lewiston 83501
Twin Falls, Twin Falls 83301

Illinois
Champaign, Urbana 61801
Cook, Chicago 60602
Du Page, Wheaton 60187
Kane, Geneva 60134
Kankakee, Kankakee 60901
Knox, Galesburg 61401
Lake, Waukegan 60085
La Salle, Ottawa 61350
McHenry, Bloomington 61701
Macon, Decatur 62525
Madison, Edwardsville 62025
Peoria, Peoria 61602
Rock Island, Rock Island 61201
St. Claire, Belleville 62222
Sangamon, Springfield 62706
Tazewell, Pekin 61554
Vermilion, Danville 61832
Will, Joliet 60434
Winnebago, Rockford 61104

Indiana
Allen, Fort Wayne 46802
Delaware, Muncie 47302
Elkhart, Goshen 46526
Lake, Crown Point 46307
La Porte, La Porte 46350
Madison, Anderson 46011
Marion, Indianapolis 46204
Monroe, Bloomington 47401
Porter, Valparaiso 46383
St.Joseph, South Bend 40601
Tippecanoe, Lafayette 47902
Vanderburg, Evansville 47708
Vigo, Terre Haute 47808
Wayne, Richmond 47374

Iowa
Black Hawk, Waterloo 50705
Cerro Gordo, Mason City 50401
Clinton, Clinton 52732
Des Moines, Burlington 52601
Dubuque, Dubuque 52201
Johnson, Iowa City 52240
Linn, Cedar Rapids 52401
Polk, Des Moines 50307
Pottawattamie, Council Bluffs 51501
Scott, Davenport 52801

Story, Nevada 50201
Woodbury, Sioux City 51101

Kansas
Douglas, Lawrence 66044
Johnson, Olathe 66061
Leavenworth, Leavenworth 66048
Reno, Hutchinson 67501
Riley, Manhattan 66502
Saline, Salina 67401
Sedgwick, Wichita 67202
Shawnee, Topeka 66603

Kentucky
Boyd, Catlettsburg 41129
Campbell, Newport 41071
Davies, Owensboro 42301
Fayette, Lexington 40507
Hardin, Elizabethtown 42701
Jefferson, Louisville 40202
Kenton, Covington 41011
McCracken, Paducah 42001
Madison, Richmond 40475
Pike, Pikeville 41501
Warren, Bowling Green 42101

Louisiana*
Acadia, Crowley 70526
Bossier, Benton 71006
Caddo, Shreveport 71101
Calcasieu, Lake Charles 70601
East Baton Rouge,Baton Rouge 70801
Jefferson, Gretna 70053
Lafayette, Lafayette 70501
Orleans, New Orleans 70112
Ouchita, Monroe 71201
Rapides, Alexandria 71301
St. Landry, Opelousas 70570
St. Mary, Franklin, 70538
St. Tammany, Covington 70433
Tangipahoa, Amite 70422
Terrebone, Houma 70360

Maine
Androscoggin, Auburn 04210
Aroostook, Houlton 04730
Cumberland, Portland 04111
Kennebec, Augusta 04330
Penobscot, Bangor 04401
York, Alfred 04002

---

* In Louisiana, counties are generally called
"parishes."

Maryland
Allegany, Cumberland 21502
Anne Arundel, Annapolis 21401
Baltimore, Baltimore 21202
Carroll, Westminster 21157
Frederick, Frederick 21701
Harford, Bel Air 21014
Howard, Ellicott City 21043
Montgomery, Rockville 20850
Prince Georges, Upper Marlboro 20870
Queen Annes, Centreville 21617
Washington, Hagerstown 21740

Massachusetts
Barnstable, Barnstable 02630
Berkshire, Pittsfield 01201
Bristol, Taunton 02780
Essex, Salem 01970
Hampden, Springfield 01101
Hampshire, Northampton 01060
Middlesex, Concord 01742
Norfolk, Dedham 002026
Plymouth, Plymouth 02360
Suffolk, Boston 02201
Worcester, Worcester 01601

Michigan
Bay, Bay City 48706
Berrien, St. Joseph 49085
Calhoun, Marshall 49086
Genesee, Flint 48502
Ingham, Mason 48854
Jackson, Jackson 49201
Kalamazoo, Kalamazoo 49003
Kent, Grand Rapids 49502
Macomb, Mt. Clemens 48043
Monroe, Monroe 48161
Muskegon, Muskegon 49440
Oakland, Pontiac 48053
Ottawa, Grand Haven 49417
Saginaw, Saginaw 48601
Washtenaw, Ann Arbor 48108
Wayne, Detroit 48226

Minnesota
Anoka, Anoka 55303
Dakota, Hastings 55033
Hennepin, Minneapolis 55415
Olmstead, Rochester 55901
Ramsey, St. Paul 55802
St. Louis, Duluth 56301
Washington, Stillwater 55082

Mississippi
Forrest, Hattiesburg 39401
Harrison, Gulfport 39501
Hinds, Jackson 39201
Jackson, Pascagoula 39567
Lauderdale, Meridian 39301
Washington, Greenville 38701

Missouri
Boone, Columbia 65201
Buchanan, St. Joseph 64501
Clay, Liberty 64068
Greene, Springfield 65802
Jackson, Kansas City 64106
Jefferson, Hillsboro 63050
St. Charles, St. Charles 63301
St. Louis, Clayton 63105

Montana
Cascade, Great Falls 59401
Flathead, Kalispell 59901
Gallatin, Bozeman 59715
Lewis and Clark, Helena 59601
Missoula, Missoula 59801
Silver Bow, Butte 59701
Yellowstone, Billings 59101

Nebraska
Douglas, Omaha 68102
Hall, Grand Island 68801
Lancaster, Lincoln 68509
Sarpy, Papillon 68046

Nevada
Clark, Las Vegas 89114
Ormsby, Carson City 89701
Washoe, Reno 89501

New Hampshire
Cheshire, Keene 03431
Grafton, Woodsville 03785
Hillsborough, Nashua 03060
Merrimack, Concord 03301
Rockingham, Exeter 03833
Strafford, Dover 03820

New Jersey
Atlantic, Mays Landing 08330
Bergen, Hackensack 07602
Burlington, Mt. Holly 08060
Camden, Camden 08101
Cape May, Cape May 08210
Cumberland, Bridgeton 08302
Essex, Newark 07102
Gloucester, Woodbury 08096

Hudson, Jersey City 07302
Mercer, Trenton 08625
Middlesex, New Brunswick 08903
Monmouth, Freehold 07728
Morris, Morristown 07960
Ocean, Toms River 08753
Passaic, Paterson 07505
Somerset, Somerville 08876
Union, Elizabeth 07207

New Mexico
Bernalillo, Albuquerque 87102
Chaves, Roswell 88201
Dona Ana, Las Cruces 88001
Lea, Lovington 88260
McKinley, Gallup 87301
Otero, Alamogordo 88310
San Juan, Aztec 87410
Santa Fe, Santa Fe 87501

New York
Albany, Albany 12207
Broome, Binghamton 13901
Bronx, Bronx 10451
Chatauqua, Mayville 14757
Chemung, Elmira 14902
Dutchess, Poughkeepsie 12602
Erie, Buffalo 14202
Jefferson, Watertown 13601
Kings, Brooklyn 11201
Monroe, Rochester 14614
Nassau, Mineola 11501
New York, New York 10007
Niagara, Lockport 14094
Oneida, Utica 13503
Onondaga, Syracuse 13202
Orange, Goshen 10924
Oswego, Oswego 13126
Queens, Jamaica 11434
Rensselaer, Troy 12180
Richmond, St. George 10301
Rockland, New City 10956
Saint Lawrence, Canton 13617
Saratoga, Ballston Spa 12020
Schenectady, Schenectady 12307
Suffolk, Riverhead 11901
Ulster, Kingston 12401
Westchester, White Plains 10601

North Carolina
Alamance, Graham 27253
Buncombe, Newton 28658
Cleveland, Shelby 28150

Craven, New Bern 28560
Cumberland, Fayetteville 28301
Davidson, Lexington 27292
Durham, Durham 27702
Forsyth, Winston-Salem 27101
Gaston, Gastonia 28052
Guilford, Greensboro 27402
Mecklenburg, Charlotte 28202
New Hanover, Wilmington 28401
Onslow, Jacksonville 28540
Pitt, Greenville 27834
Robeson, Lumberton 28358
Rowan, Salisburg 28144
Wake, Raleigh 27611

North Dakota
Burleigh, Bismarck 58501
Cass, Fargo 58102
Grand Forks, Grand Forks 58201
Ward, Minot 58701

Ohio
Allen, Lima 45802
Ashtabula, Jefferson 44047
Butler, Hamilton 45012
Clark, Springfield 45501
Clermont, Batavia 45103
Columbiana, Lisbon 44432
Crawford, Bucyrus 44820
Cuyahoga, Cleveland 44114
Erie, Sandusky 44870
Fairfield, Lancaster 43130
Franklin, Columbus 43215
Greene, Xenia 45385
Hamilton, Cincinnati 45202
Jefferson, Steubenville 43952
Lake, Painesville 44077
Licking, Newark 43055
Lorain, Elyria 44035
Lucas, Toledo 43624
Mahoning, Youngstown 44503
Medina, Medina 44256
Miami, Troy 45373
Montgomery, Dayton 45402
Muskingum, Zanesville 43360
Portage, Ravenna 44266
Richland, Mansfield 44902
Ross, Chillicothe 45601
Stark, Canton 44702
Summit, Akron 44308
Trumbull, Warren 44482
Warren, Lebanon 45036

Ohio (Cont'd)
Wayne, Wooster 44691
Wood, Bowling Green 43402

Oklahoma
Cleveland, Norman 73069
Garfield, Enid 73701
Oklahoma, Oklahoma City 73105
Payne, Stillwater 74074
Tulsa, Tulsa 74103

Oregon
Clackmas, Oregon City 97045
Douglas, Roseburg 97470
Jackson, Medford 97501
Lane, Eugene 97401
Marion, Salem 97310
Multnomah, Portland 97205
Washington, Hillsboro 97123

Pennsylvania
Adams, Gettysburg 17325
Allegheny, Pittsburgh 15219
Beaver, Beaver 15009
Berks, Reading 19601
Blair, Hollidaysburg 16648
Bucks, Doylestown 18901
Butler, Butler 16001
Cambria, Ebensburg 15931
Centre, Bellefonte 16823
Chester, West Chester 19380
Cumberland, Carlisle 17013
Dauphin, Harrisburg 17101
Delaware, Media 19063
Erie, Erie 16501
Fayette, Uniontown 15401
Franklin, Chambersburg 15723
Lackawanna, Scranton 18503
Lancaster, Lancaster 17602
Lawrence, New Castle 16101
Lebanon, Lebanon 17042
Lehigh, Allentown 18101
Luzerne, Wilkes-Barre 18703
Lycoming, Williamsport 17701
Mercer, Mercer 16137
Montgomery, Norristown 19404
Northampton, Easton 18042
Northumberland, Sunbury 17801
Philadelphia, Phildelphia 19107
Schuylkill, Pottsville, 17901
Somerset, Somerset 15501
Venango, Franklin 16323
Washington, Washington 15301

Westmoreland, Greensburg 15601
York, York 17405

Rhode Island
Kent, East Greenwich 02818
Newport, Newport 02840
Providence, Providence 02903
Washington, West Kingston 02892

South Carolina
Aiken, Aiken 29801
Anderson, Anderson 29621
Charleston, Charleston 29401
Florence, Florence 29501
Greenville, Greenville 29601
Lexington, Lexington 29072
Orangeburg, Orangeburg 29115
Spartanburg, Spartanburg 29301
Sumter, Sumter 29150

South Dakota
Hughes, Pierre 57501
Minnehaha, Sioux Falls 57102
Pennington, Rapid City 57701

Tennessee
Davidson, Nashville 37210
Hamilon, Chattanooga 37402
Knox, Knoxville 37902
Shelby, Memphis 38103
Sullivan, Blountville 37617

Texas
Bell, Belton 76513
Bexar, San Antonio 78205
Brazoria, Angleton 77551
Cameron, Brownsville 78520
Dallas, Dallas 75201
El Paso, El Paso 79901
Galveston, Galveston 77550
Harris, Houston 77002
Jefferson, Beaumont 77704
Lubbock, Lubbock 79404
McLennan, Waco 76887
Nueces, Corpus Christi 78401
Potter, Amarillo 79101
Reeves, Pecos 79772
Smith, Tyler 75701
Tarrant, Fort Worth 76102
Taylor, Abilene 79601
Travis, Austin 78767
Wichita, Wichita Falls 76301

Utah
Davis, Farmington 84025
Salt Lake, Salt Lake City 84110

Utah, Provo 84601
Weber, Ogden 84401

Vermont
Chittenden, Burlington 05401
Rutland, Rutland 05701
Washington, Montpelier 05602

Virginia
Arlington, Arlington 22210
Fairfax, Fairfax 22030
Henrico, Richmond 23219
Prince William, Manassas 22110
Virginia Beach, Virginia Beach 73458

Washington
Clark, Vancouver 98660
King, Seattle 98101
Pierce, Tacoma 98402
Snohomish, Everett 98201
Spokane, Spokane 99201
Thurston, Olympia 98501
Walla Walla, Walla Walla 99362
Whatcom, Bellingham 98225
Yakima, Yakima 98901

West Virginia
Harrison, Clarksburg 26301
Kanahwa, Charleston 25301

Monongalia, Morgantown 26505
Ohio, Wheeling 26003
Wood, Parkersburg 26105

Wisconsin
Brown, Green Bay 54301
Dane, Madison 53701
Eau Claire, Eau Claire 54701
Fond du Lac, Fond du Lac 54935
Kenosha, Kenosha 53140
La Crosse, La Crosse 54601
Manitowoc, Manitowoc 54220
Marathon, Wausau 54401
Milwaukee, Milwaukee 53202
Outagamie, Appleton 54911
Racine, Racine 53403
Rock, Janesville 53545
Sheboygan, Sheboygan 53081
Waukesha, Waukesha 53186
Winnebago, Oshkosh 54901

Wyoming
Albany, Laramie 82070
Laramie, Cheyenne 82001
Natrona, Casper 82601

INDEX